Understanding the Male Temperament

Other Books by Tim LaHaye

The Act of Marriage (with Beverly LaHaye)
Anger Is a Choice (with Bob Phillips)
Beginning of the End
How to Be Happy Though Married
How to Study Bible Prophecy for Yourself
How to Study the Bible for Yourself
How to Win over Depression
I Love You, but Why Are We So Different?
Revelation—Illustrated and Made Plain
Spirit-Controlled Temperament
Transformed Temperaments
What Everyone Should Know about Homosexuality
Why You Act the Way You Do

Understanding the Male Temperament

What Women Want to Know about Men but Don't Know How to Ask

Second Edition

TIM LAHAYE

Fleming H. Revell
A Division of Baker Book House Co
Grand Rapids, Michigan 49516

Published by Fleming H. Revell
a division of Baker Book House Company
P.O. Box 6287, Grand Rapids, MI 49516-6287

Published in association with the literary agency of
Alive Communications, Inc.
P.O. Box 49068
Colorado Springs, CO 80949

Paperback edition published 2001

Second printing, August 2001

Printed in the United States of America

Library of Congress Cataloging-in-Publication Data

LaHaye, Tim F.
    Understanding the male temperament : what women want to know about men but don't know how to ask / Tim LaHaye.—2nd ed.
        p.   cm.
    ISBN 0-8007-1719-8 (cloth)
    ISBN 0-8007-5754-8 (paper)
        1. Men. 2. Masculinity (Psychology) 3. Men—Religious life. I. Title
HQ1090.L34   1996
305.31—dc20   95-40963

For current information about all releases from Baker Book House, visit our web site:

http://www.bakerbooks.com

Contents

1

The Death of the John Wayne Myth

For more than thirty years, six-foot-four John Wayne stalked through the American imagination as the embodiment of manhood: rough, tough, and sometimes crude but always fair. He was the fast-shooting, bigger-than-life hero of more men and women than any other celluloid idol in history. Even today he can be seen on late-night movie channels dispensing his version of frontier justice and perpetuating the myth of the macho cowboy.

He left not only a trail of broken hearts and jaws everywhere, but also millions of fractured male egos that could never quite measure up to the two-fisted, ramrod-backed character who conquered the Old West. The truth of the matter is that no man could measure up to that myth in real life—not even John Wayne.

The masculine standard of the John Wayne myth was never authentic, even prior to 1900. But today's technological world has placed entirely different pressures on twentieth-century manhood that to a large degree demand even greater courage and stamina than were needed by the old pioneers. Admittedly, it takes courage to drive a herd of cattle from southern Texas to Abilene, only to find one's deadly enemies waiting at the O.K. Corral for a shoot-out to the death. But it also takes courage for a man to head doggedly to work every day at a job he despises—to support his wife and three children—and then take on a second job to pay those nagging bills that somehow have accumulated, or to earn the money to pay for his kids' college tuition.

Having counseled both men and women for twenty-eight years, I think I know something about manhood, its essential characteristics and its influence on conduct. I'm convinced that most men of our generation are as good as men have ever been. Oh, I have to admit that we hear frequent reports of cop-outs, dissenters, and deserters of wives, children, and country, but what's new about that? Western history reveals that we have always had "yellow-bellied hoss thieves" and wife beaters. No doubt the liberal policies of current humanistic thought, including leniency toward criminals, welfare subsidies that may encourage laziness, and an educationally bankrupt public-school system that produces an irresponsible citizenry have increased the number of modern cop-outs. But we can also identify millions of red-blooded he-man types in all walks of life who can look at their reflections in the mirror and confidently say, "I am a man!"

Instead of thinking about the two million quitters who either divorced their wives or just walked away from them last year, what about the seventy-five million or more men who remained faithful to their families? Do you think they all had an easy time of it? Doubtless many were mighty unhappy at home, but they stuck it out anyway!

Every generation has its real live heroes—like Roger ("the Dodger") Staubach, who quarterbacked the Dallas Cowboys to stardom in the sixties and seventies and led his team to two Super Bowl wins. Or the 1976 Olympic decathlon champion, Bruce Jenner, who in order to win his most coveted award became "the greatest living athlete" of his decade. In order to win, he trained six hours every day for one year and, according to his wife, "never ran less than ten miles a day for the ten months preceding the Olympics."

Many other modern-day heroes come to mind readily. Ronald Reagan, who after the age when most men retire, became the forty-second president of the United States, battled a hostile Congress every day, reversed the "malice" of his predecessor, ushered in the strongest economic recovery in fifty years, and stood up to the Soviet Union in space and technology expansion. Many people accredit him to be the number one reason that the "Evil Empire" collapsed into near bankruptcy.

There are many real-life heroes in the nineties. Another is the current leader of the U.S. Senate, Robert Dole, who returned as a true war hero from World War II with a paralyzed right hand and health threatened by an infection that reduced him to ninety-seven pounds. Refusing to give up, he finished law school, won a seat in the U.S. Senate from his state of Kansas, and became the most powerful member of his party. At the age of seventy-three he is seriously considering himself a candidate for president. Even those who may not agree with his outspoken ways or conservative politics admit he is a man's man.

But beyond the celebrated national hero, we can look to the more than one million unsung, equally courageous men who every day brave the crime jungles of "civilized" cities as police officers; another 450,000 firemen who, although their profession holds the record for the highest professional mortality rate, still attend to their work every day; thousands of coal miners who jeopardize their lives eight hours a day in underground caverns; the many dedicated teachers who volunteer for inner-city school positions so they can give underprivileged students the chance denied their parents; or the honest businessmen who relinquish secure positions with high incomes to enter the political jungle, often for less salary, just to do what they can to improve government in Washington, Sacramento, or Atlanta.

If you thought this book was going to be a diatribe against manhood or an exposé of the failures of modern man, you have bought the wrong book. I am writing this to men who are men, to men and boys who want to be men, and to women who want to understand and appreciate manhood in all its complexity. Though subject to extensive criticism, men are doing many things right, and they need to be reassured of that. Those who misuse or abuse their manhood need some of the suggestions offered here in order to experience the fulfillment of their manhood. The women in their lives will profit from this analysis by discovering the mainsprings of man's actions and the means by which he can be helped. I don't pretend to know all the answers to what makes a man tick, but I've heard most of the questions and have drawn on the counsel of many of the best experts in the field for practical solutions. I have written five other books on human temperament and realize how important an understanding of human temperament is. It is temperament that makes individuals, both men and women, different. And since temperament influences everything we do in life, it has a profound effect on the expression of manhood. As we shall see, it can even affect how a man feels about his own manhood.

When the first edition of this book was written in 1977, both the publisher and the author noted that many books had been written about understanding women, but books about understanding men were almost unheard of. Even today most books are about women. To our knowledge, this is the only book that applies the unique characteristics of manhood to temperament. At the time of its first publication, the study of human temperament was in its infancy in this country. Today, however, the study of temperament is well established. Many popular speakers, both secular and Christian, talk about temperament. Gary Smalley and John Trent present temperament types as animals; Florence Littauer presents them as personalities. Businessmen see them as management styles. We are all talking about the same thing—human temperament, which can be the most fascinating subject in the world, particularly when applied to manhood. This book, newly revised and updated, is prepared for the twenty-first-century man—perhaps the most complex person in the world and certainly living in the most complex era of history. Like its original version, the truths herein are greatly needed and long overdue.

Since the Garden of Eden, where Adam followed Eve's example and disobeyed God, it has never been so difficult to be a man. In recent years, men have created a more competitive world for themselves mentally through technology, emotionally through women and family, and physically through time-consuming social luxuries and a sedentary lifestyle unshared by previous generations. But I still believe that in the beginning God made them male and female and intended every man to be a man. I hope the concepts in this book will help men (and the women who love them) to realize their maximum potential in manhood while living in a technologically advanced and often impersonal society.

An interesting phenomenon that began building in the early nineties leads me to believe that millions of men seriously want to be better men, fathers, and husbands. This phenomenon is called Promise Keepers. From a small group of seventy men called together by Bill McCartney and Dr. Dave Wardell, it has spread like wildfire, packing giant crowds of men into the largest football stadiums in the country. McCartney, "the winningest coach in Colorado University history" according to sportscasters, has put his reputation on the line for this movement of gathering men to "worship, praise, pray, and study the Word of God together." In 1991 and 1992 the crowds grew to thousands of men. In 1993, fifty thousand met in the Boulder, Colorado, stadium. In 1994 they hoped to gather thirty-five thousand in skeptical, fast-paced Los Angeles, but fifty-five thousand men showed up! Only God knows where this phenomenal movement of our time will end, but the vice president of the organization told me they plan to bring the largest group of men in American history to the nation's capital in 1997 to pray for the spiritual revival this country so desperately needs. That's good timing! That will be only one year after the 1996 presidential election—the election of the century, for it will decide whose policies will prepare this nation to enter the twenty-first century. Will we continue to allow secularizers to make our laws and set our policies, or will we elect God-fearing men with a commitment to the moral traditions of our Christian forefathers? Many are already calling it "a watershed year in America's history."

The phenomenon of seeing huge stadiums filled with men gathered to worship God in the name of his Son Jesus Christ gives us an indication of the real intent of men's hearts. Many of these men dedicate themselves to God's Word and to keeping his promises (thus the name Promise Keepers) and to becoming better men, husbands, and fathers. The celebrated Million Man March on Washington in the fall of 1995 was not a referendum on the leadership of the group but rather exposed the deep-rooted desire in the hearts of tens of thousands of black men to be better men, husbands, and fathers. Millions of men of all races want to reach their full potential, starting with manhood. That is what this book is all about: helping men become the best they can be for God, family, and country according to the temperament God has given them.

Admittedly, it is harder to be a man today than it was in our father's or grandfather's time, for conditions and customs have changed. But the basic ingredients of manhood will never change—character, personality, leadership, productivity, courage, mind, emotions, sexuality, body, and boyishness. They go on for generation after generation. The John Wayne myth is dead! Some men are dead, others are dying, and all will one day pass away, but manhood will never die. Long live manhood!

The Complexity of Manhood

A man once said, "There is nothing more complex than a woman!" He was wrong. Men are every bit as complicated as the fairer sex. We tend to preserve the strange notion that a man is open, candid, perceptible, and easily understood. That is nonsense! Men are just as mysterious as women, but they hide their complexity behind the impenetrable mask of their masculinity. In this chapter we will remove that mask and examine the major characteristics that produce this creature—man.

The circle on the following page records the ten major characteristics that comprise a man. To fully understand him, you must consider each of these traits carefully, noting its influence on his behavior. Later, after studying the four temperaments and the various blends of temperaments with their natural strengths and weaknesses, we shall verify that all men are created different. The influence of each of the ten characteristics shown on the Complexity of Manhood circle will vary with the individual's temperament, making humans in general and men in particular an extremely fascinating subject to study. As we shall see, tem-

The Complexity of Manhood

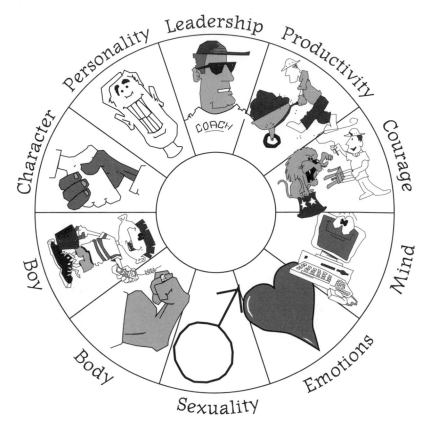

perament will determine the degree of influence each of these ten characteristics has on an individual.

From the beginning of time more male babies than female have been born. Perhaps our Creator knew that man's more aggressive tendencies would make him a greater mortality risk than woman and consequently he would have to produce more of them. Now, several millennia and hundreds of wars later (almost all of which were started by men), we total 9 percent more women than men in the United States. Had it not been for this higher male birth rate, the race would probably be extinct by this time. Since these creatures called men comprise such an enormous part of the world's population, they deserve careful scrutiny to see what makes them tick. To do so, we must examine the ten qualities of manhood.

Character

What a person does is the result of what he is. If a man is weak and without principle, he will follow the path of least resistance to an early grave. If he is hostile, self-centered, overbearing, or domineering, he will become aggressive, troublesome, and in most cases, lawless, respecting the laws of neither man nor God. Remember, what you are determines what you do.

At your core lies your character, the real you, the individual's Supreme Court. It is what you are when no one else is around, determining your actions when no one else is there to observe. Character is what a person is when the lights are out. Next to the spiritual side of a person's makeup, nothing else is more influential in his life—because character affects the way he uses all the other nine facets of his nature.

Many significant qualities combine to produce a man's character, beginning with moral principles, integrity, self-discipline, determination, responsibility, dependability, motivation, and a sense of justice and mercy that makes him considerate of the rights and feelings of others. Men of bad character lack this normal sense of justice and mercy that should have been instilled in them in their youth. It is this deficiency that enables them to run roughshod over the rights and feelings of others.

Men today fall into three basic categories of character based on this definition: (1) good or strong character (those who manifest these qualities most of the time); (2) bad or weak character (those who seldom reveal any of these qualities); and (3) mediocre character (those who utilize some of these qualities some of the time). Of the three, the mediocre character is the least predictable; one is never sure just how this man will react to a given situation.

Three Things That Influence Character

Strength of character is not entirely innate at birth, although every man receives some of these qualities genetically from his parents. The most powerful influences on a man's character for good or bad are temperament, conscience, and childhood training.

Temperament

The combination of inherited traits a man receives from his parents at the time of conception will determine his eventual temperament. We shall study this in detail in chapter 4. Nothing except a genuine conversion to a Christ-controlled life has a greater impact on his behavior than his temperament.

Intuitive Moral Standards and Conscience

Contrary to humanistic philosophical teaching, every human being is born with an intuitive sense of right and wrong that distinguishes him from animals and makes him a moral creature. This intuitive moral code is not as stringent as the Ten Commandments, but it is similar. Anthropologists have found many primitive tribes where the Bible has never penetrated that nevertheless have codes similar to the Judeo-Christian ethic, attesting to its intuitive source. In each case where libertine morals were practiced, they came through the false teachings of the tribe's pagan religions. Tribal priests learned early that the easiest way to gain a following is by appealing to the passions and lusts of men in the name of religion to violate that moral code and thus "having their conscience seared with a hot iron"

(1 Tim. 4:2). But this time-honored practice does not negate the fact that men are born with an intuitive moral standard.

Humanistic teachers of our day are likewise in hopeless confusion with regard to the human conscience. They insist that man is born neutral and that conscience is a result of religion or cultural training. As long as they persist in this error, they will never be able to understand the nature of man and effect a proper means of solving his problems. The Bible is extremely clear that all men possess a conscience that is either "accusing them or else excusing them" (Rom. 2:15), although by hard practice one can sear his conscience and develop "a reprobate mind" (Rom. 1:28 KJV) given totally over to the appetites of the flesh, and thus destroy his character. People with a weak character are those who either have seared their conscience or have a guilty conscience, either of which produces misery, for the Bible warns that "the way of transgressors is hard" (Prov. 13:15 KJV).

Good character is built by allowing biblical teaching to reinforce the intuitive moral standard that all men receive at birth. Both the Old and New Testaments are filled with such principles, but of the entire sixty-six books of the Bible, the best character builder is the Book of Proverbs, which contains advice like this: "Do not be wise in your own eyes; Fear the LORD and depart from evil. It will be health to your flesh, And strength to your bones" (Prov. 3:7–8). This practical book is designed with thirty-one chapters, one for each day of most months—an ideal way to fortify and build a good character. All the wisdom literature of the Bible is pointed at the formation of character.

As a college president for six years and a pastor for more than thirty years, I have worked closely with hundreds of young people and parents. It is my studied opinion that if parents were as conscientious about infusing good character into their children when they are young as in sacrificing to give them a good education later in life, they would produce better and stronger men and women. Young people with such strength of character will have little trouble getting a proper education.

Childhood Training

God has given to each child a set of private tutors called parents. Even without the benefit of formal training, these parents are easily the most significant human force in the character building of that child and, eventually, that man. The place they command in the heart of their child gives them an enormous opportunity to build character into the lives of their children, but they must start when the child is very young.

Here are the four building blocks, offered by all tutor-parents, that produce good character:

Parental love. Before a child can focus his eyes or distinguish sounds, he can sense love. If his parents are sufficiently mature to supply that necessary affection (which some psychologists call "stroking"), his sense of self-worth and self-confidence will be enriched. Children who lack sufficient stroking are prone to become insecure and inhibited adults—if they live to grow up at all. As I pointed out in my book *How to Win over Depression,* God has made breast-feeding the ideal way for infants to be supplied simultaneously with the nutritional and emotional necessities of life. It is no accident that the enormous incidence of emotional depression among today's adults parallels the bottle-feeding craze in the days when they were infants. Fortunately, breast-feeding is now "in," so babies get both mother's milk and mother's stroking at the same time—the way God intended.

Fathers, too, can teach self-worth through tender strokes of love. My father died when I was a small boy, so I have very few memories of him. Although his mother was an alcoholic and he was educated only through the eighth grade, my dad was a great father. I could run into his heart anytime I wished. He was a strong disciplinarian with a violent temper, but I never questioned his love. Together with the undying love of my widowed mother, I have enjoyed the extreme luxury of never knowing what it is like to be unloved. To this I attribute my natural sense of self-confidence and self-worth (which I have enjoyed as long as I can remember). The greatest legacy any parent can bestow on his child is love that expresses itself in stroking. No child ever received too much of it. Perhaps that is why the Bible refers to *love* as the "royal law" (James 2:8).

Parental discipline. The present rebellious, griping, undisciplined, and unhappy generation is a constant reminder that parental discipline is absolutely essential to character building, as the Bible has taught for centuries. Dr. Benjamin Spock's "permissivism" of the last four or five decades—which even he later repudiated on national television—has produced the most undisciplined, most self-centered and self-indulgent generation of adults in American history. That should not be difficult to comprehend, for only with great effort can anyone make the transition from a lack of parental discipline to self-discipline, whereas it is relatively easy to proceed from good family discipline to self-discipline. And one can never overestimate the importance of self-discipline, for without it there is no success in any field—and certainly no character.

Parental instruction. From the earliest days of childhood, it is hard to distinguish the instructional voice of a parent from the voice of God. The tutor-parent's voice is bigger than life and of more value than all other voices combined. Happy is the child whose parent's voice is synonymous with the voice of God. If he heeds it—and he usually does when it is administered with the other three parental building blocks—he is enriched in this life and the eternity to come.

Parental example. In young children, "more is caught than taught." The old adage "What you do speaks so loudly I cannot hear what you say!" is particularly true of tutor-parents. Nothing negates good parental teaching faster than a poor parental example. The most mixed-up children do not come from excessively strict homes, but from those where teaching and example live in conflict. I have heard people say that they would not force their children to attend church for fear that they would become antagonistic to the church. Save yourself that fear. Most kids have to be forced to go to church at some stage in their lives, just as they must be compelled to act correctly in other situations. What turns young people against Christ and his church is to hear parents give lip service to Bible standards of morality but practice the opposite in the home.

This is one area in which the father's influence is especially important. He sets the pace for both his wife and children. If he says with Paul, "Imitate me, just as I also imitate Christ" (1 Cor. 11:1), they will most likely follow both him and his Lord. But if he teaches one thing and lives another, his home will become a disaster area—unless his wife's good character and godliness provide that element of Christian example all second-generation Christian children need. Happy is the family where father and mother agree on living a good example before their offspring.

The prestigious influence of the tutor-parents in building character into the lives of children has long been known to Christian authorities on the raising of children. From them I learned years ago that "50 percent of a child's character is formed by the time he is three years old and 75 percent by the time he is five."

Make no mistake about it—the most important people in the life of any child are his tutor-parents. If they take advantage of their God-given position in the early years of their children's lives, they can teach the principles of character, integrity, and a reverential awe of God that no mind bender can take from them later.

Character is not born within a person. It is formed into him by loving and concerned parents who will establish within his life those principles that God has instilled within their own.

Is There Hope for Those Weak in Character?

So far we have considered only those human building blocks for producing good character—temperament, innate moral principles, and parental training. What about the person who was raised by non-Christian parents, grew up in a broken home, or was brought up by self-indulgent, cop-out parents? Is there any hope for him? Certainly! With God all things are possible. Remember, it is God's will that all men and women be "conformed to the image of His Son" (Rom. 8:29), who was the embodiment of good character. Since God wills that all his children develop a good character, you can be confident that he will enable even the most disenfranchised in their youth to become the men and women of character he intends them to be.

Modern psychology often cripples man emotionally and mentally by tying his potential so tightly to his background, often used as a crutch to excuse a weak or mediocre character. As we shall see later on, God has made provision for even the most emotionally crippled to "rise up and walk" by the power of the new nature he introduces into a person's life when he has a born-again experience with his Son, Jesus Christ. That power is so real that it has transformed many a character dropout into a productive human being. I have seen it happen scores of times, but it doesn't happen immediately; it is a long growth process that affects every area of a person's life.

Personality

The expression of one's self to other people—personality—is usually the basis on which first impressions are built. The field of psychiatry has long distinguished between the introvert, or passive personality, and the extrovert, or active personality. As we shall see in chapter 4, that twofold separation is incomplete, for each can be divided into two further categories—superextrovert and ordinary extrovert as compared to superintrovert and ordinary introvert.

Many forces combine to mold one's personality, not the least of which is temperament. However, like character, personality can be seriously influenced by childhood training. This is particularly true of the ordinary extrovert (Choleric) and the ordinary introvert (Melancholy). The

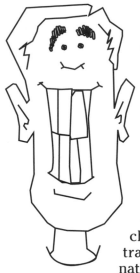

"supers" (Sanguine and Phlegmatic) are so ingrained with their respective outgoing and internal traits that all the training and experience in the world do not usually subdue their inherited characteristics. This may explain why some children can adopt a personality similar to someone they admire or associate with, while others cannot. Their natural temperament traits are not as severe as others.

Ideally, your personality should be an external expression of your character. That is the "transparent character" referred to in the Phillips translation of the Scriptures. Unfortunately, many people so despise or lightly esteem their real selves that they adopt false personalities that are quite unrelated to their character traits. Such individuals often develop mental or emotional problems. It is much better to let the Spirit of God make you internally into the kind of person you can approve of and love so you can relax in the Spirit and be yourself. Such a personality projection is a "good personality"—not because it is ideal, outgoing, or some other preferred quality, but because it is *you*. To quote Shakespeare, one of the keys to mental health is "To thine own self be true." When you understand your own temperament, you will be better able to analyze your personality to see if it is indeed a genuine reflection of the real you.

Leadership

All men possess leadership tendencies, some more than others. Those with strong leadership abilities are designated in the business world as SNLs—Strong Natural Leader. SNLs comprise 25 percent or less of the world's population. Most men are just ordinary leaders to one degree or another, but every man has both the capability and the desire to be a leader, particularly in his own home and marriage. I am convinced that this is a need in every man that, if not realized at least in his home life, will leave him unfulfilled. In some cases it may cause him to act irrationally. This characteristic is one of the many areas where a man differs from most women. While some strong-willed women (Cholerics) do enjoy leadership, they are in the minority. Instead, most women seem to shun leadership by nature, particularly in the home, and prefer the husband to take the lead. Unfortunately, the harmful teaching of feminine assertiveness of the feminist movement has produced an unnatural lifestyle of female-dominated homes that is making husbands irresponsible, wives frustrated, and children abnormal. Most men could solve this problem by asserting themselves and assuming the role of leadership God intended for them.

There is no question in the Bible as to the leadership capability of man. The first verse of Scripture that refers to man includes the statement that he should have "dominion over the fish . . . birds . . . cattle, over all the earth" (Gen. 1:26). Man's first sin occurred when he followed woman in disobedience, after which God said to her, "Your desire shall be for your husband, and he shall rule over you" (Gen. 3:16). All through the Bible, God used men to communicate his will to mankind. He used women when he could not get a man to do his work. That does not mean, of course, that women are unimportant! They have a vital role to play in God's scheme of things, but not in leadership, particularly in the home.

The most frustrated men I know are those whose naturally passive temperaments have been dominated by more aggressive wives. Such homes are incapable of happiness!

I have never met a happy henpecked husband—nor, for that matter, have I met a happy henpecker. You can count on this: In his frustration, a henpecked man will dedicate himself to making his henpecker miserable.

One goal every loving wife should have is to help her husband realize his subconscious need to be the leader of his home. No matter how passive he is, he will love her more and treat her better if he serves as their leader. Specific suggestions on becoming a good leader are discussed in chapter 11.

Productivity

The well-known Puritan work ethic is not just an ethic; it is a work compulsion—productivity. Deep within man is the God-given necessity to work, to accomplish, to be productive. It may surprise you to know that this has nothing to do with sin or the fall but is part of the Creator's design in the male being. According to Genesis 2:5, before man was created "there was no man to till the ground," so God made man with this in mind. After the creation of man and before the intrusion of sin, God placed man in the Garden of Eden "to tend and keep it" (v. 15). Obviously, then, God fashioned man with an original capacity to work. He did not set him in the Garden with the expectation of living freely off the land. Even before the fall, he was to tend it and keep it.

After the fall, God's command to Adam was even more specific, for he decreed, "In the sweat of your face you shall eat bread" (Gen. 3:19), and man has earned his livelihood by toil ever since. It is further instructional that the first two children born on earth are initially mentioned in relation to their areas of productivity: "Abel was a keeper of sheep, but Cain was a tiller of the ground" (Gen. 4:2).

Originally, and for centuries thereafter, the responsibilities of men and women were distinct, understood, and accepted. Women were to bear children and be "keepers at home"; men were to be the breadwinners, providers, and leaders of the home. Today our technologically sophisticated society is revamping those roles and creating more frustration and misery than the world has ever known—modern luxuries and conveniences notwithstanding. Later we shall consider the necessity of men to be productive and the various areas to which it should extend. Of one thing you can be certain—it is impossible for a man to accept himself unless he is productive.

Courage

Another basic ingredient in the complex nature of masculinity is courage. This trait varies with a man's temperament, as we shall see, but all men have it to one degree or another. Originally, it was this trait that made man the protector of his family, home, and country. A study of history is replete with illustrations of millions of men who had the courage to engage in mortal combat to protect those they loved. Courage is a trait both men and women possess but tend to manifest differently Women will courageously sacrifice themselves for their children, and history has recorded many female martyrdoms or voluntary slaveries to spare their young. When threatened, a woman may throw her body over her child for protection; not necessarily so for a man, for he might be more inclined to engage in combat with his aggressor.

This courageous spirit of man sent Columbus to sea to discover America. It induced Magellan to sail around the world, Lindbergh to fly to Europe, Neil Armstrong to walk on the moon, and many established businessmen to risk life and fortune in pursuit of some new goal.

Courage does not always involve risking one's physical safety, of course. Sometimes it means a professional venture or challenge against all kinds of odds. Many times it involves the courage to stand by one's convictions when to do so means standing alone. Admittedly, this is easier for some than for others, but for all it takes courage.

One distinctive aspect of courage that may be overlooked is that it does not preclude the presence of fear. In fact, most courageous men acknowledge that they were frightened prior to a feat of heroism. Whenever life is endangered or the future is threatened, one commonly entertains fear, but courage overcomes fear and compels a man to disregard this natural apprehension.

Mind

The mind of man easily sets him apart from all other living creatures. No animal has a brain that even remotely resembles man's; man's brain is more than twice as large as that of any other creature and possesses many times the thinking capacity. Scientists tell us that the average brain contains twelve billion cells, but most people use only 10 percent of its potential during a lifetime. A recently published book explains research indicating a relationship between a child's IQ and that of his parents. IQ is, in the words of the authors, "heritable,"[1] that is, it is passed on from parent to child. This thinking mechanism that we call the mind, together with the heart or emotional center, which we shall consider next, comprises the motor of man. Although scientists have made great strides in brain research, they admit to discovering only a fraction of its intricacies.

Somehow the mind of a man is different from that of a woman. This becomes apparent in childhood when most little boys lose interest in dolls very early and gravitate to trucks, cars, and sporting toys long before girls cease playing house enthusiastically. Certainly some of that is cultural and some is influenced by the child's temperament, but the differences of the sexes appear less in their genitalia than in their brains.

Nowhere is this distinction more apparent than in the masculine problem of the mental attitude of lust. After he has passed the "latency period" (the preadolescent years, usually around fourth to seventh grade), a boy begins puberty. At that time he starts to develop physically as a man and mentally cultivates an absorbing interest in girls. It is not uncommon for him to fantasize exploits with girls and young women, and he is highly susceptible to lust to a degree women find difficult to comprehend. Easily the most beautiful, fascinating, and intriguing sight in most men's brains is a woman's body. Jesus Christ knew about this uniquely male problem when he challenged men not to lust after women lest they commit adultery in their hearts (Matt. 5:28).

During his campaign for the White House, former President Jimmy Carter stirred up national interest when in a *Playboy* magazine article he inadvertently admitted that like every other man, even he had engaged in lust. This natural male weakness is related to his sex drive, which is intrinsically linked to his manhood and must be kept in control. The primary means of control include marriage, a good character, a strong spiritual life, and the avoidance of any suggestive or pornographic literature that would incite his mind or inflame his passions. The Bible teaches us that we must bring "every thought into captivity to the obedience of Christ" (2 Cor. 10:5).

It is a wise woman who understands this problem unique to men and keeps it in mind as she chooses her wardrobe and as she conducts herself around the opposite sex. When she marries, she will recognize that since the dawn of human history one of the primary purposes of marriage has always been to provide mutual sexual satisfaction. A good sex life in marriage can enable a man to control his sex drive and his thoughts, which in turn can improve his spiritual life.

Another mental area that usually distinguishes men from women involves a male's goal-oriented thinking pattern. Some would have us believe it is cultural, but I prefer to deem it a result of the male psyche mechanism. In either case, it is real. Women by nature tend to think vocationally of the home—the things that pertain to it, child raising, and the needs of her family. Men are apt to become absorbed in their vocational pursuits. A man's vocation, we must understand, is more than a means of livelihood, for if he likes his work, it often becomes the focal point of his life. If he doesn't keep his priorities in focus, his vocation may cease to be a means to an end and become an end in itself. As a result, his home life suffers, and he may even neglect fathering his children properly at a crucial time in their lives. Most men should take an objective look at themselves occasionally and restructure their priorities. In some instances—where an individual's work is seasonal or he experiences periods of unusually high pressure—vocational necessity may temporarily demand excessive time. But if he becomes a workaholic, something is wrong. The bull's-eye in every man's target should be the training of his children for the day they will graduate from his home. The man who lets his children take second place to his work lives to regret it.

Emotions

As indicated in the previous chapter, the notion that in their emotions men are stoics who face the dangers of life unafraid and never indulge intemperate passions is not derived from the real world. Men are probably not as emotional as women of the same temperament combinations, but they do have strong feelings. It is extremely important that both men and women understand their emotional potential, for it affects every area of their lives.

Scientists tell us that between our temples and behind our foreheads we possess an emotional center that is neurologically tied to every organ of the body. All physical action starts in that emotional center. If a person is upset, his condition originates in the emotional center and is carried to other areas of the body. That is why a tense person is so susceptible to all kinds of physical diseases. Dr. S. I. McMillen in *None of These Diseases,* an excellent book which all Christians should read, specifies fifty-one diseases to which the body is vulnerable because of protracted tension in the emotional center. He lists high blood pressure, heart attack, ulcers, colitis, arthritis, headaches, and many others. By the same token, when the emotional center is at peace, the entire body enjoys that relaxation. Tests have proved that emotionally relaxed individuals live longer and enjoy better health than those who are tense.

When Jesus Christ walked this earth, he addressed himself repeatedly to problems of the emotional center, which he called "the heart." He indicated that the heart causes the mouth to speak, that an evil heart produces evil thoughts, that a greedy man has a greedy heart. In short, to quote Solomon, "Keep your heart with all diligence, for out of it spring the issues of life" (Prov. 4:23). Consequently, you are what is in your heart! If your heart is evil, you are evil; if you are pure in heart, you will be pure in body. For this reason, every man should guard his heart, or emotional center, carefully.

Everyone knows that the human heart contains all kinds of feelings, both good and bad. As we shall see in analyzing manhood in light of the blends of temperament, the basic ingredients for feelings are inherited, but what we do with them is our responsibility. In some people, love and fear predominate; in others, hate and bitterness. But all have the basic ingredients for full feelings, and each adult is responsible for those that dominate him. We shall later clarify how to cultivate the best feelings, but it is sufficient here to note that feelings are not spontaneous. They are the products of thoughts. If your thoughts are good, so will be your feelings. If you sow the seeds of bad thoughts, you will reap a crop of evil feelings. Test yourself right now by examining your present feelings. They will identify the nature of your recent thoughts. Do you want to change your feelings? Then modify your thoughts, and *gradually* your feelings will be transformed.

Since we are talking primarily about manhood in this chapter, we should note an important difference between men and women that every man wishes his wife understood. Generally speaking, women have a greater capacity for love and affection than men. In fact, a woman's love has a height, depth, breadth, and elasticity that confounds most men. Perhaps it was divinely created as a part of the maternal instinct. But of this I am certain: Men have to work at manifesting love far more than women do. Not only does my counseling experience indicate this, but even more important, the Bible commands men four times to love their own spouses, where it only indirectly demands that of women. This difference between men and women should be understood by a husband and wife and diligently heeded by both. Every married man, realizing this male weakness, should seek God's help in deepening his love for his wife. Every wife should learn to accept this masculine weakness and avoid becoming bitter when, on occasion, his love for business, sports, or anything else seems to supersede his love for her. If she remains her loving, affectionate self, she can gradually cultivate a greater love in his heart for her. The male capacity for learning to love is evident in the lives of men in their mature years of life. Love and affection can be learned. But more of that later.

Body

The most obvious aspect of manhood and the one best understood is the body. Consequently, it is in need of the least comment here. I should point out that the many differences existing between men and women are clearly discernible in their bodies. Men tend to be taller, heavier, and bigger boned than women. An examination of a doctor's weight charts will indicate that the ideal poundage for women is considerably less than for men of the same height. Men have beards and coarser features; women tend to have smoother complexions and delicate features. Our terms *beautiful* and *handsome* certainly highlight the difference between the sexes—a man ceases to be handsome when he becomes beautiful, and no manly appearing woman is ever identified as beautiful. To further accentuate the bodily differences between men and women, one need only consider their entirely opposite yet complementary reproductive systems.

Man's body needs regular physical exercise. In recent years, insurance companies have alerted us to the fact that women tend to live seven to ten years longer than men. If you visit a senior-citizens' home, you will find far more octogenarian women than men, in spite of the fact that more boy babies are born than girl babies. Several known reasons are offered for this phenomenon, one of which is that men are faced with more pressures today than most women, or at least seem less able to endure stress. I'm not sure that is a satisfactory answer. I believe a man's body was designed for hard work and physical exercise. For most of the world's history this was routinely exacted by the rigors of life. Today a man is more apt to drive his power-equipped car to an automated office where he will push a few buttons, experience a variety of stress-producing emotions, and return home without even challenging his deodorant. He probably overeats more to appease his stress level than his hunger drive, and his diet of refined sugar, flour, and artificially prepared foods gradually transforms his magnificent physical machine into a sluggish relic in need of constant repair, long before he has much mileage on his odometer.

Fortunately, today we are becoming nationally health conscious. Men are jogging, jumping rope, cycling, and swimming; they are engaging in handball, racquetball, tennis, golf, and many other activities that will prolong their lives. Finally realizing that if their work does not provide them sufficient daily exercise they must look for it elsewhere, men are searching for programs of physical exercise. It is a matter of life or death.

One of my dearest friends is Dr. Kenneth Cooper, the famous aerobics specialist of Dallas, Texas. We ski together for a week each year at his winter home in the Colorado mountains. On some of our long ski lift rides he has talked about the increased interest in well-being today as compared to thirty years ago, especially for heart patients. Some doctors who thought him a quack then are now his patients. In fact, one day out on the slopes we met a surgeon who credited Dr. Cooper with saving his life: his heart problem was detected early by Dr. Cooper's famous treadmill stress test, and the man's health improved when he adhered to the follow-up fitness program. Thousands of men and many women are enjoying healthier, more active, and longer lives through regular jogging more than any other exercise. I have jogged over three miles a day, four or five times a week, for more than twenty-eight years, and I thank God that I enjoy near perfect health at an age twice as old as my father's when he died of a heart attack. I look forward to water- and snow-skiing in my eighties (many years from now!) and still play touch football with our grandsons. Even more important than the future it promises, jogging helps men to feel good about their manhood.

The failure of wives to understand man's basic need for regular exercise often produces a bone of contention in many fine homes. Instead of encouraging her husband in his athletic pursuits, his wife may resent the time it takes away from the family, particularly if she is confined much of the day to their home and children. Expecting her man to go to work every day and come straight home each night, she becomes resentful at his taking any time off "to play with the boys," interpreting it as an obvious indication that he doesn't love her the way he used to. If she nags him, she only increases his stress.

Admittedly, men can abuse their need for exercise and become physical-fitness nuts at the expense of the family. They may even use it as an excuse to avoid family responsibilities or, if a conflict has arisen, resort to the spa or health club instead of resolving marital difficulties. If time spent gaining physical fitness often comes at the expense of conjugal harmony, one can imagine what it does to an already deteriorating relationship. Of necessity, most physical exercise for contemporary man will demand time he could otherwise spend at home, but if pursued in moderation, the sweat-producing activity will usually give him vitality around the house and will definitely help him to live longer. It might even catapult him into attacking that "Honey, do" list—but don't count on it!

Let me offer an illustration from my heart. When one of my dearest friends died at forty-four, the family asked me to conduct his funeral. As is my custom, I walked forward to view the body and pray just before going to the platform. As I looked into his face and rubbed his cold hand affectionately, I could hear his dear wife sobbing just a few feet away. Suddenly I reflected, What a waste! My friend and his wife together had both killed him before his time. He ate all the wrong foods, and though I had begged him to diet several times, he regularly replied, "My wife makes such delicious goodies that I just can't say no." In addition, he seldom, if ever, engaged in strenuous physical exercise. He was an outstanding family man—as long as he lasted, which unfortunately wasn't even until his children finished school.

Because his adoring wife indulged his weakness for deep-fried foods, white bread, sweets, and carbohydrates, encouraging him to "come straight home from work and rest," my friend has stepped off this planet for the glories of the new city our Lord had prepared for him. Nevertheless, I have a hunch that his wife would encourage him to take better care of his physical machine if she had another chance.

Sexuality

The second most obvious characteristic of manhood and the least understood by the fairer sex (and sometimes even the man himself) is his sexuality. It is a time-acknowledged fact that men possess a stronger sex drive than women. This is not to minimize the woman's sex drive, however. Modern research clearly establishes her capacity to enjoy equal lovemaking pleasures in proper consummation of the act of marriage with her husband. But as in many other areas of their lives, men and women differ sexually.

It is almost impossible to exaggerate the role of man's sexuality in his makeup, for it is an important source of his masculinity, manliness, chivalry, and aggressiveness. Stripped of his sex drive, he is reduced to a neutral in almost every vital area of life. Eunuchs rarely distinguish themselves in any field. The hidden force that colors man's thinking, giving him three-dimensional fantasies and stereophonic female perception, is the result of his natural ability to manufacture billions of sperm cells a week. One oft-quoted female comment best describes many women's confusion on this subject: "Men are sexual animals." That statement is wrong on two counts, for they are not animals and they are not abnormal, as the comment suggests. All normal men are sexual creatures. Individual temperament, however, will determine the manner of expressing sexuality.

One difference between men and women that causes undue heartache, particularly in the early years of marriage, is in the way they are aroused sexually. A woman usually enjoys a long buildup to sexual intercourse that includes many affectionate interchanges, kind acts of love, and tender expressions of approval. She enjoys a long, slow burn. Not so her partner. His route to arousal is through the eye to the brain, then to his emotional center, and directly to his sex organs. Unless he learns self-control, and she learns to interpret what she considers "passion" as really her man's way of showing love and affection, they will experience trouble. That is one of the major areas both need to work on during the adjustment stage (usually the first three years, though with some couples it comprises the first fifty). My wife and I have tried to detail some of these vital areas in our book *The Act of Marriage* because it is supremely important for both partners to know.

I have delayed a consideration of the male ego to this point because it so perfectly fits in here, for it is intrinsically tied in with a man's acceptance of his masculinity, which is linked to his sexuality. The two things that fracture the male ego most quickly are threats to his masculinity and fear of sexual inadequacy. What he fails to realize is that his emotions control his sex drive. I have counseled athletes and fantastic physical specimens of manliness who were impotent not because they were sexually deficient, but because anger at someone or something short-circuited their sexual capability on some occasion. Then fear stifled their performances, and they subsequently became emotionally induced eunuchs. The remedy for the problem was not medicine or other physical treatment, but the correction of their emotional malfunctions. Anger is often stronger in a man than love. Consequently, his sexual inability shatters his male ego and adds insecurity to his problems. As we shall see, anger and bitterness are cruel slave drivers.

Whether recognized or not, marriage is a threat to every man's sexuality and consequently to his male ego.

Fortunately, it usually occurs when his sex drive is the greatest (around age twenty-one). If he and his bride wed with the approval of his parents and no animosity exists in his heart, he can—with loving consideration, reading, and/or counseling—become a good lover. I am convinced that any man can be a dynamic lover, but success is not automatic. Like anything else worthwhile in life, love-making is an art to be learned. Unfortunately, if a man assumes that "anyone can do it," makes no preparation, indulges in hatred or bitterness, and does only what comes naturally, he will get his wife pregnant but not bring her sexual satisfaction and delight. And in the long run that will frustrate them both. Many an ordinary man is a fantastic lover in the eyes of his wife, and that is a goal every man should strive for. Such men do not have to strut their sexuality, brag about their exploits, or flex their muscles to prove their manhood, for they are secure in their masculinity.

A word familiar to young people in the seventies was *machismo.* To them it signified a man who was virile and masculine, sparkling with charisma and sex appeal. I discovered in Venezuela that the word had a less distinguished meaning than our youth suspected. In Spanish-speaking countries, it stemmed from the word *macho,* which means "animal." Thus, machismo really meant "the sexual superiority and animal appeal of men." It was supposed to give the man sexual license to use the woman, obligating her to care for the children while he lived to the satisfaction of the flesh. In that culture one encountered a male-dominated world. In fact, a man may marry one woman but maintain four or five others on the side. Not only did men fulfill this role, but women expected it! In actuality, a man's machismo seems related to how many women he kept on his string— children and all. In Mexico, a man automatically gained control of the children in a divorce unless he was caught in the act of adultery. Machismo, then, served as the popular term for "Don Juan" or "Casanova," but it distinctly did not correspond with *masculinity.*

A truly masculine man has a streak of chivalry in him that causes him to control his sex drive, and instead of using a woman, he will protect her. In days of old, knights actually fought to defend a woman's virtue, honor, and life. Such actions should characterize our society today, but they are becoming rare. *Redbook* magazine published an article describing the shocking things some married men do to working women (against their will but under threat of job loss). The article reported that nine out of ten working women surveyed claimed that they had been molested, humiliated, or subjected to other forms of sexual harassment, such as lurid or insulting remarks, often by male employers.

But the age of chivalry is not dead. In fact, an engineer recently jeopardized his job in a spontaneous show of it to a superior. He had watched his attractive secretary repeatedly being embarrassed and humiliated by their lecherous department superintendent until he could stand it no longer. He went into the boss's office, closed the door, very calmly objected to these unprovoked advances, and warned that if they didn't stop, he would meet the superintendent outside and teach him "some respect for womanhood." Now that is masculinity!

You may say, "What if he's bigger than I?" Organize a task force! You will find others who agree with you, but don't shirk your responsibility. Something inside you will begin to die if you do.

I have long admired my missionary brother-in-law, Bill Lyons, for something he did as a GI during the invasion of Germany in World War II. After his unit secured a small village, he was searching for hidden enemy troops when he heard a scream. Kicking open the door of a small house, he caught sight of his own sergeant in the process of trying to rape a young German woman. Pointing his rifle at the man, Bill commanded, "Leave her alone!" and nodded to the girl to leave. At the risk of making an enemy of a superior or of taking a bullet in the back someday, his manly instincts impelled him to protect a helpless woman he didn't know and with whom he couldn't even communicate. Somewhere in Germany today, a woman knows that some American men love and respect womanhood and will instinctively rise to protect it. Otherwise she might have harbored the bitter thought that Americans are animals masquerading as men—sergeant stripes notwithstanding.

One dictionary equates masculinity with manliness, for it defines manliness as "that which pertains to masculinity" and adds "as opposed to femininity." I would be remiss not to point out the importance of men being men and women being women—starting with early childhood. Due to the emphasis on legitimizing homosexuality by many in education, media, and the entertainment industry, we already find too many young men, insecure or dissatisfied with their role as men, who adopt female attire and mannerisms. A television documentary recently stated that over ten thousand such men have indicated a desire to have their sex changed surgically. They could offer no biological reason why they felt "more comfortable as women," but ever since Christine Jorgensen's well-publicized operation more than thirty years ago, such requests have been on the increase. The sex direction of a young person is not set by the genes or glands. It is determined largely by inherited temperament plus the influences of very early childhood. The last thing a sensitive child needs is a smother-love relationship with mother, or an unaffectionate, ever-rejecting father. The following are needs all children share in order to grow up with the proper sex direction:

1. Affectionate parents who freely show their children love and acceptance.
2. Parents who accept the sex of their children and let them know it.
3. Proper masculine role models.
4. The early wearing of clothes of their sex.
5. Learning to accept their own sex and to be thankful for it.

Developing manliness in boys was scarcely a problem in past generations. A boy had to become rugged to survive.

If he didn't get manliness training in school, he certainly received it at home on the business end of a plow or while chopping a cord of wood or going hunting with Dad. Today it is more difficult for boys to cultivate such manly traits and mannerisms because of our less physical ways. But it is good therapy for every lad to try his hand at sports, outdoor activities, and arduous chores.

In defense of the sensitive, quiet, artistic man or boy: One does not have to be a rugged, overbearing extrovert to be a real man. History reveals that many genuine men who helped mold our destiny were not particularly robust. James Madison, our nation's fourth president, would never have made it as an NFL football player. Frail and sickly by nature, doctors did not predict a normal life span for him. In fact, they advised against his going into the ministry, which was his first desire. Instead, they suggested that this brilliant young man study law. He did, and became the father of the Constitution and lived to be eighty-one years of age. His main contribution to America was the First Amendment to the Constitution, which has guaranteed freedom of religion for more than two hundred years. You don't have to be a six-foot-six, three-hundred-pound behemoth to be a giant of a man. And you don't have to possess a Choleric temperament to be forceful and effective.

We shall see that these outward manifestations are primarily a result of inherited temperament, not necessarily an indication of manhood. But sensitive individuals, particularly those cheated out of a proper masculine example in the home, would be advised to avoid excessively graceful mannerisms and gestures and cultivate more manly deportment—not to enrich their manhood but to avoid giving a false impression.

A high school teacher who went out of his way to help me provides a timely illustration. A gifted mathematician and philosopher, he was highly cerebral—a truly dedicated teacher. His father died shortly after the teacher was born, and he was raised in the city by his mother and two older sisters. Because he was such a good man, it always grieved me that the kids mocked him behind his back because of his gentle spirit and graceful gestures. One day in study hall the situation got out of hand and some obnoxious rowdies taunted him openly. He tried to ignore it, but finally his boiling point was reached, and he gave three boys some hot blasts with the paddle he kept hidden in his desk. That solved the problem for the rest of that year, but I've often thought that such a dedicated teacher would have been more productive had he adopted more masculine mannerisms. Unfortunately for him, he didn't have a masculine role model or a man who showed interest in him to encourage him to take up weight lifting or other athletic pursuits in his youth. In today's culture, with so many single women raising children, millions of boys need male companionship from time to time. My good fortune was that my masculinity was set before my father's death when I was nine. But I was also blessed by men in our church who took me under their wing to help nurture me. I treasure the memory of one particular Sunday school teacher who really helped me when I was in the sixth grade. Any Christian man who wants a ministry helping boys today doesn't have to look very far. Next to sharing your faith with a boy, the best thing a good man can do for a boy is help him develop his manhood.

The Boy in Every Man

Beneath the folds of every man's complex nature lurks a fun-loving boy. At times the boy in him may dominate, so that, in spite of adult responsibilities that stifle these boyish tendencies, sooner or later this boy within will surface like a cork under water.

Some men are practical jokers; others are adventuresome lovers of excitement. Still others never forget their exploits as star quarterback on the Pop Warner football team or as sixth-grade sprint champion. Some think the freeway is a glorified version of the Saturday night stock car races, while others let the boy in them take over while attending a sporting event, enjoying the circus, or tramping the golf course. The boy in every man makes him seek some element of excitement. A sixty-seven-year-old psychiatrist who rode horseback every morning justified it to a reporter by saying, "Every man has a need for excitement to perpetuate his manhood. For some it is contact sports, hunting or fishing, or perhaps some form of competition. For me it is horseback riding. This diversion helps keep me young."

You have no doubt noticed that young fathers like to give their sons toys that they can play with themselves. For our son Larry's second Christmas I bought him an electric train—just what I needed to renew my boyish ways. Several years ago I had a mental flashback to my youth, recalling an experience when I was only five years old. Sneaking downstairs the night before Christmas, I had peeked into a long cardboard box that contained a splendid model airplane. What startled me in the flashback was that for the first time it dawned on me that I never saw the airplane again. During the next visit with my mother, I asked her about it, and she immediately started to laugh. It seems that my father had succumbed to the insatiable desire to put that plane together and fly it the night before Christmas. He flew it all right—out into the night and lost it forever!

There seems to be a streak in every man in which the boy in him takes over and the woman in his life thinks he is just a boy grown tall. Although a man may indulge this boy within him so much that he never grows up, he will normally use it for a welcome diversion. That's what makes him play so hard on a holiday that he can barely pull his stiff, aching body out of bed to go to work the next day. Occasionally he needs that kind of diversion.

During one of our treks to the desert, my wife commented, "I don't understand you men. You work for two days packing and getting ready for a three-day outing, then struggle for two more days of cleaning up when you get home. You ride off on your motorcycle through the hot desert sand for miles and return a sweaty, muddy mess!" Fortunately for me, she understood as I said, "Honey, when I throw my leg over that motorcycle seat and kick the starter, it takes only thirty seconds for me to roar off into my boyhood again for a few hours and leave behind the responsibilities of the church, college, and everything else. It's good for the four of us [our two sons, our son-in-law, and me] to act like boys trying to stay ahead of each other or just grabbing a few thrilling moments together. I guess I need that kind of excitement once in a while." She must have understood, because later when I bought a new motorcycle, I overheard her say to our daughter-in-law, "Kathy, there's only one difference between a man and a boy—the man's toys are more expensive." Further proof that she understood the need to keep that boy alive in me came on my sixtieth birthday. She gave me a new off-road dirt motorcycle that I thoroughly enjoy. It's really unfortunate that all wives don't understand that the boy in every man is a necessary part of his nature. They would both be happier if she did.

This part of the book was written during the holiday season, as both college and professional football seasons were coming to an end. As one wife said, "An end? There's no end to bowl games—there's Cotton, Sugar, Orange, Rose, and Super Bowls. Why don't they have a Wife Bowl so we can get reacquainted with our husbands?" Her wail is not so uncommon today, as ninety-seven million TV viewers concentrate on the tube Monday nights, Saturdays, and Sundays. (Be grateful for one thing: Thursday-night Canadian football didn't make it on American TV.)

It may be hard for wives to understand, but the boy in every man is what makes him a sports lover. The world over, every country or culture has its own favorite sports, from hockey to soccer and rugby to tennis. While men are young enough, they participate in the competition. As they get older, they become spectators and enjoy the game vicariously. Now that TV brings such events into our homes, it is understandable that it becomes a bone of contention when the wife doesn't share her husband's enthusiasm for the game. Many homes start each new year off in bitterness because football has generated so much hostility on New Year's Day. If that happens in your house, consider the following suggestions. Not all of them will work for everyone. Find those that best fit your home.

1. *If you can't beat 'em, join 'em.* Most women who don't like football fail to understand it. Remember, you can't enjoy anything until it becomes intelligible. (That's probably why Wagnerian operas have never sent me into ecstasy—I don't understand German.) Many wives (including my own) have learned the significance of four downs to gain ten yards and the importance of the third-down play. After that, football is a breeze. My wife is as big a football nut as I am now that she has learned to understand the game. It has become a significant occasion for family enjoyment. Many a wife has cheated herself out of hours of fun with her family by just never learning to understand the game. Look at it this way— 50 years of marriage times 3 NFL games a week times 17 weeks in a season totals about 2,550 professional games in a lifetime. (It is estimated that 10 billion man-hours were spent watching Super Bowl XXV.) Couples might as well have 2,500 mutually enjoyable experiences instead of that many reasons for conflict. But that will happen only if the wife learns to understand the game.

2. *If you can't learn to enjoy it with him, try to accept his interest cheerfully.* After all, there are thirty-five other weeks in the year. Doing something practical or pleasurable while he is watching his favorite game and maintaining a positive spirit will produce a more appreciative husband the rest of the year. According to my experience, a wife is more likely to incur a fifteen-yard penalty for unsportsmanlike conduct than score a touchdown when she pressures her husband into giving up football "for the old lady." The one man I knew who discarded his favorite pastime for that reason died a little inside. He didn't fight her, but the inner stress that mounted when he was forced to give up something he enjoyed has taken a toll on the boy inside. Someday she may not like the boyless man he is becoming.

3. *The Bible teaches, "Let your moderation be known unto all men" (Phil. 4:5 KJV).* Admittedly, there is a point in most men when the boy gets out of hand. If something occurs repeatedly, a wife should have a frank talk with her husband in love, gently suggesting that he may be indulging his "boy" or hobby too much. He needs to use the boy within him to relax and unwind from the usual pressures of life, but when it becomes an excuse to hide behind or selfishly indulge his own pleasure at the expense of the family or his spiritual life, it has been converted from a healthy diversion to a harmful obsession.

4. *Don't nag him!* Solomon said that a nagging wife annoys like constant dripping (Prov. 19:13). Nothing turns a man off faster. I suspect that the boy in the man is responsible for making him react to nagging with violence, sarcasm, sullenness, or silence, depending on his temperament. Perhaps he finds it detestable because it reminds him of his mother or reduces him to a mother-son relationship with his wife. Nagging is one of the worst habits a wife can adopt. Unfortunately, unless a wife overcomes that bad habit when she is young, she becomes worse later in life. For as women grow older, they often become more verbal. That can be good or bad, depending on the communication habits she has gathered along the way. As a husband of forty-five years said after divorcing his wife, "I just wanted some peace and quiet. That woman would never shut up."

5. *Submit yourself to God, your husband, and prayer.* If your husband's indulgence of his boy nature is indeed excessive, your heavenly Father knows it. He will fight for you by convicting your husband and giving you grace. Though it will take practice on your part, submission will be worth it in the long run as you build a sound marriage relationship. Always remember, you cannot change either the man (or the boy) you are married to, but God can! Give him time.

6. *Even in football, "give thanks."* Millions of widows, divorcées, and singles wish they had your problem.

Can a man offer a reasonable explanation for his oftentimes boyish actions? Of course not. It is the boy in him that motivates some deeds that a woman may label immature, whereas to a man they are natural.

It's the boy in the man that makes it impossible for him to resist the challenge of that sports car revving its engine at a red light.

It's the boy in the man that makes the middle-aged father offer to play quarterback for the neighborhood kids on the front lawn.

It's the boy in the man that makes him go out fishing when they're not biting, in hopes that he'll get that big one.

It's the boy in the man that makes him scare his wife with a dead mouse.

It's the boy in the man that makes him put salt in the sugar on April Fools' Day.

It's the boy in the man that makes him punch the tops of the chocolates in search of a caramel.

It's the boy in the man that brings home that puppy his wife has absolutely forbidden, consoling himself all the way home with, "When she sees it, she just can't help but love it!"

It's the boy in the man that makes it impossible for him to walk by a construction project without looking into the hole or over the fence.

It's the boy in the man that makes him send his wife on a treasure hunt to find her Christmas present.

It's the boy in the man that makes him lift, shake, and poke at his Christmas present when no one is looking.

It's the boy in the man that threatens his wife, "When you turn forty, I'll trade you in on two twenties."

Here is an interesting aside to women. When collecting the above list of boyish traits, I found eighteen women who unanimously agreed that men act more like babies when they get sick than women do. This impression echoes a comment by the wife of an outstanding Christian leader when she was asked about her husband's greatest weakness: "When he gets sick, he turns into a big baby." One

Melancholic wife declared, "We women were made to suffer pain. When you men get sick, you can't handle it." I'm
not sure women were meant to suffer any more than men,
except in childbirth as a result of the fall, but it certainly
becomes apparent that they suffer with greater maturity.
A doctor friend once told me, "If God had created us so
that the wife bore the first child and the husband the second, I am confident that most couples would likely have a
third, but I guarantee there would never be a fourth!"

The boy in the man frequently causes trouble early in a
marriage. A woman enters marriage intent upon giving herself so much to her husband that she anticipates a gradual
exclusion of her old girlfriends. When his failure to follow
suit is reflected by plans to "go skiing with the boys" or continue his hunting, fishing, golfing, or bowling, the young
bride is often offended and can become resentful. It is a
wise young woman who understands his boyish needs to
get together with his old friends occasionally. If she makes
it unpleasant, she may create unnecessary bitterness.
These things, if given enough time, usually take care of
themselves just by virtue of the complexity of life. Besides,
occasional absences are good for couples. Send him on a
fishing trip for a weekend with your blessing, and he will
return to you a much more loving and grateful person.

It's the boy in the man that gives him that trapped feeling after a few weeks of marriage. He often fantasizes about
bachelor freedom in "the good old days." With most men,
however, a few such outings with the boys convince him
that, except in rare instances, it's more enjoyable to be with
his wife and family. If your church holds annual men's and
women's retreats, be sure you both attend, for you both
need the companionship of your own sex and an occasional
rest from each other.

One couple I know found they were entirely different in
one major area. He loved outdoor activities such as hunting and skiing, whereas she disdained any form of camp-
ing. A motor home with hot and cold running water was her
idea of roughing it. She refused to join him on any outdoor
activity and became resentful when he went with his dad.

Needless to say, they have endured unnecessary stress in their marriage, and even now I fear for their future.

Many a wise woman has learned to camp out and rough it just to build a relationship with the man (boy) she loves. Gradually, she can wean him away from some of these activities and learn to share others with him. But it is most important that she not expect him to quench the boy inside the man quickly or entirely. A man without the boy inside becomes a boring man!

Conclusion

Well, there he is in all his complex splendor, all ten parts of him. If you recall, I warned that he is not as easy to understand as most people think, but you haven't seen anything yet. Just wait until we begin to apply the various temperaments to these ten areas of manhood. Then you will understand why some characteristics predominate in some men and seem incidental in others.

Before that necessary application can be made, however, we must take careful note of the very core of human nature. In the Complexity of Manhood circle at the beginning of this chapter, the center is blank. Because that core is so basic in both men and women, I chose to place it in a chapter by itself.

The illustration in the next chapter replaces that blank center with man's "self"—the core of personhood without which man is incomplete.

3

The Core of Human Nature

he heart and core of all human nature, both male and female, is one's unseen spiritual life. Because it is invisible and impossible to locate scientifically, humanists deny its existence. They do not comprehend it, but its significance is so great that unless man takes it into account, he will never fully understand or explain the complexities of human behavior.

The spiritual side of man's nature was placed in the center of the Complexity of Manhood circle because it is the very core of personhood. Located there, it touches all ten of the other areas of your complex nature, drawing upon and influencing each. It would be impossible to exaggerate the importance of this spiritual core of man, for it can illuminate one or more parts of manhood at the exclusion of others and, more important, strengthen a man's weakest areas. No other area of human nature has the potential, with God's help, for positive change in a person like the spiritual core.

This vital core of man, the spirit (called the *ego* and/or *id* by Freud and his disciples), is the seat of self-consciousness.

The Complexity of Manhood

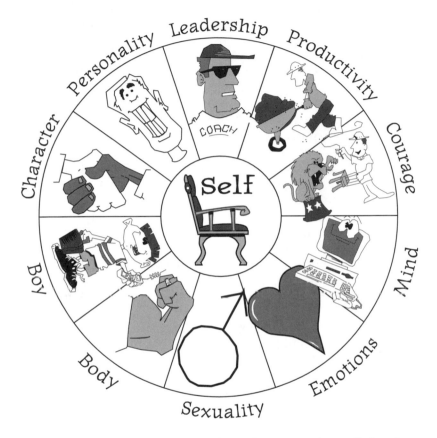

The most influential aspect of man's spirit is his will, for the manner in which he exercises his will determines the way he utilizes all other aspects of his nature. For example, two men of identical temperament and general characteristics will be as different as their degrees of selfishness, for self-ishness determines how we use our will.

Because man has will, he can obey God or disobey him as he wishes, for God in his sovereignty has chosen to give man that prerogative. History bears ample evidence to the fact that the majority of people have chosen the broad road of self-will, though some have elected the narrow road that leads to life. The spirit of man, the part of personhood that is eternal, is the victim of the decision of his will, for where the spirit spends eternity is determined by whether the will submits to God.

Although most modern philosophers, psychiatrists, and educators say little about this all-important spiritual core of man, the Bible refers to it on many occasions. Why should we turn to God's Book to diagnose this core of personhood? Because Zechariah 12:1 tells us that the Lord "forms the spirit of man within him." From the spirit's location at the center of the manhood chart, you can readily see how it can draw on the mind, emotions, sexuality, productivity, or other aspects of a person's nature. It can rightly be said that as the spirit goes, so goes the person. Because the will is the most powerful single aspect of a person in determining behavior, we will profit in this study by examining it carefully.

The best symbol to communicate this unique human characteristic of will is a throne, for like a king on his throne, the self in every man sits astride that throne, making the decisions of life—what you wear, eat, do, and so on. If you are a self-centered person, you make all these decisions with only yourself in mind—without realizing that you have chosen the best means to destroy yourself. You will never find a happy selfish person—not for long, anyway.

Everyone has a self-life. That is perfectly normal. Jesus Christ even took it for granted when he said, "Love your neighbor as yourself." There is nothing wrong with self-love, for you would be abnormal if you didn't love yourself. That, in part, is the seat of self-preservation, self-respect, self-acceptance, and self-confidence. The apostle Paul even approved of loving your own body, for he said, "Husbands ought to love their own wives as their own bodies" (Eph. 5:28). But in both these passages, self-love is *not* to exceed neighbor-love or wife-love. The man who treats his body better than his wife is selfish! The man who loves himself more than his neighbor is self-indulgent.

Who's Normal?

In a crazy, mixed-up world, it would be helpful to distinguish between the normal and the abnormal. Based on the above Scriptures, a person who loves himself as he does his neighbor and, if married, loves his wife as he does his own body is normal. The abnormal man or woman will fall into one of two categories—he will hate or reject or depreciate himself, or he will overevaluate himself. The first is called a self-deprecator, the latter an egotist. Naturally there will be degrees of both, as shown on the following chart.

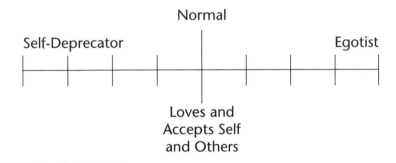

Being an extreme self-deprecator usually so immobilizes a person that he makes no use of his natural talents or capabilities. In desperate straits he may even take his own life. At the other extreme, a strong egotist is such an obnoxious, unlikable person that he tempts others to take his life for him.

Just weeks before his daughter left for college, a super-selfish father, separated from his wife, phoned the house and asked his daughter to call his wife to the phone so he could—under the threat of suicide—demand a reconciliation. Failing in that, he killed himself while they were both listening. His selfishness had reached such obsessive proportions that he actually lost his self-preservation instinct. Selfishness is a destroyer that devours in direct proportion to its intensity—in either direction.

Selfishness is the supreme sin! Consequently, the pursuit of the so-called normal amount of self-acceptance, love, and self-interest is every individual's supreme quest. It is essential to a well-balanced life, for it provides self-preservation—without self-centeredness—to sustain life, self-acceptance—without pride or arrogance—to make good use of one's talents, and self-confidence—based on a growing vital faith in God—that envisions the impossible and scoffs at pessimism. None of these predominates at the expense of other people, however. A normal, or unselfish, person will always be others-conscious; he will genuinely desire to help and serve his neighbor. A selfish, or abnormal, person is so self-interested that he makes all decisions strictly on the basis of "what is good for me." We accept that attitude in babies; we expect far more from adults. As an experienced marriage counselor, I can say without hesitation that the number one cause of marital disharmony is selfishness. Never do I have to counsel normal people who are others-conscious. Furthermore, I have noticed that the intensity of the problems of the self-centered people is in direct proportion to their selfishness. Only those with adult bodies and childish hearts or spirits find it impossible to resolve their differences.

The Normal Maturing Process

One universal trait shared by all babies is selfishness; they are controlled by it. It matters not to a baby that mother is tired at 3:30 A.M. If his tummy is empty, he screams out his discomfort until his exhausted mother attends to his need. Babies think they are the only creatures on earth and by the painful process of maturing must learn that others exist. That's why we call this process growing up.

The home was designed by God to be a haven of love, but each child needs to learn that he cannot always have his own way or his wants supplied immediately. He needs to learn the art of unselfishness when playing with other children. You undoubtedly have seen a child grab toys from others and cry, "Mine!" embarrassing his parents but not the selfish child himself. Fortunately, God has given him two parents who love him enough to teach him tenderly, but firmly, that he must share and give—in short, think of someone besides himself. The first five years are the most important for any child, for during this period he must practice unselfishness. Failure to learn during this preschool period makes it more difficult to learn unselfishness with each passing year. The parent that falters in teaching his child to become others-conscious—and to obey authority—lives to regret it later.

Adolescent

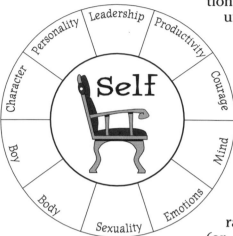

The oil that reduces the friction of interpersonal relationships is maturity, or unselfishness. Parents who have made some headway in this area during the early years of life will find the traumatic teen years almost a delight. All teens experience a variety of emerging forces as their bodies (including hormones), minds, and emotions mature rapidly. If they are normal (or appropriately others-conscious for their age level) and have a positive attitude, they will be able to face the natural turmoil of insecurity, sex drive, unstable emotions, rebellion, seeking for approval, and a host of other growing pains, and thus they will ride out the storm. At best, adolescence is a period of tribulation. The last thing a young person needs is an infantile self-life. Christian parents have a distinct advantage here if they set goals to lead their children to Christ early in life, provide a loving Christian atmosphere in the home, and see that they remain active in a spiritually alive, Bible-teaching church during those tempestuous years of a youngster's life.

"How old do you have to be to get married?" many young people ask. I always answer, "When you are old enough to think about someone besides yourself." In some young people that occurs around the ages of 18 to 23; in others 95 to 125. Let's face it, many adults have never grown up.

By examining the four selfishness diagrams, I'm sure you will grasp the principle. When the hub or core of a person is so selfish that it almost engulfs the entire wheel, creativity and natural talents are all but stifled; all close, vital interpersonal relationships become ineffective. But when a per-

Adult

son matures or becomes normal, others-conscious, or unselfish (I use these terms interchangeably), he will make maximum use of his God-given potential and will be loved and accepted by others. But no man can do this without God's help! In addition, a good home life and loving parents who exercise proper discipline are a great asset to any young man or woman. Such a background will help one adjust to life and other people better than unconcerned or absentee parents, but no man can realize his creativity and potential independent of God.

The Universal Need for God

No matter how good a person is, no matter how mature or unselfish he may be, the Bible declares that "all have sinned and fall short of the glory of God" (Rom. 3:23) and "there is none righteous, no, not one" (Rom. 3:10). In all my travels and conversations with people, I have never met anyone who claimed to be perfect. Better than others, perhaps, but not perfect.

The good news to such individuals is that "God so loved the world that He gave His only begotten Son, that whoever believes in Him should not perish but have everlasting life" (John 3:16). That verse confers the best possible news to all human beings and, like many other passages, makes it clear that because of his love for mankind, God has made ample provision for forgiving our sins and errors through the death of his Son, Jesus Christ, on the cross. Because he rose bodily from the tomb on the third day, God now offers forgiveness and cleansing to everyone who will believe or trust in his Son. This offer is open to every person who will by faith receive Jesus Christ as Savior and Lord by personal invitation.

The Natural Spirit

No man was ever born with Christ in his life. As symbolized here, Christ is outside the individual's spirit life—or core. It doesn't matter that this person was blessed with ideal parents who raised him to be a mature, unselfish individual because, as we have seen, no one can claim perfection, for "all have sinned." He needs to personally invite Jesus Christ to come into his life as Lord and Savior. Jesus explained in Revelation 3:20, "Behold, I stand at the door and knock. If anyone hears My voice and opens the door, I will come in to him and dine with him, and he with Me." The Bible also promises in John 1:12, "But as many as received Him, to them He gave the right to become children of God, even to those who believe in His name."

The Natural Man

In the eyes of God it really doesn't matter if the individual is like the one pictured above—a good man but not perfect, with Christ on the outside of his life—or a superselfish individual who has turned to a life of crime. Both must face the reality that Christ remains on the outside of their lives.

Eventually the natural man pictured here will begin to feel guilty before God because of his sins. In addition, his transgressions will rob him of the blessings and potential that God designed him to enjoy. The greater the sin, the greater the misery. Such a man needs to receive Jesus Christ as Savior and Lord.

You no doubt have noticed that emphasis has been placed on receiving Christ both as Savior *and* Lord. You need a *Savior* from past sins, but you also need a *Lord* for your future! The one element of conversion least understood by people today is that receiving Christ is not some easy experience of believing and having their sins forgiven without surrendering their will. If it were, believers would go right on running their own lives with little or no change of conduct. Be sure of this: When you accept Jesus Christ, making him your Savior and Lord, your conduct will change. The Scripture tells us that old things—habits and attitudes—will pass away and all things will become new to those who are *in* Christ (2 Cor. 5:17).

The Christ-Controlled Man

The man who blasphemed God prior to becoming his child will stop using the Lord's name in vain, as a curse or in a disrespectful manner, after he receives him as Lord and Savior. This will not likely occur instantaneously (habit is a cruel taskmaster), but gradually he will clean up his speech, behavior, and other old vices.

God is interested in the whole of an individual's life. He wants to forgive it, bless it, and use it. That is why salvation involves repentance from self-will. Whenever a person truly receives Jesus Christ, he exchanges the seat of authority in his life from one of self-will to Christ's will. That is, he voluntarily turns the control of his life over to Christ and at that moment becomes his servant. Notice the exchange of roles in the next diagram.

Christ is now the Lord of the man's life, and the new believer has voluntarily become the servant of Christ. Initially the individual receives *pardon*—forgiveness for all his sins—which produces a new *peace* with God in place of his previous guilt and fear. In addition, he now possesses a new *power*, for Christ has actually come into his life with a new Spirit that, as we shall see, offers a whole new dimension of strength that will enable the man to overcome his natural weaknesses. In addition, he has gained *joy* and *love* and a new purpose for living that can unbelievably expand his entire life, and he can enjoy the "abundant life" that Jesus Christ offers mankind. He said, "I have come that they may have life, and that they may have it more abundantly" (John 10:10).

Before you read another page, carefully examine the next two diagrams and ask yourself which one represents you *right now*.

If you find that your life is represented by the diagram on the left, then I urge you right now to bow your head and ask Jesus Christ into your life as Lord and Savior, just as the Bible teaches that you should. If you do not know how to pray but would like to, please consider the following sample prayer: *Dear God, I realize I am a self-willed sinner and*

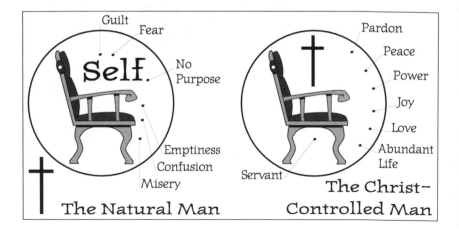

*ask Jesus Christ to come into my life as Savior and Lord. I give
myself to you.*

If this prayer adequately expresses the attitude of your
heart, I urge you to stop right now and pray it. If you have
done so sincerely, the Bible guarantees that you are now a
saved, or born-again, Christian.

> If you confess with your mouth the Lord Jesus and believe in your
> heart that God has raised Him from the dead, you will be saved.
> For with the heart one believes to righteousness, and with the
> mouth confession is made to salvation.
>
> Romans 10:9–10

> For "whoever calls upon the name of the LORD shall be saved."
>
> Romans 10:13

Born to Live

According to our Lord himself, if you have prayed that
prayer in faith, you are a born-again Christian. In John 3
(thought by many to be the most important chapter in the
Bible) there are several comparisons between physical
birth and spiritual birth. For example, no one is ever born
into adulthood. We all begin life as helpless babies and need
a mother's love and nurturing to get us started on the road
to physical adulthood. It takes years of food, rest, exercise,
training, education, and effort to grow up just to be normal.
We have all seen the tragedy of children devoid of adequate
care and feeding. Many eventually make it but often show
the marks of malnutrition throughout life.

Similarly, many newborn Christians do not understand
that it is equally as essential for them to feed their new spiritual life on a regular basis in order to grow into a strong
mature Christian. The Scripture says, "as newborn babies,
desire the pure milk of the word, that you may grow
thereby" (1 Peter 2:2). Just what mother's milk is to the newborn baby so is the Word of God to baby Christians. In fact,
on the basis of my experiences in training hundreds of men
in small groups or one on one, I can emphatically say that

if you do not follow up your conversion experience with regular feeding—mentally and spiritually—on the Word of God, you will never be a strong Christian.

Mr. America Was Not Born That Way

I recall an experience I had when I was in the Air Force, stationed at Las Vegas Army Air Base (now Nellis Field). One of our physical training instructors was an ardent weight lifter; Clancy Ross was the first person I ever saw pump iron. One weekend he went to Los Angeles and won the Mr. America title. I was not surprised, for he had a magnificent body. But Clancy Ross was not born with the body of Mr. America—he built it. Admittedly, he inherited the potential for a good body from his parents at birth, but he cooperated with nature, ate the right foods, got enough rest, and exercised his body into that beautifully muscled man of twenty-five that won that coveted award.

That is a near-perfect comparison to us as Christians now that God has given us the gift of spiritual life. We must feed and exercise that spiritual life, and God will cause us to grow into strong and effective Christians. It won't happen overnight, and it won't happen without your cooperation.

The importance to growth of regular, continuous feeding on the Word of God cannot be overemphasized. I have never seen a strong, effective Christian who did not regularly read the Bible. Unfortunately, however, our churches are full of baby Christians who have been attending the services for years, but are more like three-year-old children walking around in thirty-year-old bodies. That is okay if you were converted three years ago, but if you accepted Christ thirty years ago, that is a disgrace. So important is the need for growth in the Christian life that I wrote a book on the subject especially for men titled *How to Study the Bible for Yourself*. In fact, I was teaching the San Diego Chargers' Bible study at the time and dedicated the book to them. It emphasizes the five major methods of feeding on the Word of God.

1. *Hearing the Word.* This is the method the average Christian uses most at church or by listening to the radio or cassettes. It is imperative that all new Christians find a Bible-teaching church home where they can feed on the Word of God regularly by hearing it taught. It is also there that they will make many new friends who share their new-found faith.

2. *Reading.* The daily reading of the Scriptures is indispensable to all Christians, especially new converts. It is like milk for babies.

3. *Study.* The Bible can be studied in many ways, from chapter or book analysis to comparing many passages on a given subject.

4. *Memorizing.* Committing Scripture to memory is the fastest way to learn the Word and to grow in your new-found faith.

5. *Meditate on the Scripture.* This just means to think about it. I enjoy reading a passage and thinking about it as I jog in the mornings.

Success Is Not Automatic

Assuming that you have received Jesus Christ as Lord and Savior, either before reading this book or as a result of it, I must warn you of one thing. Success in the Christian life is not automatic. God has just saved your spirit and soul for eternity and has also inserted a new nature into your life—his Holy Spirit. The success of your Christian life depends now on two basic things: (1) how regularly you feed this new nature, or spiritual life, the Word of God and (2) how successfully you learn to turn everything in your life over to Christ's control. Becoming a Christian does not end the decision-making process of life! You will still have many choices to make, but if by force of habit your determination is based on self-will, you will be miserable. If you learn to seek Christ's will and ask him through prayer and the regular study of his Word what you should do, you will be controlled by his Spirit, which is now within you. Consider the following diagrams:

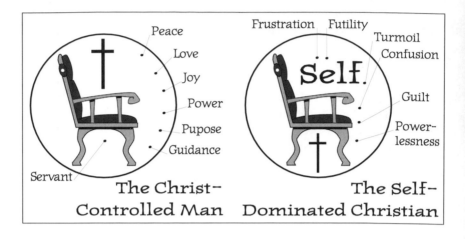

The Christ-Controlled Man

The Self-Dominated Christian

Many Christians live the life pictured on the right—they were sincere when they received Christ and he does reside within, but force of habit and evil temptations soon find them making their own choices as though he were no longer accessible. Consequently, the core of their lives is as miserable (or sometimes more so) as that of non-Christians. Always remember, Christ is now your Lord and you are his servant. A good servant delights in obeying his master. If you approach every decision in life the way the apostle Paul did after his conversion—"Lord, what would you have me do?"—you will make maximum use of your life and be a blessing to those with whom you come in contact.

While conducting a seminar in Hamilton, Ontario, an enormous man spoke to me during a break period. He was a good-looking, manly type, and because I had noted his broken nose, I was not surprised when he introduced himself as a boxer—the Canadian boxing champion who had fought Archie Moore, the great American light-heavyweight champion of the '60s, for the light-heavyweight world championship. It was a fierce fight, but Archie knocked him out in the tenth round. After the fight, my new friend admitted, "I was so depressed that I turned to booze and became an alcoholic." He went on to relate how his self-concern and disappointment made him a problem to himself, his family, and the government. Two years before the seminar, he had experienced the transformation pictured above, receiving Jesus Christ as Lord and Savior, and was now a different man. God had restored his home and made him a new creature. Who but Jesus Christ could have caused what two years before was a self-centered boxer, wallowing in self-pity, to attend a seminar advertised to help make him a better person, husband, and father?

Jesus is a master at producing such changes! Now that you understand the complexity of manhood—the core that makes it work and the divine Spirit of God who is able to empower your spirit to make full use of your creativity—we are ready to proceed. We shall next examine the fascinating subject of temperament. Then we shall see how it relates to manhood and clarify what God can do to help you fulfill your destiny and enable those you love to fulfill theirs. Every man and woman, father and mother, and particularly every husband and wife needs to know what you are about to learn.

4

Why You Act the Way You Do

Humanly speaking, nothing has a more profound influence on your behavior than your inherited temperament. The combination of your parents' genes and chromosomes at conception, which determined your basic temperament nine months before you drew your first breath, is largely responsible for your actions, reactions, emotional responses, and to one degree or another, almost everything you do.

Most people today are completely unaware of this extremely powerful influence on their behavior. Consequently, instead of cooperating with and using it, they often try to make something of themselves that they were never intended to be. This not only limits them personally and vocationally, but it also affects their immediate family and often spoils other interpersonal relationships. It is one of the reasons so many people say, "I don't like myself," or "I can't find myself." I have noticed that when people discover their own basic temperament, they can usually figure out rather easily what vocational opportunities they are best suited for, how to get along with other people, what natural weaknesses to watch for, what kind of husband or wife they should marry, and how in a number of ways they can improve the effectiveness of their lives.

What Is Temperament?

Temperament is the combination of traits we inherit from our parents. No one knows where it resides, but I think it is somewhere in the mind or emotional center (often referred to in the Bible as the heart). From that source it combines with other human characteristics to produce our basic makeup. Most of us are more conscious of its expression than we are its function. For example, sports lovers are familiar with Deion Sanders and Bo Jackson (prior to his injury), whose inherited temperament and physical condition made them into super football players in the '90s. Both men have aggressive temperaments with a strength of discipline that has enabled them to be the only two athletes in their time to excel in both football and baseball.

It is a person's temperament that makes him outgoing and extrovertish or shy and introvertish. Have you ever noticed how some adults have an anger problem? It just seems to flare up at the slightest provocation. Yet other people rarely ever get angry, but they may have a tendency to worry or feel fear. People didn't just become that way accidentally; they inherited those traits or temperaments with a predisposition toward anger or fear. You may know both kinds of people who were born to the same parents. Similarly, it is temperament that makes some people art and music enthusiasts while others are sports or industry minded. I have met outstanding musicians whose brothers were tone deaf, and I know a professional football player whose brother has never watched him play a game because, as he tells it, he just can't stand to watch violence.

Temperament is not the only influence on our behavior, of course. One must consider early home life—parental love (or the lack of it), moral character training (or the lack of it), role models—as well as traumatic experiences, educa-

tion, and motivation that contribute to our actions throughout life. Temperament is, however, the number one influence on a person's life, not only because it is the first thing
that affects us, but also because, like body structure, color
of eyes, and other physical characteristics, we're born with
it and it stays with us all through life. An extrovert is an
extrovert. He may tone down the expression of his extroversion, but he will always be an extrovert. Similarly,
although an introvert may be able to come out of his shell
and act more aggressively, he will never be transformed
into an extrovert. Temperament sets broad guidelines for
everyone's behavior, patterns that will influence a person
as long as he lives.

Of one thing I am certain after studying and teaching
about temperament for thirty years. Everyone can benefit
from learning as much as he can about his own temperament, particularly his strengths and weaknesses. The primary advantage of learning about the four basic temperaments is to discover your most pronounced strengths and
weaknesses so that with God's help you can overcome your
weaknesses and take maximum advantage of your
strengths. In this way you can fulfill your potential. After
testing more than thirty thousand people and giving them
a fifteen- to seventeen- page personalized analysis of their
strengths and weaknesses, I am more convinced than ever
of the validity of the concept and its potential for helping
people.

Temperament and Modern Psychology

Shortly after my first public lecture on the four temperaments, I became painfully aware of the fact that much
of modern psychology is extremely hostile to this theory.
Even the psychologists who have attended my Family Life
Seminars, if not hostile, appeared totally uninformed on the
subject. At first their attitude caused me considerable concern, but after years of research, I am thoroughly convinced
of the validity of the four-temperaments theory (with my

adaptation of the blends of temperament, which will be presented in chapter 6) and unimpressed with their reasons for rejecting the concept.

My first book, *Spirit-Controlled Temperament,* has exceeded half a million copies in print and to date has been translated into seventeen languages. Thousands of people have written or told me personally what an extraordinary tool this concept has been in understanding themselves, and many others have found it a handy guide in overcoming their weaknesses through the Spirit-controlled life. I have found it to be the best instrument ever devised for helping other people. Until modern psychologists can establish a replacement that will be equally beneficial for people, I will not pay much attention to their objections. Their reasons for opposing it are not really scientific. But because 35 percent of our population have attended college, and 80 percent of those have taken psychology (a favorite collegiate course), you should consider at the outset the following reasons why psychology as a rule rejects the theory of the four temperaments.

1. *Modern psychology is obsessed with the notion that man is an animal.* Since animals are born neutral, psychologists assume (through the unscientific process of evolution) that man evolved equally neutral.

2. *Since the passing of Sigmund Freud, every major psychological theory has assumed and taught that inherited characteristics do not influence a person's behavior.* Recently, while reviewing a new psychology textbook, *Theories of Personality* by Duane Schultz, I was again impressed with the uniform insistence on this thesis, from Jung and Adler to Rogers and Skinner. Because our society has tended to place psychiatrists and psychologists on an intellectual pedestal, and since psychiatrists and psychologists don't believe in inherited temperament, many people conclude that their position must be true. What people don't realize is that the four-temperaments theory was rejected not on the basis of scientific reasoning, but because it conflicts with one of psychology's pet theories that men are born neutral and thus behavior is a result of environment.

An extremely interesting news report to students of the four temperaments appeared in *Time* magazine on December 13, 1976. It seems that a growing number of anthropologists were being attracted to a science called sociobiology. Some of its advocates believe that "at most, 10% or 15% of human behavior is genetically based." As Dr. Robert L. Trivers, a Harvard biologist, said, "I think that every field that deals with humans is going to have to change sooner or later." The author of the article concludes by adding, "In other words, mankind must learn to understand the drive of its selfish genes." Those of us who accept the four basic temperaments today have been saying that for years! In fact, Christians have been dealing with that problem for two millennia. The secular community is still dragging its feet on accepting the four temperaments theory in spite of its practical application to laypeople.

3. *Their obsession with racial equality makes them blind to the natural differences of the races.* Culture did not produce the races—races produced the contrasting cultures of the world. They can claim there is no difference in the temperament of a fun-loving Italian Sanguine and a serious-minded German Choleric, but anyone unencumbered by sophomore psychology can see it plainly.

4. *They are committed to personal irresponsibility.* The truth is, humanistic psychologists do not understand human nature. They state that all people are born good and it is their environment that makes them what they are. It is this philosophy that liberals espouse to contend that government should solve all of man's problems, rather than admonishing each person to take responsibility for his own behavior. Until the last few years, most psychologists have taught that society was to blame for the behavior of people. There are still those who say that problem individuals should be considered victims. If a child is "abnormal" or acts as a criminal, it is probably because his parents sent him to school with his jacket buttoned up the wrong way or some other equally traumatic experience occurred during his formative years. They would have us believe that if a child or man steals, it is because "he didn't have a

chance." Such notions gave rise to permissivism and behaviorism, which robbed the individual of the opportunity of taking full responsibility for his own behavior. The leniency of our courts toward criminals and their disregard for law-abiding citizens that this leniency engenders can be traced to such teachings. And it has made our nation the crime capital of the world. Fortunately, a new breed of psychologist, disenchanted with such futile reasoning, has produced reality therapy, integrity therapy, and other concepts that call for the placing of responsibility back where it belongs—on the individual. Only when we face the fact that a man steals because he is dishonest, or lies because he is deceitful, or is immoral because he is lustful and selfish will people hold every individual accountable for his behavior. Only then will some people be forced to improve themselves.

The recognition that we possess an inherited temperament that needs improvement is helpful to everyone. It is good for a person to be aware of his natural weaknesses so he can take the necessary precautions to avoid being overcome by them. Dr. Henry Brandt, a Christian psychiatrist whose basic philosophy is deeply grounded in the Bible, advances an interesting concept regarding maturity. He has said, "A mature man is one who is sufficiently objective about himself to know both his strengths and his weaknesses and to create a planned program for overcoming his weaknesses." No man needs to be conquered by his weaknesses! The Bible says, "We are more than conquerors through Him [Jesus Christ] Who loved us" (Rom. 8:37). Knowing your temperament will help you to appropriate the power of Jesus Christ to overcome your natural weaknesses, so you can be the kind of person God and you want you to be.

You are about to embark on a most exciting journey into understanding yourself. It could change your life! Read the next three chapters carefully.

5

The Four Basic Temperaments

T he heart of the temperament theory, as first conceived by Hippocrates over twenty-four hundred years ago, divides people into four basic categories, which he named Sanguine, Choleric, Melancholy, and Phlegmatic. Each temperament has both strengths and weaknesses that form a distinct part of a person's nature and characterize him throughout life. Once a person diagnoses his own basic temperament, he is better equipped to ascertain what vocational opportunities he is best suited for and what natural weaknesses he must work on to keep from short-circuiting his potential and creativity.

The chart on the facing page summarizes the strengths and weaknesses of each temperament. You may find your predominant temperament by marking each word that describes one of your strengths or weaknesses. The quarter of the circle with the highest number will indicate your primary temperament.

By way of introduction to the four basic temperaments, consider the following descriptions. No doubt you will identify several of your friends in one or another of these clas-

The Four Basic Temperaments

Strength

Weakness

Introvert

Extrovert

Sanguine
Actors
Salesmen
Speakers

outgoing
charisma
warm
friendly
responsive
talkative
enthusiastic
carefree
compassionate
generous

undisciplined
weak-willed
restless
disorganized
unproductive
undependable
obnoxious-loud
egocentric
exaggerates
fearful
insecure

Choleric
Leaders
Producers
Builders

determined
strong-willed
independent
productive
decisive
practical
visionary
optimistic
courageous
self-confident
leader

cold
unsympathetic
insensitive
inconsiderate
hostile-angry
cruel-sarcastic
unforgiving
self-sufficient
domineering
opinionated
prejudiced
proud
crafty

Phlegmatic
Diplomats
Accountants
Teachers
Technicians

calm and quiet
easygoing
likable
diplomatic
efficient and organized
dependable
conservative
practical
reluctant leader
dry humor

unmotivated
blasé
indolent
spectator
selfish
stingy
stubborn
self-protective
indecisive
fearful

Melancholy
Artists
Musicians
Inventors
Philosophers
Doctors

gifted
analytical
perfectionist
conscientious
loyal
aesthetic
idealistic
sensitive
self-sacrificing
self-disciplined

moody
negative
critical
rigid and legalistic
self-centered
touchy
revengeful
theoretical and
impractical
persecution-prone

sifications, and if you look carefully, you may even discover one that reminds you of yourself.

Sparky Sanguine

Sparky Sanguine is a warm, buoyant, lively, and "enjoying" person. He is receptive by nature, and external impressions easily find their way to his heart, where they readily cause an outburst of response. Feelings rather than reflective thoughts predominate to form his decisions. Sparky is so outgoing that I call him a superextrovert. Mr. Sanguine has an unusual capacity for enjoying himself and usually passes on his fun-loving spirit. The moment he enters a room he tends to lift the spirits of everyone present by his exuberant conversation. He is a fascinating storyteller, and his warm, emotional nature enables him to relive the experience as he tells it.

Mr. Sanguine never lacks for friends. One writer noted, "His naive, spontaneous, genial nature opens doors and hearts to him." He can genuinely feel the joys and sorrows of the person he meets and has the capacity to make him feel important, as though he were a very special friend—and he *is,* as long as he is looking at him or until he fixes his eyes with equal intensity on the next person he meets. The Sanguine has what I call "hanging eyes." That is, his eyes hang or fix on you until he loses interest in you or someone else comes along to attract his attention.

The Sanguine is never at a loss for words, though he often speaks without thinking. His open sincerity, however, has a disarming effect on many of his listeners, causing them to respond to his mood. His freewheeling, seemingly exciting, extrovertish way of life makes him the envy of the more timid temperament types.

The apostle Peter in the Bible was much like Sparky Sanguine. Every time he appears in the Gospels he is seen talking. In fact, I read through the Gospels one time to verify my suspicion and found that Sanguine Simon Peter talked more in the four Gospels than all the other disciples put together—and that's typical for Sparky. As my minister friend, Ken Poure, says, "A Sanguine always enters a room mouth first." And like most Sanguines, Ken Poure is loved by everyone.

Sparky Sanguine enjoys people and detests solitude. He is at his best surrounded by friends where he is the life of the party. He has an endless repertoire of interesting stories, which he tells dramatically, making him a favorite with children as well as adults. This trait usually gains him admission at the best parties or social gatherings.

His noisy, blustering, friendly ways make him appear more confident than he really is, but his energy and lovable disposition get him by the rough spots of life. People have a way of excusing his weaknesses by saying, "That's just the way he is."

Vocational Potential of the Sanguine

The world is enriched by these cheerful people with their natural charisma. They usually make excellent salesmen and are often attracted to that profession. You have doubtless heard the cliché, "He could sell refrigerators to the Eskimos." Sparky is so convincing that he could sell rubber crutches to people who aren't even crippled. If you ever want to watch Mr. Sanguine in action, just visit your local used-car dealer. Two-thirds of his salesmen are probably Sanguines.

In addition to being good salesmen, Sanguines make excellent actors, entertainers, and preachers (particularly evangelists). They are outstanding masters of ceremonies, auctioneers, and sometimes leaders (if properly blended with another temperament). Because of our mass media today, they are increasingly in demand within the political arena, where natural charisma has proved advantageous— and Sanguines have charisma to burn.

In the area of helping people, Sanguines excel as hospital workers. Doctor Sanguine always has the best bedside manner. You may be on the verge of death, as white as the sheet you are lying on, when he bubbles into the room, but before he leaves, he will have lifted your spirits by his natural charm. His obvious compassion in response to your tale of woe will almost make paying his exorbitant bill easy. (Sanguines are never moderate about anything.) Nurse Sanguine is equally enthusiastic about helping sick folks, and her radiant smile as she enters the room always gives you a pickup. In fact, most sick people respond to the Sanguine's question of "How are you today?" by saying, "Fine," whereas Nurse Melancholy asking the same question would probably receive the self-pitying lament of "Miserable."

No matter what work the Sanguine enters, it should always give him extensive exposure to people. I think his chief contribution to life lies in making other people happy. Certainly someone should be assigned that task in these uncertain times. Sanguines are happy, fun-loving people who enjoy life to the hilt—if they are not destroyed by their weaknesses.

Weaknesses of the Sanguine

Every temperament has its natural set of weaknesses that keep people from living up to their potential. I have skimmed lightly over the Sanguine's strengths because they are not the cause of serious problems. In an attempt to help the reader personally, I will deal more specifically with each temperament's weaknesses.

Weak-Willed and Undisciplined

Sanguines are often voted "most likely to succeed" in college, but they often fail or fall short of their potential in life. Their tendency to be weak-willed and undisciplined will finally destroy them unless it is overcome. Since they are highly emotional, exude considerable natural charm, and are prone to be what one psychologist called "touchers" (they tend to touch people as they talk to them), they commonly have a great appeal for the opposite sex. Consequently, they usually face sexual temptation more than others. Unfortunately, their weak will makes it easy for them to give way to such temptations unless they are fortified by strong moral principles and possess a vital spiritual power.

This weakness of will and lack of discipline makes it easier for them to be deceitful, dishonest, and undependable. They tend to overeat and gain weight, finding it most difficult to remain on a diet; consequently, a thirty-year-old Sanguine will often be thirty pounds overweight and gaining rapidly.

Someone has said, "Without self-discipline, there is no such thing as success." I couldn't agree more. Consider athletes, for example—no man is so gifted that he can excel without self-discipline. In fact, many a potential superstar has fizzled because of lack of discipline. On the other hand, many an ordinary athlete has excelled because he has disciplined himself.

Mike Fuller, a dedicated Christian who was largely responsible for our weekly San Diego Chargers' Bible study, was the Chargers' exciting safety and sure-handed punt return specialist. (He averaged only one or two fumbles per season from high school through college and into the pros.) Mike stood only a little under five feet ten and weighed a muscular 185 pounds. Admittedly, he had above-average speed and coordination, but had he not been willing to discipline himself to many hours of weight lifting to build muscle onto his upper body, he would not have developed into such a deadly tackler. In one memorable game, he made eleven unassisted tackles and was the main reason that the Houston Oilers' running attack was almost completely shut off. Without self-discipline, Mike would never have become a pro football player or lasted in the league for ten years.

Lack of will and discipline are mentioned here first in considering Mr. Sanguine's weaknesses because I am convinced that if he will conquer this inherent tendency by the power of God, he will make progress toward strengthening all his weaknesses and realizing his incredible potential.

Emotionally Unstable

The only temperament more emotional than a Sanguine is a Melancholy, but he isn't anywhere near as expressive as Sparky. Not only can Sparky cry at the drop of a hat (one such pro football player's wife won't watch a sad film on TV with her husband because his blubbering embarrasses her!), but the spark of anger can instantly become a raging inferno. You have no doubt heard the expression "He was livid with rage." That's Sparky Sanguine when he gets angry. His face turns beet red and he explodes.

There is one thing about his anger that is comforting— he never carries a grudge. Once he blows up all over you, he forgets about it. *You* may not, but he does. That's why he doesn't get ulcers; he gives them to everyone else!

This lack of emotional consistency usually limits him vocationally, and it certainly destroys him spiritually. When filled with the Spirit, however, he becomes a new creature, an emotionally controlled Sanguine.

Egotistic

Every human being is plagued with ego, but Sanguines have a double dose of the problem. That's why a Spirit-filled Sparky is easily detected; he will reflect an unnatural spirit of humility that is refreshing. A carnal Sanguine is not so, for he continually vies for the limelight. To him, "All the world's a stage," and he is the supreme actor. Listening to his endless supply of stories, you will notice that he is his favorite character. The more Sanguine he is, the more egotism he manifests.

One subtle ego habit of Mr. Sanguine involves name-dropping. I noticed that a friend of mine who is a supersalesman and basically a fine Christian always called great people by their first names. He would never introduce a person by referring to his title, qualifications, or accomplishments, but in his introduction always worked his own relationship to the person into focus and then presented him to an audience by his first name. It seems that his personal egotism so clouded his judgment that he was blind to the discourtesy to which he was subjecting his guest. Such public displays may be greeted by nervous laughter but are seldom appreciated by an audience.

Restless and Disorganized

Sanguines are notoriously disorganized and always on the move. They seldom plan ahead and usually take things as they come. They are happy most of the time because they rarely look back (consequently not profiting from past mistakes) and they seldom look ahead. It has been said of them, "They are a disorganized accident waiting to happen."

Wherever Sparky works or lives, things are in a disastrous state of disarray. He can never find his tools, even though they are right where he left them. Keys are the bane of his life—he is forever losing them. One Sanguine I know solved that problem very simply; he made it the rule of his life when away from home *always* to put his keys in his right pants pocket, and when at home to hang them on a hook in the kitchen *every time* he entered the house. It worked so well that his key-loss rate dropped from 90 percent of the time to only 10 percent. His attitude toward the 10 percent? So who's perfect!

Sparky's garage, bedroom, closet, and office are disaster areas unless he has an efficient wife and secretary to pick up after him. His egotism usually makes him a sharp dresser, but if his friends or customers could see the room where he dressed, they would fear that someone had been killed in the explosion. How does Sparky get by with that kind of living? The way Mr. Sanguine handles all confrontations caused by his temperament weakness—a disarming smile, a pat on the back, a funny story, and a restless move to the next thing that sparks his interest.

The Sanguine will never become a perfectionist, but when the Spirit of God controls him, more planning and order will be brought into his life. And when that happens, Sparky is a much happier person—not only with others but also with himself. In addition, planning and organization will multiply the effectiveness of his tremendous personality and charm.

Insecure

Behind that superextrovertish personality that frequently overpowers other people, giving him a false reputation as a self-confident person, Sparky Sanguine is really quite insecure. His insecurity is often the source of his vile profanity. He is a name-dropper anyway, so why shouldn't he drop the biggest name of all, particularly when he is angry or frustrated? This habit made one Sanguine so profane that his barber commented (after Sparky had walked out of his shop), "If you took all the profanity out of his conversation, he wouldn't have said a thing."

Sanguines are not usually fearful of personal injury and often resort to outlandish feats of daring and heroism. Their fears can, however, entertain the area of personal failure, rejection, or disapproval. That's why they often follow an obnoxious display of conversation with an equally mindless statement. Rather than face your disapproval, they are hoping to cover up the first goof with something that will gain your approval. The Sanguine married to a loving and thoughtful wife soon learns that she has the power to encourage or discourage him. He is like a giant inner tube—easily inflatable with a tire pump, or instantly deflated with a needle. It is a wise wife, regardless of her temperament, who avoids criticism and faultfinding and accepts her husband as he is and reassures him verbally of her love. (That also is great therapy for a husband to extend to his wife—particularly if *she* is a Sanguine. The last thing she needs is criticism from her partner. Women always respond better to approval and acceptance than to criticism.) As has been said many times, every human being craves approval and recognition. That goes double for Sparky Sanguine.

Flexible in Conscience

Perhaps the Sanguine's most treacherous trait, one that really stifles his spiritual potential, is his weak or flexible conscience. Since he so capably talks others into his way of thinking, earning him the reputation of being the world's greatest con artist, he has no difficulty convincing himself that anything he wants to do is perfectly all right. As a little boy, he can look you right in the eye and tell the biggest yarn you have ever heard. When he grows up, he learns to bend the truth or exaggerate until any similarity between his story and the facts is totally coincidental. Yet this rarely bothers him, for he cons himself into believing that the end justifies the means. Sometimes you might ask, "What end?" His answer, whether spoken or thought, is usually the same—"*My* end." Others often find it incredible that he can lie, cheat, or steal, yet seldom endure a sleepless night. That is why he frequently walks all over the rights of others and rarely hesitates to take advantage of other people.

Several years ago a great leader founded a much-needed organization that he had dreamed about for years. A younger man, quite a Sanguine by nature, talked him into taking his own organization into the new one "because our objectives are so similar." He was so personable and insistent and the founder so trusting that he agreed. Within a few months the original founder knew that he had made a mistake, and within two years that man was on the outside of the very organization he had founded, forcing him to establish yet another. Subsequently it was discovered that the younger man had a history of deception and seemingly didn't know the difference between right and wrong. As with most Sanguines, surface repentance was easy for him, of course, but his repentance never seems to produce restitution as the Scripture teaches. Such individuals can look you in the eye and say, "If I've ever done anything wrong, I'm sorry," and expect you to be spiritual enough to forgive them.

Honesty is not only a biblical virtue but the best policy in life. Sooner or later, Sparky Sanguine often weaves a web of deceit that eventually produces his own destruction. The Bible says, "Do not be deceived; God is not mocked; for whatever a man sows, that he will also reap" (Gal. 6:7). The only way to conquer that problem is to concentrate on truth and honesty. Every time a man lies or cheats, it becomes easier, and the next temptation is bigger. I have found in counseling men guilty of infidelity that I can expect them to lie, cheat, and steal, if necessary, to cover up their adultery.

Ross Perot, the wealthy computer expert whose run for president in 1992 helped elect candidate Bill Clinton with only a 43 percent vote, said in a national magazine interview that in his company, adultery was grounds for dismissal. When asked why, he simply replied, "The man who will cheat on his wife will cheat on our firm." In other words, the man who cannot be trusted to keep his marriage vows cannot be trusted in anything else. The Sanguine who learns to accept full responsibility for all his actions has taken the first giant step toward victory over his natural tendency toward situation ethics.

Sparky Sanguine's penchant for exaggeration, embellishment, and plain old-fashioned deceit catches up with him most quickly in his marriage and family. While he may fool those who see him occasionally, it is impossible for him to cheat and deceive his way through life without teaching his wife and children that they cannot depend on his word. One of the nine necessary building blocks in any love relationship, according to 1 Corinthians 13:4–8, is trust. Consequently, though his family may *like* him, it is difficult for either his wife or children to love and respect him completely unless he overcomes this habit. Part of the reason our Lord and the Scriptures speak so frequently on the subject of truth or honesty is that it not only produces the necessary clear conscience all men need, but it also creates the kind of foundation on which lasting and enjoyable interpersonal relationships are made.

Conclusion

If you are a Sparky Sanguine by nature, you may think I am particularly hard on this temperament. (Wait until we get to the other temperaments, who usually level the same accusation.) Actually, I love Sanguines and have many as friends. I do get perturbed at them, however, when I see their tremendous talents slowly go down the drain because of their lack of self-discipline. By contrast, it is beautiful to see a Spirit-filled Sanguine whose talents are used by God because he recognizes the need to walk in the Spirit. But as we shall see, that is the need of every temperament.

Sanguine Simon Peter offers hope for every defeated Sanguine. He was an overtalkative, extrovertish, weak-willed, and defeated Christian who even denied his Lord three times. But we read in Acts 2 how he became a Spirit-controlled Sanguine and an effective leader of the early Christian church for more than fifteen years.

Rocky Choleric

Rocky Choleric is the hot, quick, active, practical, and strong-willed temperament type who is self-sufficient and independent. He tends to be decisive and opinionated, finding it easy to make decisions for both himself and other people. Like Sparky Sanguine, Rocky Choleric is an extrovert, but he is not nearly so intense.

Mr. Choleric thrives on activity. In fact, to him, "life is activity." He does not need to be stimulated by his environment but rather stimulates his environment with his endless ideas, plans, goals, and ambitions. He does not engage in aimless activity, for he has a practical, keen mind capable of making sound, instant decisions or planning worthwhile projects. He does not vacillate under the pressure of what others think but takes a definite stand on issues and can often be found crusading against social injustice.

Rocky is not frightened by adversities; in fact, they tend to motivate him. His staunch determination usually allows him to succeed where others fail, not because his plans are better than theirs, but because where others may become discouraged and quit, he doggedly keeps pushing ahead. If there is truth to the adage that leaders are born, not made, then he is a natural-born leader—what management experts call the SNL (Strong Natural Leader).

Mr. Choleric's emotional nature is the least developed part of his temperament. He does not sympathize easily with others, nor does he naturally show or express compassion. He is often embarrassed or disgusted by the tears of others and is usually insensitive to their needs. Reflecting little appreciation for music and the fine arts, unless his secondary temperament traits are those of the Melancholy, he primarily seeks utilitarian and productive values in life.

The Choleric is quick to recognize opportunities and equally as quick to diagnose the best ways to make use of them. He has a well-organized mind, though details usually bore him. Not given to analysis but rather to quick, almost intuitive appraisal, he tends to look at the goal for which he is working without recognizing the potential pitfalls and obstacles in the path. Once he has started toward his goal, he may run roughshod over individuals who stand in his way. He tends to be domineering and bossy and does not hesitate to use people to accomplish his ends. He is often considered an opportunist.

Rocky's attitude of self-sufficiency and willfulness makes him difficult to reach for Christ in adulthood. For this reason I urge Sunday school teachers to never let a fifth-grade Choleric out of your class until he finds Christ as his Lord and Savior. That is also good advice for parents. The stronger the Choleric tendencies in a child, the more intense should be your prayers for his conversion between third and fifth grades while he still retains sensitivity to spiritual things.

Vocational Potential of the Choleric

Any profession that requires leadership, motivation, and productivity is open to a Choleric, provided it does not require too much attention to details and analytical planning. Committee meetings and long-range planning bore him, for he is a doer. Although he is not usually a craftsman (which requires a degree of perfection and efficiency usually beyond his capability), he often serves well in supervising craftsmen. He usually enjoys construction because it is so productive, and will frequently end up as a foreman or project supervisor.

Rocky is a developer by nature. When he and his wife drive through the countryside, he cannot share her enjoyment of the beautiful rolling hillsides, for he envisions road graders carving out streets and builders constructing homes, schools, and shopping centers. Most of today's cities and suburbs were first envisioned by a Choleric. You can be sure, however, that he hired a Melancholy as the architect with the analytical and creative ability to draw the plans he has outlined, for he could never do that himself. He still cannot understand why a few lines on the back of an envelope aren't sufficient to gain the city planning department's approval. No one fights City Hall harder than a Choleric, who bitterly laments, "Why all this business of detailed plans, anyway? I've built enough projects to know that the best of plans have to be modified during construction, so why not make up your mind as you go along on the little issues? I know what I want to accomplish!" It is a wise Choleric who hires a Melancholy as his assistant or goes into business partnership with a Melancholy. Together they make an unbeatable team. Of course, since everyone has both a primary and secondary temperament, occasionally one meets a person with both traits.

Most entrepreneurs are Cholerics. They formulate the ideas and are venturesome enough to launch out in new directions. They don't limit themselves to their own ideas either, but sometimes overhear a creative idea from someone who is not sufficiently adventurous to initiate a new business or project. Once Rocky has started a new business, however, it is not unlike him to get bored soon after its success. There are two reasons for this. First, as the business grows under his dynamic leadership, of necessity it creates more detail work. But since Cholerics are not by nature good delegators of responsibility (although with proper training they can learn) and tend to prefer the fruits of their own productive and capable industry, the efforts of others are evaluated as somewhat inadequate. Consequently, they end up trying to do everything themselves. Second, when Rocky discovers that he is busier than the proverbial "one-armed paperhanger with the seven-year itch," he looks for someone to buy his business. Thus, the average Choleric can be expected to start four to ten businesses or organizations in a lifetime.

Once a Choleric learns to delegate responsibility to others and discovers that he is able to accomplish more through other people, he can complete an amazing amount of work. Other people cannot believe that he can be involved in so many things and keep his sanity, but to Rocky Choleric it is really very simple. Since he is completely performance-conscious and has no perfectionist hang-ups, he will reason, "I'd rather get a number of things finished 70 to 80 percent than a mere few things 100 percent." As Charley "Tremendous" Jones says in his talks to businessmen, "Your motto should be 'From production to perfection.'" Cholerics love that philosophy—perfectionist Melancholies reject it vigorously.

Rocky Choleric is a natural motivator of other people. He oozes self-confidence, is extremely goal-conscious, and can inspire others to envision his goals. Consequently, his associates may find themselves more productive by following his lead. His primary weakness as a leader is that he is hard to please and tends to run roughshod over other people. If he only knew how others look to him for approval and encouragement, he would spend more time patting them on the back and acknowledging their accomplishments— which would generate even greater dedication from his colleagues. The problem is that the Choleric subconsciously thinks that approval and encouragement will lead to complacency, and he assumes that an employee's productivity will fall off if he is too complimentary. Thus he may resort to criticism and faultfinding in the hope that this will inspire greater effort. He must learn that criticism is a *de*motivator. Once Rocky discovers that people require reassurance and stimulation in order to perform at the height of their potential, his role as leader will radically improve.

Rocky Choleric could learn an important lesson by watching outstanding middle linebackers just before a crucial play. They walk up and down the line, patting their teammates encouragingly. That touch silently urges, "I'm counting on you to do your best; don't let me down." One lineman said of his defensive captain, "I'd lay down my life for that man!" Interestingly enough, the captain was a perennial back patter.

In the early days of American industry, when business production and manufacturing were not so technical, our industrial complexes were largely built by Cholerics. Today, as technology demands greater sophistication and creativity, it is gradually turning for leadership to Melancholies or at least Choleric-Melancholies or Melancholy-Cholerics. Now Cholerics are more apt to build the factory buildings or the streets and highways that furnish the supply routes used by industry, whereas complex organization increasingly requires a more analytical leader.

Don't feel sorry for the Choleric of the future; he will figure out something worthy of his talents. He always lands on his feet. Cholerics have a built-in promotional ability and do well in sales, teaching (but always practical subjects), politics, military service, sports, law enforcement, and many other endeavors. Like the Sanguine, Rocky Choleric makes a good preacher, although he is much less emotional.

I have noticed that many of the most successful churches in the country have a preacher in the pulpit who is predominantly Choleric. Not only is he a dynamic Bible teacher, but his organizational and promotional ability together with his strong leadership gifts make it hard for the average fearful congregation to slow him down. An old saying characterizes him well: "Fools rush in where angels fear to tread." No one ever accused a Choleric of being an angel. He launches into many projects and, with proper motivation and the blessing of God, usually enjoys a successful ministry.

Western civilization has benefited much from its Rocky Cholerics (Nordic, Teutonic, Germanic, Gallic, or Frankish people often had a high degree of Choleric temperament). But it has suffered much from them also. The world's greatest generals, dictators, and gangsters have been predominantly Cholerics. What made the difference? Their moral values and motivations. If there is such a thing as a success tendency, Cholerics have it. That doesn't mean they are smarter than other people, as is often assumed, but that their strong will and determination drive them to succeed where other, more gifted, people are prone to give up in the midst of their superior projects. If a job requires industry, hard work, and activity, Rocky Choleric will usually outperform the other temperaments. If it demands analysis, long-range planning, meticulous skills, or creativity, that's a different ball game. Rarely will you find a predominant Choleric as a surgeon, dentist, philosopher, inventor, or watchmaker. Rocky's interests thrive upon activity, bigness, violence, and production. He is so optimistic, rarely anticipating failure, that he seldom fails—except at home.

Weaknesses of the Choleric

Like all the other temperaments, Rocky Choleric has his own unique set of weaknesses that can seriously limit his effectiveness. To further complicate things, he rarely likes to change himself. As one such attorney urged in my counseling room, "Tim, I want you to explain my temperament to my wife so she can learn to accept me the way I am." Needless to say, their marriage didn't last long after that.

Fortunately, Cholerics are extremely practical people, so once they realize what they are doing wrong, they can be motivated to improve themselves. But how can one get them to objectively face their shortcomings? It is my hope that the following description of the most common weaknesses of the Choleric will be given an objective appraisal by every Choleric who reads this book.

Angry and Hostile

Cholerics are extremely hostile people. Some learn to control their anger, but eruption into violence is always a possibility with them. If their strong will is not brought into control by proper parental discipline as children, they develop angry, tumultuous habits that plague them all through life. It doesn't take them long to learn that others are usually afraid of their angry outbursts and thus they may use wrath as a weapon to get what they want.

The anger of Cholerics is quite different from that of Sanguines. Rocky's explosion isn't always as loud as Sparky's because he is not quite as extrovertish as the Sanguine, but it can be much more dangerous. Sanguines have a gentle streak that makes it hard for them to injure others purposely (although they can hurt them thoughtlessly). Not so with a Choleric; he can purposely cause pain to others and enjoy it. His wife is usually afraid of him, and he tends to terrify his children.

Rocky Choleric often reminds me of a walking Mount Vesuvius, constantly gurgling until at the right provocation he spills out his poisonous or bitter lava all over someone or something. He is a door slammer, table pounder, and horn blower. Any person or thing that gets in his way, retards his progress, or fails to perform up to the level of his expectations will soon feel the eruption of his wrath. And unlike the Sanguine, Rocky doesn't get over his anger right away but can carry a grudge an unbelievably long time. Maybe that's why he often gets ulcers by the time he is forty years old.

Several years ago I felt led to talk to an angry friend whose tremendous grasp of the Scriptures impressed me. He was a gifted teacher who probably knew the Bible better than any layman I have ever encountered, yet we could not let him teach in our Sunday school because we never knew when he might explode at someone, ruining both his testimony and ours. Having had no small anger problem myself until God convicted me of it and began to change my life by his Holy Spirit, I thought he would accept from me the suggestion that his uncontrolled anger was seriously limiting

God's use of his life. Without being insulted or displaying anger, he responded, "That's the way I am. I'm a striker and I don't intend to change." I watched helplessly as that man drove his five children away from him, the church, and the things of God. Finally, his long-suffering wife of over thirty years left him, and at fifty-five he died of a heart attack— which I am confident was brought on prematurely by his anger.

It has been my observation that few young people who have grown up in angry, hostile homes dedicate their lives to Christ. They usually get so angry at the Choleric parent that they tend to hate God. When the parent is their father, they usually find it difficult to love their father's God. They envision God as an angry tyrant, always watching them to discover a word or deed that is displeasing to him, much as did their human father. Such individuals have a difficult time accepting the love of God. In addition, they often take on the angry traits of their Choleric parents. The wisdom given us in Proverbs 22:24–25 warns about the contagion of anger, explaining why angry children come out of angry households.

This tendency of angry Cholerics to destroy their children was graphically illustrated in an event at our church several years ago. The Board of Deacons was trying to sell a program to the church at a business meeting when a few predominantly Choleric men took violent issue with the plan. (Cholerics either cooperate enthusiastically with others' ideas or oppose them vehemently. They are rarely neutral.) On the way home that night, my wife asked me, "Did you notice what those men who opposed the program had in common?" "Yes," I said, "they are either predominant Cholerics or Melancholies in temperament or a combination of both." "No," she replied, "that's not what I mean. They all have had trouble with rebellious teenagers in their homes." As I called the roll in my mind, I found that she was absolutely correct—and unfortunately, that is not uncommon. The Bible warns that the "forcing of wrath produces strife" (Prov. 30:33), which explains why angry children usually come out of angry homes. Yes, anger is contagious.

Unless Rocky faces the wickedness of this sin and lets God's Holy Spirit replace his bitterness of spirit with love and peace, he will never attain the level of spiritual maturity and leadership that God desires for him.

Cruel, Cutting, and Sarcastic

No one utters more acrid comments with his mouth than a sarcastic Choleric! Sometimes it makes me wonder whether he inherited a tongue or a razor blade. As an extrovert, he is usually ready with a cutting comment that can wither the insecure and devastate the less combative. Even Sparky Sanguine is no match for him, because Sparky isn't cruel or mean. Rocky will rarely hesitate to tell a person off or chop him to bits. Consequently, he leaves a path of damaged psyches and fractured egos wherever he goes.

It is a happy Choleric (and his family members) who discovers that the tongue is either a vicious weapon of destruction or a tool of healing. Once he learns the importance of his verbal approval and encouragement to others, he will seek to control his speech until he gets angry, whereupon he discovers with the apostle James that "no man can tame the tongue. It is an unruly evil, full of deadly poison" (James 3:8). Ready speech and an angry spirit often combine to make a Choleric profane. His language is not only improper for female company, but also often unfit for man or beast. Jesus taught that "out of the abundance of the heart the mouth speaks" (Matt. 12:34). If a person is angry, he says unkind, hurtful things, with profanity being the most common speech that comes from an angry heart.

Cold and Unaffectionate

The milk of human kindness has all but dried up in the veins of a Choleric. He is the least affectionate of all the temperaments and rarely makes any public show of emotion. Marital affection to him means a kiss at the wedding and on every fifth anniversary thereafter. Except for anger, his emotions are the most underdeveloped of all the temperaments. One wife of a Choleric for twenty-four years lamented in the counseling room, "My husband is terribly cold and unaffectionate. He lets me use his lips, but there is never any real feeling to it. Kissing him is about as exciting as kissing a marble statue in a cemetery on a cold winter day!"

His emotional rigidity rarely permits him the expression of tears. He usually stops crying at the age of eleven or twelve and finds it difficult to understand others when they are moved to tears. One day I lost a great handball partner and friend while trying to comfort this Choleric at his father's funeral. He sat stony-eyed through my message, but when everyone had left the chapel, he came unglued and burst into tears as his natural grief finally overcame him. He wept so hard that tears poured through his fingers. All I could do was put my arm around him and let him put his head on my shoulder and sob. Suddenly he stopped crying, stood up, and walked out of the room and out of my life. He has avoided me ever since. Apparently he was so ashamed of breaking down in front of me that he can't bear the thought of facing me again.

What my Choleric friend doesn't realize is that tears or crying are a God-given means of flushing out the emotional system in times of stress. If he hadn't broken down at that funeral, his heart might well have burst from pent-up grief.

Being predominantly a Choleric myself, I think I can understand his problem. My tears ceased about three years after my father's death, when I was about twelve years old. Something snapped inside, and I have never wept since. It's not that I don't feel for others or wish I could cry, but evidently my tear ducts have shut off. The closest I have come to tears was several years ago in a motel room in Miami, during the time when I was still pastoring a church. When the phone rang, my wife and I received the tragic news from Fred and Betty that their seven-year-old son, Russell, had drowned in the Colorado River at our high-school youth camp's skiing trip while the parents were cooking breakfast. For years these two dedicated young people had been almost like a son and daughter to us. In fact, Bev and I called in their home years ago before they even began a family, and I dedicated each of their four lovely children shortly after birth. Coupled with the realization that this was the first such accident we had ever experienced as a church and the responsibility I naturally felt, I too came unglued. After hanging up the phone, my heart ached so intensely that I threw myself across the bed and sobbed into the pillow. Even though no tears came, I cried uncontrollably. My wife didn't know what to do, for she had never seen me cry in twenty-eight years of marriage. Finally I gained control of myself, and my overpowering grief passed. For the first time in my adult life I realized that tears and crying have their rightful place in any man's life. After all, did not the perfect man, Jesus Christ, weep at the death of his friend Lazarus, even though he knew Lazarus would soon be brought back to life? Unfortunately, I had no such power.

Many men (and some women) contend that crying is not manly, which is why some men are ashamed of shedding tears. That is ridiculous! Regardless of his temperament, every man and boy has his breaking point. Sanguines can cry when telling a sad story or hearing one. Melancholies are usually sensitive to the sufferings of humanity, and Phlegmatics are normally tenderhearted. I am suspicious that, although it takes much more provocation, Cholerics feel deeply also. Rocky may rub his nose or slap his leg self-consciously to release the pressure, but he too can be moved to tears, particularly if he is a Christian filled with the Spirit.

Cholerics are so transparent that they are about as successful at concealing their feelings as a fat man hiding behind a telephone pole. One telltale sign that they are walking in the Spirit is compassion—a characteristic of love that is one of the nine strengths of the Holy Spirit (Gal. 5:22–23).

It was an exciting experience for me in Grand Rapids, Michigan, when I was confronted by two men (independently) who asked the same question: "In your book *Transformed Temperaments,* you mentioned a gracious Choleric gentleman who impressed you so much that you hoped when you were his age you would be as gracious. Then you went on to explain that he had been a hard-driving Choleric in his younger years, but God had mellowed him until today he is a model of Christian manhood. Was that Mr. _____?"

and they proceeded to name the same man. I gulped, not knowing whether my illustration held up in real life, but both men acknowledged that they knew him in his aggressive days when he bought the bankrupt business that he built into one of the largest of its kind in the world. Then they added, "And I agree with you—God has brought a supernatural compassion and sensitivity into his life that is beautiful." The first characteristic of the Holy Spirit in the life of a person will be love, which produces compassion. That will become particularly pronounced in a Choleric, for he is much more apt to bulldoze over the feelings of others and manipulate people rather than serve them until the Holy Spirit implants that love in his heart.

Insensitive and Inconsiderate

Similar to his natural lack of love is the Choleric's tendency to be insensitive to others' needs and inconsiderate of their feelings. One dynamic Choleric shared with me that at a seminar he had rededicated his life to Christ and was convicted of his "insensitivity to the needs of my family." Consequently, when he returned home he called his family together and announced, "God has convicted me that I should be more sensitive to the needs of every member of my family." Whipping out his notebook, he turned to each one and demanded, "What are your needs?" Needless to say, their minds went blank. Gradually, however, he had improved, learning to read their spirits and anticipate their needs.

When a Choleric is sensitive and considerate, he can be a great blessing to others, for as we have seen, what he thinks of others is of vital importance to them. By nature, Rocky Choleric has the hide of a rhinoceros. The Spirit of God, however, will make him kind and tenderhearted.

Opinionated and Bullheaded

The Choleric's natural determination is a temperament asset that stands him in good stead throughout life, but it can make him opinionated and bullheaded. Since he has an intuitive sense, he usually makes up his mind quickly (without adequate analysis and deliberation), and when once made up, it is almost impossible to change. No temperament type more typifies the old cliché "Don't confuse me with the facts; my mind is made up." Being an extrovert, he will openly argue to uphold his position and often lose ground and time rather than simply acknowledge that he has made a mistake, regroup, and set off in a better direction.

Cholerics are neutral about few subjects and are opinionated about everything. One Choleric, his best friend, and their wives were enjoying an afternoon at the fair when they spotted a computer that analyzed handwriting. The Choleric challenged them all to invest fifty cents. They agreed, if he would go first. After he signed his name, the computer spit out five cards with data about him. The first one sent his friends into peals of laughter as they read, "You are highly opinionated and inclined to be blunt and sarcastic." Their laughter signaled that the machine was right on target.

This highly opinionated tendency often stereotypes the lives of these dynamic people, for their actions or reactions are almost predictable to those who know them. It is a happy day for him when Rocky learns to deliberate before making decisions and admits that his first impressions and prejudices often limit his enjoyment of life and inhibit productivity. Most Choleric husbands would do well to listen more to the thoughts, opinions, and feelings of their wives. Since opposites attract, his partner usually commands a broader perspective on life, is more deliberate when forming conclusions, and would be an asset to him in making decisions *before* he jumped into things. When he listens to her, they are usually both happier!

Crafty and Domineering

One of the undesirable characteristics of the Choleric involves his inclination to be crafty if necessary to get his own way. He rarely takes no for an answer and will often resort to any means necessary to achieve his ends. Since he never gives up, he regards a "No" decision as "Wait!" and can be counted on to bring it up again. If he has to juggle his figures and bend the truth, he rarely hesitates, for to him the end justifies the means. When he needs a favor, he can be almost a Sanguine in his persuasiveness, but as soon as you give him what he wants, he forgets he ever met you. It is probably this trait that gains him a reputation for using people.

Since he easily comes to conclusions, he finds great delight in making decisions for other people and forcing them to conform to his will. If you work for a Choleric, you rarely wonder what he wants you to do, for he tells you five times before 8:30 in the morning—and usually at the top of his lungs. Impatience personified, he gives instructions in such staccato style and abbreviation that one needs to hear them five times to know what he means. Reading his inter-office notes is even more difficult. He writes so fast, skipping half the letters and some of the words, that you cannot be sure what he wants and are usually afraid to ask questions.

Conclusion

Rocky Cholerics are effective people if their weaknesses are not indulged until they become a dominating lifestyle. When they are filled with the Spirit, their tendencies toward willfulness and harshness are replaced by a gentleness that verifies clearly that they are controlled by something other than their own natural temperament. From the days of the apostle Paul until the present, both the church of Jesus Christ and society have benefited much from these active, productive people. Many of our great church institutions were founded by venturous Cholerics. But to be effective in God's service, they must learn the divine principles of productivity. "'Not by [Choleric] might nor by [natural] power, but by My Spirit,' says the Lord of Hosts" (Zech. 4:6).

The Choleric apostle Paul is probably the most productive Christian in the history of the church. In my book *Transformed Temperaments*, I use him as an illustration of a Choleric controlled by the Holy Spirit. That is, of course, the key for any Choleric—to be controlled by the Holy Spirit.

Martin Melancholy

Martin Melancholy is the richest of all the temperaments—an analytical, self-sacrificing, gifted, perfectionist
type with a sensitive emotional nature. No one gets
more enjoyment from the fine arts than the
Melancholy. By nature, he is prone to be an
introvert, but since his feelings predominate,
he is given to a variety of moods. Sometimes
they will lift him to heights of ecstasy that cause
him to act more extroverted. At other times
he will be gloomy and depressed, and during
these periods he becomes withdrawn and can
be quite antagonistic. This tendency toward
black moods has earned him the reputation
of being the "dark temperament."
Martin is a faithful friend, but unlike the
Sanguine, he does not make friends easily. He
seldom pushes himself forward to meet
people but rather lets them come to him. He
is perhaps the most dependable of all the
temperaments, for his perfectionist tendencies do not permit him to be a shirker
or let others down when they are count-
ing on him. His natural reticence is not an indication
that he doesn't enjoy people. Like the rest of us, he not only
likes others but has a strong desire to be loved by them.
Disappointing experiences make him reluctant to take
people at face value; thus he is prone to be suspicious when
others seek him out or shower him with attention.

His exceptional analytical ability causes him to diagnose
accurately the obstacles and dangers of any project he has
a part in planning. This is in sharp contrast to the Choleric,
who rarely anticipates problems or difficulties but is confident he can cope with whatever crises may arise. Such a
characteristic often finds the Melancholy reticent to initiate some new project or take on a new venture. Vocational
change is a decision that is hard to make for a Melancholy.
He prefers the status quo—even if it is a deep rut. Whenever a person looks at obstacles instead of resources or

goals, he will easily become discouraged before he starts. If you confront a Melancholy about his pessimistic state, he will usually retort, "I am not being pessimistic! I'm just being realistic." In other words, his usual thinking process makes him realistically pessimistic. Occasionally, in one of his exemplary moods of emotional ecstasy or inspiration, he may produce some great work of art or genius (e.g., Edgar Allen Poe), but these accomplishments are often followed by periods of great depression.

Martin Melancholy usually finds his greatest meaning in life through personal sacrifice. He seems desirous of making himself suffer, and he will often choose a difficult life vocation involving great personal sacrifice. But once it is chosen, he is prone to be thorough and persistent in his pursuit of it and more than likely will accomplish great good if his natural tendency to gripe throughout the sacrificial process doesn't get him so depressed that he gives up on it altogether. No temperament has so much natural potential when energized by the Holy Spirit as the Melancholy.

Vocational Potential of the Melancholy

As a general rule, no other temperament has a higher IQ, creativity, or imagination than a Melancholy, and no one else is as prone to perfectionism. Most of the world's great composers, artists, musicians, inventors, philosophers, theoreticians, theologians, scientists, and dedicated educators have been predominantly Melancholies. Name a famous artist, composer, or orchestra leader and you have identified another genius (and often eccentric) Melancholy. Consider Rembrandt, van Gogh, Beethoven, Mozart, Wagner, and a host of others. Usually the greater the degree of genius, the greater will be the predominance of a Melancholy temperament.

Any vocation that requires perfection, self-sacrifice, and creativity is open to Martin Melancholy, but he tends to place self-imposed limitations on his potential by underestimating himself and exaggerating obstacles. Almost any humanitarian vocation will attract Melancholies to its staff.

For years I have watched doctors, and although there are bound to be exceptions, almost every doctor I know is either predominantly or at least secondarily Melancholic. A Melancholy's mind is an advantage for getting through the rigors of medical school, for a doctor has to be a perfectionist, an analytical specialist, have a near photographic memory, and be a humanitarian propelled by a heart that yearns to help other people.

The analytical ability required to design buildings, lay out a landscape, or look at acreage and envision a cohesive development usually requires a Melancholy temperament. In the building trades the Melancholy may want to supervise construction, but he would be better off hiring a project supervisor who works better with people and then spend his own time on the drawing board. He becomes frustrated by the usual personnel problems and, with his unrealistic perfectionist demands, adds to them.

Almost every true musician has some Melancholy temperament, whether he is a composer, choral conductor, performing artist, or soloist. This often accounts for the Melancholy's lament that seems to find its way into so much of our music, both in and out of the church. One day as my wife and I were driving to the airport, a country-western tune crooned (or warbled, depending on your point of view) over the radio. We looked at each other and laughed as the wail of the obvious Melancholy became so apparent, and that song is one of today's top tunes.

The influence of temperament on a person's musical ability was apparent several years ago as our church evaluated a gifted minister of music and his piano-playing wife, obviously a Choleric. On the way home I reflected to my wife that I couldn't understand how a Choleric could be such a good pianist. Beverly replied, "She is a mechanical musician. It's her strong willpower that forces her to play the piano well, but she doesn't feel her music." As it turned out, the fantastic arrangement she used that night had been written by her husband, a Melancholy. Although he was not a pianist, he could feel music.

Not all Melancholies, of course, enter the professions or arts. Many become craftsmen of a high quality—finish carpenters, bricklayers, plumbers, plasterers, mechanics, engineers, and members of almost every profession that provides a meaningful service to humanity. One vocation that seems to attract the Melancholy, surprisingly enough, is acting, for we tend to identify this profession with an extrovert. On stage the Melancholy can become another person and even adopt that personality, no matter how much extroversion it requires, but as soon as the play is over and he comes down from his emotional high, he reverts back to his own more introverted personality. Some great preachers have been criticized for their lack of personal charm when not in the pulpit, which shouldn't be surprising if they are predominantly Melancholic in temperament. But it is that trait of perfection that propels them to study hard so they can deliver good sermons.

Weaknesses of the Melancholy

The enemies of every temperament are his natural weaknesses. These tendencies often prevent him from fulfilling the tremendous potential for which he was created. The following list catalogs the Melancholy's most pronounced weaknesses. If he concentrates on gaining victory over these problems, he can be a most effective and productive human being.

Negative, Pessimistic, and Critical

The admirable qualities of perfectionism and conscientiousness often carry with them the serious disadvantages of negativism, pessimism, and a spirit of criticism. Anyone who has worked with a gifted Melancholy very long can anticipate that his first reaction to anything will be negative or pessimistic. The reaction of the numerous Melancholies in our college and church organizations to most things is quite predictable. Their favorite response echoes, "Impossible!" or "It won't work!" or "It can't be done!" The statements that always bug me the most: "We've tried that once and it failed!" or "The other people will never go for it!"

This one trait limits a Melancholy's vocational performance more than any other: The minute a new idea or project is presented, his analytical ability ignites and he begins to concoct every problem and difficulty that may be encountered in the effort. This is an advantage for industry because by using that trait the Melancholy can anticipate problems and prepare for them. But to himself it is a distinct disadvantage because it keeps him from venturing out on his own and taking advantage of his creativity. Rarely does a predominantly Melancholy person start a new business or privately instigate an untried program. Instead, he is more apt to be used by less gifted but more enterprising temperaments.

The bachelor is a good example. He thinks he is a Melancholy because he is a bachelor, but in reality he is a bachelor because he is a Melancholy. The reason is simple: He forms a mental vision of the ideal wife. When he meets her, he falls instantly in love but soon observes that she exhibits weaknesses. (A Melancholy discovers before marriage what other temperaments do not learn until after—that *every* human being has weaknesses.) He then faces the $64,000 question: "Can I love someone who is so obviously imperfect?" All too often his ladylove tires of waiting and marries someone else.

A lovely young woman counselor at a youth camp asked for counseling and surprised me by requesting, "When you are at _____ Church next month, would you tell the youth pastor either to marry me or get out of my life?" This twenty-seven-year-old woman had dated this twenty-eight-year-old dedicated Christian worker for eight years. They had been engaged seven times (twice their wedding invitations had been sent out), but each time he had called it off as their wedding day approached. When I saw him a month later, he confirmed everything she said and added, "No other girl appeals to me, but I'm unsure whether I'm doing the right thing." (Almost everyone experiences buyer's remorse, but Melancholies usually get it before they even make the purchase or decision.) I advised him, "Tom, the next time you get the urge to marry that girl, don't tell a soul. Just drive her to Yuma and marry her." I forgot about the experience until Christmastime when I received a postcard from Yuma, Arizona, that simply read, "We did it!" signed, Mr. and Mrs. Tom _____. Six months later I met him again. Thanking me, he admitted ruefully, "I wish someone had told me to do that five years ago."

This pessimistic, negative, indecisive tendency may be maddening to others, but it has nothing to do with manhood. *Temperament* causes it. A friend of mine represents a similar case. A top linebacker in college and an outstanding player for two years for the Oakland Raiders, he hung up his spikes to study for the ministry. Today he is pastoring in Southern California. He led his wife to Christ when they were in college, but many times this giant of a man broke their engagement and almost her heart. Several times Ken Poure and I encouraged him to ignore his fears and marry the girl. Finally he did—and today he has three beautiful children and no regrets.

In his favor, I should add that once married, Martin Melancholy is more apt to be loving, sensitive, and faithful than any other temperament—*if* he doesn't let his negative thought patterns dominate. Sometimes, for instance, they can make him obsessively suspicious for no reason. One negativistic Melancholy became so obsessed with doubt that he accused his wife of having an affair with his father—though not a shred of evidence verified his suspicions.

The most damaging influence upon a person's mind, in my opinion, is criticism, and Melancholies have to fight that spirit constantly. It is bad enough to entertain negative thoughts, but even worse to verbalize them, for they not only reinforce the critical spirit of his mind but also devastate his wife and children. I have observed that the most psychologically disturbed children come from homes of predominantly Melancholy or Choleric parents. Cholerics are hard to please; Melancholies are impossible to satisfy. Even when the children bring home Bs and B+s, the parent will grimace with dissatisfaction because they didn't get

As. Instead of commending their wives and encouraging them, Melancholies criticize, carp, and censure—or if they don't verbalize their attitudes, they puff up with a disapproving spirit that is equally as destructive. Even when they realize the importance of their approval to both wife and children, it is hard for them to offer it because they cannot endure the hypocritical taint of saying something that isn't 100 percent true. To commend the 95 percent of a person that is acceptable is most difficult for one whose magnifying glass of perfectionism seems to concentrate on the 5 percent of his family's imperfections.

This same high standard is usually turned inward by a Melancholy, making him dissatisfied even with himself. Self-examination, of course, is a healthy thing for any Christian who wants to walk in the Spirit, for through it he gains the realization that he must confess his sins and seek the Savior's forgiveness (1 John 1:9). But the Melancholy is not satisfied to merely examine himself; he dissects himself with a continuing barrage of introspection until he has no self-confidence or self-esteem left. It is not uncommon for Melancholies who have heard my talk on the four temperaments to respond, "I don't think I'm on your chart, for I have all of the weaknesses of all of the temperaments and none of the strengths."

Accepting Jesus Christ as his Savior and walking in the control of the Holy Spirit is the best remedy for the weaknesses of any temperament. It is particularly beneficial for the Melancholy because the indwelling of the Holy Spirit communicates a new power to this normally defeatist, pessimistic person, enabling him to look forward to success instead of failure. This one concept can change the critical mouthings of a griping Melancholy (man or woman) whom people inwardly shun and outwardly avoid, into a complimentary, commending person who gains and enjoys the love and fellowship of others, particularly his own family. This new confidence is the result of his growing faith in God and the many promises in his Word, such as: "Do not let your hearts be troubled. Trust in God; trust also in me";

"Fear not"; "Do not be anxious about anything"; and a host of others.

One of the most direct challenges to the negative thinker is found in Philippians 4:8: "Brethren, whatever things are true, whatever things are noble, whatever things are just, whatever things are pure, whatever things are lovely, whatever things are of good report, if there is any virtue and if there is anything praiseworthy—meditate on these things." Notice carefully that the challenge to "think" in that verse is totally positive—not one negative concept is permitted. When a Christian Melancholy realizes that he is out of the will of God whenever he permits his mind to indulge in negative and pessimistic criticism, worry, or fear, his personality, character, and life are transformed.

Self-Centered, Thin-Skinned, and Touchy

The Melancholy is more self-centered than any other temperament. Everything in life is interpreted by him in relation to himself. He is most likely to accuse the minister of "preaching at me." If a new work regulation is announced, he responds with alarm, "They're out to get me!" He tends to compare himself with others in looks, talent, and intellect, invariably feeling deficient because it never occurs to him that he compares himself to the best of another's traits and fails to evaluate their weaknesses.

He is everlastingly examining his spiritual life and typically coming up short—in his own mind—in spite of the fact that he is most likely to be more devoted than others. As one Melancholy said to me, "I've confessed all the sins I can remember, but I know there must be others that I just can't recall." This kept him from enjoying any confidence with God. He needed to comprehend that one of the works of the Holy Spirit is to convict us of sin, so that if we examine ourselves and do not find sin, we should take God at his promise and enjoy his forgiveness and peace. A Melancholy, quite unlike all the other types, finds it difficult to believe he is "approved of God," basically because he can seldom approve himself.

After I had preached on "all have sinned and fall short of the glory of God" (Rom. 3:23), one Melancholy I had counseled mirrored his self-centered trait in his response. "See, just like I told you. I'm a sinner—all have sinned." Only after he realized that the verse was speaking of men before conversion and attempting to draw them to Christ was the Christian Melancholy able to enjoy peace with God.

This self-centered tendency, together with his sensitive nature, makes a Melancholy thin-skinned and touchy at times. You can offend him by merely looking at him. Then again, you can offend him by *not* looking at him. It is not uncommon for him to be personally affronted when he is passed over in a church or club election. When I confronted one Melancholy about his bitter and obviously injured spirit, he reluctantly confessed that it was because he was not elected to a church office. Immediately he launched into a tirade about how he had been a tithing, active, and faithful member and "deserved better treatment." When I explained that the nominating committee had just set a policy of giving a year's rest to every person who had served the previous three years, he was incredulous. In fact, he refused to believe me until he had gone over the list carefully and verified that all last year's officers had been rested. Even then he wanted me to understand that that was a "stupid decision."

As I travel over one hundred thousand miles a year, holding Friday and Saturday Family Life Seminars, I am often confronted with disgruntled church members who criticize their pastor. At least 90 percent of the critics are Melancholies who are impossible to please. Although I realize ministers are not perfect, if they were half as bad as these critics make them out, the church would have been out of business years ago. If you have ever contacted a person who was driven away from a church by some tragic blunder or offense, he was probably of a Melancholy temperament. Other temperaments seem to accept such adversity in stride, but Melancholies tend to become disillusioned.

One word to parents: Be extremely careful when raising children who are Melancholies! You can wound their sensitive spirits very easily. It will take all the love and compassion the Holy Spirit can provide to enable you patiently to instruct, discipline, and love them into maturity without unnecessary scars on the psyche, for all Melancholies, young or old, carry their feelings on their sleeve. In my wife's book *How to Develop Your Child's Temperament*, she points out that more conflicts between parents arise over the discipline of such children than any other. One parent usually thinks the other is too strict.

Revengeful and Persecution-Prone

The gifted mind of a Melancholy can be either the spawning ground for creative and worthwhile concepts or the cause of harmful thoughts. Although not at all as expressive of his anger as the Sanguine or Choleric, he is capable of long-term seething and slow-burning anger in the form of revengeful thinking patterns and self-persecution reveries.

If indulged long enough, they can make him manic-depressive, or at least erupt into an angry outburst that is unlike his normally gentle nature. Many an outstanding athlete has ruined his career by thinking the coach had it in for him. One professional quarterback became so obsessed with such thoughts that he was convinced the coach sent in plays from the bench that were designed to make him look ridiculous. Naturally, he was so upset that he did poorly. This problem is so basic that it explains why some great athletes will do better after being traded to another club. It isn't really the new coach's superior techniques, but the athlete's change of attitude.

Negative thought patterns cause a Melancholy to make unrealistic decisions. I have seen a Martin Melancholy resign from a good job, leave his wife and children, estrange himself from a relative or neighbor, or drop out of school for completely inadequate reasons. No temperament is more apt to "throw the baby out with the bath water" than the Melancholy, and ninety-five times out of a hundred, his revengeful, oppressive thinking pattern has blown the problem all out of perspective. But he usually doesn't wake up to his error until it is too late.

A Melancholy finds it most difficult to forgive an insult or injury. He may appear calm over the matter and will occasionally say "I forgive you," but in his heart he will carry a grudge. One couple I counseled provides a good illustration. The Melancholy husband had so criticized his Sanguine wife for her "inefficiency, weak will, and tendency to flit all over" that he stripped her of any self-respect. Consequently, when a man came along who was kind to her, it was only a matter of time until he enticed her into his bed. A few weeks later she was so guilt stricken that she confessed to her husband and he brought her to me. After their confession to God, I gave them some suggestions for spiritual safeguards in order to avoid a repetition. At first the husband was solicitous and acknowledged that he had not treated his wife properly. But when he went home, he started thinking about her infidelity. Within three months they were back, and she tearfully accused him of not forgiving her because, except for the first week, he had not made love to her since. His revengeful thoughts and self-martyrdom had stifled his normal sex drive. What a price to pay for revenge!

After confronting him with the fact that he had not forgiven his wife, he responded, "Yes, I forgave her, but I can't forget it." That is an old dodge that amounts to a lie. God not only forgives our sins but remembers them no more (Heb. 10:17). He further tells us not only to forgive those who sin against us but also to forgive others as Christ forgave us (Eph. 4:32). Only after this self-righteous man who wanted to throw the first stone was convinced that he possessed a revengeful heart and that he had an obligation to God to forgive his wife did he go home and try. I am happy to say that with God's help he did. His reward? Spiritual growth, an exciting family life, and hundreds of exciting lovemaking experiences with his wife. Because of *his* forgiveness, she was able to forgive herself and today is a different woman. Forgiveness never hurt anyone and is a great emotional healer, whereas condemnation always destroys.

Moody, Depressive, and Antisocial

One of the most prominent characteristics of a Melancholy's temperament is mood swings. On some occasions he is so high that he acts like an international Sanguine; on others he is so down that he feels like sliding under the door rather than opening it. The older he gets (unless transformed by a vital relationship to Jesus Christ), the more he is prone to experience black or dark moods. During such times he is gloomy, irritable, unhappy, and all but impossible to please. Such moods make him particularly vulnerable to depression.

Several years ago I read an article on depression in *Newsweek* magazine that stated, "Depression is the emotional epidemic of our times. 50,000 to 70,000 depressed individuals attempt suicide annually." Having counseled over one thousand depressed people by that time, I felt compelled to write a book called *How to Win over Depression*, which became a best-seller in only three months. Today there are nearly one million copies in print, and it has been translated into at least twenty-nine languages. Evidently *Newsweek* did not exaggerate the problem, which must be international. Certainly any thinking person who looks realistically at the mess this world is in will be depressed unless he has the hope in Christ that he alone provides. But depression is not necessarily the result of external circumstances. The inward contemplation of self-pity often produces that awful mood.

Anyone with a depression problem, particularly a Melancholy, should make 1 Thessalonians 5:18 a way of life: "In everything give thanks; for this is the will of God in Christ Jesus for you." It is the best antidote available for the problem. You cannot rejoice and give thanks over something while maintaining your state of depression.

Legalistic and Rigid

No other temperament is so apt to be rigid, implacable, and uncompromising to the point of unreasonableness as the Melancholy. He is a natural martyr to his cause, viewing a group compromise "to keep the peace" as an insufferable lack of principle or integrity. He never speaks in exaggeration and often corrects himself in the middle of a statement in an attempt to be scrupulously honest. He would never cheat on his income tax and often looks down on those who make legitimate business deductions as being dishonest. He is intolerant and impatient with those who do not see things his way; consequently, he finds it difficult to be a team player and is often a loner in the business world. Usually his gifted mind and creativity can get him by in business, but his tendency to be an unreasonable purist tends to complicate personnel problems. Because he is only there for eight working hours a day, he can maintain a career. But at home it is a different matter. A wife and children subjected to such rigid standards will often become insecure and unhappy and sometimes give up on him. Once he learns that flexibility and cooperation are the oil that makes interpersonal relationships run smoothly and begins to loosen up, he is a much happier person—and so are those around him.

Impractical and Theoretical

We have already seen that the Melancholy is an Idealist, a trait we list as a strength. But he is also apt to be impractical and theoretical. Just as the Choleric has an innate tendency to be utilitarian and practical, so the Melancholy will usually campaign for an ideal that is so altruistic it will never work. Nowhere is this more apparent than on the college campus, where brilliant professors present humanistic ideals of socialism to our young people, in spite of the fact that such theoretical concepts are so impractical as to be historically nonfunctional—primarily because they destroy human initiative.

The first time I had a chance to observe this tendency was on a trip over the polar cap to Amsterdam, long before the collapse of the Soviet Union. Seated next to me for nine hours was a seventy-year-old college professor who had retired after thirty years of teaching political science in state colleges. Although I was dog tired after a whirlwind schedule in preparation for a tour through Europe and the Holy

Land, he brought me straight up in my chair. At first I
thought he was an outright Communist, but later I decided
he was just a theoretical Marxist intellectual. (*U.S. News and
World Report* once indicated that there were more than ten
thousand such Marxist professors in the American college
and university system.) He was on his way to visit Russia
for the first time, "anxious to see socialism in action." When
I registered surprise at his obvious approval of a govern-
ment-controlled economy, he began to extol its ideals. As
soon as I could interrupt, I reasoned with him that such a
program has never worked in any country successfully
because it stifles human initiative and responsibility. For
three hours we argued until finally I reminded him that Com-
munism and socialism are twins, except that Communists
use brute force in confiscating privately owned land, which
is why over thirty million Russians were killed after the Bol-
shevik revolution. He flushed in the face and screamed at
me, "They had to kill those people because of capitalism.
If the capitalists would stop resisting, the Communists
wouldn't have had to kill anyone, and we could have peace
instead of war." Even summoning all the self-control I could
muster, it was impossible for me not to point out that the
result would be a Communist dictatorship, to which he
replied, "You capitalists are hopeless!" He refused to speak
to me again all the way to Holland.

I wonder what mental gymnastics he uses now to explain
the utter failure of socialism in Russia after seventy years.
Or maybe he was cured by his visit there.

I hope such exaggerated idealism is not typical, but when
one discovers that far too many collegians favor interna-
tionalism over American patriotism, a guaranteed income
over self-reliance, and responsibility and dependence on
government instead of on God, one has to wonder. Students
seldom derive such ideas from the home, but they are bom-
barded with them on college campuses.

Such idealism could account partially for today's humanistic ecology lovers who are more interested in whales
trapped under ice than thirty million unborn children
aborted by the "choice" of their mothers, or that saving owls

is more important than the vocations of over twenty-five thousand lumberjacks. These examples of idealism are typical of the Melancholy. In the office, factory, or home, it can be a serious deterrent to harmony. One such employee counted the discarded materials in his fellow employees' wastebaskets over a period of time and reported the wastefulness to his boss. He overlooked the possibility that the time he spent on the project (and that which his associates consumed in altering their policy so as to salvage otherwise discarded materials) plus the interpersonal hostility thus generated might cost more than the suggested savings.

A Melancholy should always subject his plans to the practicality test. In addition, he would be wise to associate with a partner of another temperament, for complementary temperaments often accomplish more together than if they operated individually. One might get the impression from all of this that I am opposed to idealism or altruistic values, but that is not true. I commend the Melancholy for his idealistic tendency but urge him to analyze it carefully lest it devise theoretical and impractical programs. After all, the Bible challenges us with "Let your gentleness be known to all men" (Phil. 4:5). This world has benefited greatly from the lofty ideals of Melancholies who were practical enough to package their ideas in such a way as to appeal to the people of their day. The planet earth has been beautified and enriched by many Melancholies who have used their creativity for the good of humanity. Unfortunately, equally as many have done nothing worthy of their talents, while others have even been detrimental. The reason some were successful and others were not is quite simple—some triumphed over their weaknesses, whereas others were enslaved by theirs.

Conclusion

God has used many Melancholies who made their talents available to him. In fact, many of the characters recorded in the Bible were Melancholies. Name a prophet and you have probably identified a Melancholy, for all the prophets were predominantly of that temperament. But the key to their success was not their temperament, talents, or gifts, but their commitment to the Holy Spirit. Moses, the doubtful, hesitant, nonspeaker ("I am slow of speech"—Exod. 4:10), became the greatest leader the world has ever seen—*after surrendering his will to God.* He led three million griping Jews through the wilderness for forty years.

Philip Phlegmatic

Philip Phlegmatic is the calm, easygoing, never-get-upset individual with such a high boiling point that he rarely becomes angry. He is without question the easiest person to get along with and is by nature the most likable of all the temperaments.

Philip Phlegmatic derives his name from what Hippocrates thought was the body fluid that produced that "calm, cool, slow, well-balanced temperament." Life for him is a happy, unexcited, pleasant experience in which he avoids as much involvement as possible. He is so calm and unruffled that he never seems agitated, no matter what circumstances surround him. He is the one temperament type that is consistent every time you see him. Beneath his cool, reticent, almost timid personality, Mr. Phlegmatic has a capable combination of abilities. He feels much more emotion than appears on the surface and has the capacity to appreciate the fine arts and the better things of life.

The Phlegmatic does not lack for friends because he enjoys people and has a natural, dry sense of humor. He is the type of individual who can have a crowd of people in stitches, yet never cracks a smile. Possessing the unique capability for seeing something humorous in others and the things they do, he maintains a positive approach to life. He has a good, retentive mind and is capable of being a fine imitator. One of his great sources of delight is needling or poking fun at the other temperament types. For instance, he is annoyed by the aimless, restless enthusiasm of the Sanguine and disgusted by the gloomy moods of the Melancholy. The former, says Mr. Phlegmatic, must be confronted with his futility, the latter with his morbidity. He takes great delight in throwing ice water on the bubbling plans and ambitions of the Choleric.

Phil Phlegmatic tends to be a spectator in life and tries not to get involved with the activities of others. In fact, it is usually with great reluctance that he is ever motivated to any form of activity beyond his daily routine. This does not mean, however, that he cannot appreciate the need for action and the predicaments of others. He and Rocky Choleric may confront the same social injustice, but their responses will be entirely different. The crusading spirit of the Choleric will cause him to exclaim, "Let's get a committee organized and campaign to do something about this!" The Phlegmatic would more likely respond, "These conditions are terrible! Why doesn't someone do something about them?" Usually kindhearted and sympathetic, Phil Phlegmatic seldom conveys his true feelings. When once aroused to action, however, his capable and efficient qualities become apparent. He will not volunteer for leadership on his own, but when it is forced upon him, he proves to be a capable leader. He has a conciliating effect on others and is a natural peacemaker.

Vocational Potential of the Phlegmatic

The world has benefited greatly from the gracious nature of Phil Phlegmatic. In his quiet way, he has proved to be a fulfiller of the dreams of others. He is a master at anything that requires meticulous patience and daily routine.

Most elementary school teachers are Phlegmatics. Who but a Phlegmatic could have the patience necessary to teach a group of first-graders to read? A Sanguine would spend the entire class period telling stories to the children.

A Melancholy would so criticize them that they would be afraid to read aloud. And I can't even imagine a Choleric as a first-grade teacher. The students would leap out the windows! The gentle nature of the Phlegmatic assures the ideal atmosphere for such learning. This is not only true on the elementary level but in both high school and college, particularly in math, physics, grammar, literature, language classes, and others. It is not uncommon to find Phlegmatics as school administrators, librarians, counselors, and college department heads. Phlegmatics seem drawn to the field of education.

Another field that appeals to Phlegmatics is engineering. Attracted to planning and calculation, they make good structural engineers, sanitation experts, chemical engineers, draftsmen, mechanical and civil engineers, and statisticians. Most Phlegmatics have excellent mechanical aptitude and thus become good mechanics, tool-and-die specialists, craftsmen, carpenters, electricians, plasterers, glassblowers, and watch and camera repairmen.

Currently, the biggest problem faced by industry pertains to personnel. With wages for many jobs skyrocketing, with government bureaucrats (OSHA and EEOC) searching for civil rights or sexual harassment violations, employees can become so demotivated that employers may lose millions of dollars in productivity. In recent years as government overregulation has increased, management has begun to discover that experienced Phlegmatics in their employ often make excellent foremen, supervisors, and managers of people. Because they are diplomatic and unabrasive, people work well with them. When given positions of leadership, they seem to bring order out of chaos and produce a working harmony that is conducive to increased productivity. They are well organized, never come to a meeting unprepared or late, tend to work well under pressure, and are extremely dependable. They rarely test government rules and regulations but fulfill them. Phlegmatics often stay with one company for their entire career.

An interesting aspect of their leadership ability is that they almost never volunteer for authoritative responsibilities, which is why I label them "reluctant leaders." Secretly, a Phlegmatic may aspire for a promotion, but it would be against his nature to volunteer. Instead, he may patiently wait until more discordant and inept personalities make a mess out of things and then assume the responsibility only after it is forced upon him. Unfortunately, in many instances Phlegmatics wait their lives away and opportunity never knocks because, although employers appreciate their capabilities, they don't envision them as leaders. Consequently, both the company and the employees lose. Rarely does a Phlegmatic either live up to his full capabilities or fail in life.

Because they tend to struggle with the problem of personal insecurity, Phlegmatics may take jobs with retirement or security benefits in mind. Therefore, civil service, the military, local government, or some other "good security risk" will attract them. Rarely will they launch out on a business venture of their own, although they are usually qualified to do so. Instead they often enhance the earning power of someone else and are quite content with a simple lifestyle.

Weaknesses of the Phlegmatic

In spite of their nice-guy image and easygoing temperament, Phlegmatics are not perfect. The following list is of typical weaknesses.

Unmotivated, Slow, and Lazy

The most obvious of Phil Phlegmatic's weaknesses and that which caused Hippocrates to label him *phlegm* (slow or sluggish) is his apparent lack of drive and ambition. Although he always seems to do what is expected of him, he will rarely do more. He may give one the feeling that his metabolism is low and his blood thick, and he frequently falls asleep the moment he sits down. Rarely does he instigate an activity but thinks up excuses to avoid getting involved with the activities of others and tends to slow down with each passing year.

As a marriage counselor, I noticed long ago that opposites attract each other in marriage. Consequently, it is not uncommon for an energetic and activity-driven Sanguine or Choleric to marry a Phlegmatic. Whenever the Choleric wife of Phil Phlegmatic comes in for counseling, I usually anticipate what I call the Phlegmatic Lethargy Syndrome—and I am right over 80 percent of the time. Dynamic Clara Choleric married Phil Phlegmatic because she "felt so comfortable around this quiet, stable, easygoing man." Now, after a few years of marriage, she is going stir crazy. Why? Because this nice, faithful, gentle man seems to wind down more during each successive year. He usually wakes up early, goes off to work in a good mood, and returns at 5:30 P.M., "utterly exhausted." He often requires a nap before dinner, after which he sits in front of the TV (with a remote-control unit in his hand, of course) and falls in and out of sleep several times during the evening. Finally, after the late news, she awakens him and assists him to bed where he sleeps the sleep of death until morning. Such is the exciting life of Clara Choleric when married to Phil Phlegmatic!

One frustrated Choleric wife read my first book on temperaments, *Spirit-Controlled Temperament,* and related this story. She was so blessed by the book that she longed for her Phlegmatic husband to read it, but he would no sooner begin than he would fall asleep. Finally, one night while he was "resting" on the couch, she sat on the floor in front of him and read it to him from beginning to end. Upon finishing she asked, "What did you think of it?" His classic response was "Fine!" Then he rolled over and fell asleep. At the close of her letter the wife implored, "How can I motivate my husband?"

At a recent Family Life Seminar, a lovely Sanguine wife asked the same question, but particularly about their sex life. Like many middle-aged women, she acknowledged an increased interest in lovemaking and added that her husband was a good lover "when he's not too tired, but I always have to initiate lovemaking." Most alert wives enjoy instigating lovemaking occasionally but fear that something is undesirable about them if hubby regularly waits to be approached and rarely pursues her. After she quickly described what she did to arouse him, I thought, "Only a Phlegmatic could sleep through a scene like that."

Phil Phlegmatic can do seven positive things to improve his self-motivation:

1. Accept Jesus Christ as Savior and Lord, then walk in the control of his Spirit. One of the nine strengths of the Holy Spirit is self-control, which will motivate him.
2. Develop an "others" mentality; that is, let the Holy Spirit flood his heart with love for others so that he will think of them and their needs rather than indulge his own comforts.
3. Recognize that he is not internally motivated and thus take up activities that force him into action. I have urged several Phlegmatics to join the church couples' bowling team, go out for visitation, or participate in other programs in order to get involved. By nature a Phlegmatic is like a watch that is unwinding; he needs to take on projects that will wind him up.
4. Visualize himself in action. The last thing a Phlegmatic should do on his way home from work is to visualize and verbalize how tired he is. Naturally, sleep becomes his central desire, and that is his problem. Modern science has established that you will do what your mind has been dwelling on—so Phil should think "activity" on his way home each night. He should also develop the habit of setting goals for himself—goals for tomorrow, next week, and for life. He that aims at nothing will be sure to hit it.
5. Take vitamins. Most nutritionists suggest that our bodies lack the necessary minerals they need from food. Particularly after forty almost everyone should take vitamins.
6. See a doctor. Make sure all systems are "go."
7. Exercise regularly. Moderate exercise does not wear one out but rather tones the muscles and increases energy.

More than any other temperament, the Phlegmatic is vulnerable to the law of inertia: "A body at rest tends to stay at rest." He needs to reverse that trend with premeditated activity. Both he and his family will benefit by such efforts.

Self-Protective

No one likes to be hurt, and that is particularly true of Phil Phlegmatic. Although not as sensitive as a Melancholy, he does have a thin skin and accordingly learns early in life to protect himself. It is not uncommon for him to live like a turtle; that is, he builds a hard shell of self-protection to shield him from all outside griefs or affronts. But even a turtle could give Phil a valuable piece of advice: "You can never go anywhere unless you stick your neck out." Nor will you ever help anyone else unless you risk the possibility of an emotional injury.

Selfish and Stingy

One of the less obvious weaknesses of the Phlegmatic is his selfishness. Every temperament faces this problem to some degree, but Phil is particularly afflicted with it, though he is so gracious and proper that few people who don't live with him are aware of it. Selfishness makes him self-indulgent and unconcerned about his family's need for activity.

Nowhere is his selfishness more apparent than in his use of money. He is a penny-pincher and a miser except where clothes for himself or tools for his work are concerned. One outstanding Phlegmatic has through the years embarrassed his Sanguine wife so often in restaurants that she now expects it. When the waitress asks, "Do you want to order dessert?" he has a stock answer: "Does it come with the meal?" Naturally, Phil Phlegmatic doesn't call his tightfisted money policy selfishness; to him it is frugality. But you may wish to ask his wife sometime for her interpretation!

As a rule, Phil Phlegmatic is the lightest tipper in a restaurant, and when it comes to tithing, he is the last one to reach 10 percent. When he does, he rarely moves on to the "hilarious giving" of offerings. Consequently, he seldom enjoys

the blessings of God on his finances. Of all the temperaments, he and his wife tend to fight the most about money.

Stubborn, Stubborn, and Stubborn

No one can be more stubborn than a Phlegmatic, but he
is so diplomatic about it that he may proceed halfway
through life before others catch on. He almost never openly
confronts another person or refuses to do something, but
he will somehow manage to sidestep the demand. In church
administration I have found this gracious, kindly, placid
individual to be most exasperating at times. He will smile
as I detail the program, even nod his head as if he understands, and then walk away and ignore the mandate. He simply will do it his way—quite affably and with less contention
than any other temperament, but definitely *his* way.

In a family situation, Phlegmatics never yell or argue; they
just drag their feet or set their legs and do not budge. They
often remind me of a Missouri mule that stubbornly refuses
to follow anyone's request. Fortunately, they are not stubborn very often, and when they are it is *almost* funny. I've
already mentioned that opposites tend to attract each
other; Phlegmatics often marry Cholerics. That means the
most determined type marries the most stubborn. Perhaps
you have heard the old expression "The irresistible force
meets the immovable object." I deal with this and what to
do about it in my book *I Love You, but Why Are We So Different?* It makes for a challenging marriage!

Indecisive and Fearful

Beneath the gracious surface of a diplomatic Phlegmatic
beats a fearful heart. He is a worrier by nature who erroneously seems to misinterpret Philippians 4:6 as: "Be anxious for everything, and by worry and fear let your requests be made known unto God." This tendency often
keeps him from venturing out on his own to make full use
of his potential.

An obviously Phlegmatic man nearing retirement age
came up after a seminar to register a mild rebuke. A civil-
service mechanic for many years, he complained to me,

"You preachers always talk about the blessings of tithing. I've tithed for years and am about ready to retire, but God has not 'opened the windows of heaven' and poured out a blessing I can receive." After questioning the man, I discovered that he was not thanking God for (1) a long and healthy life, (2) a good wife and marriage, (3) four grown children and several grandchildren, and (4) an excellent job at which he had not lost a day's pay in thirty years and that provided him a government-secured retirement program (one of the best in the nation)—to mention just a few of his blessings. Evidently the Holy Spirit prompted me to ask, "In all these years, have you ever had an opportunity to go into business?" "Yes," he replied, "three times." When I inquired why he hadn't, he answered, "I was afraid it wouldn't work." Then he told me about a friend who, ten years before, tried to get him to invest three thousand dollars (which he had) and become a partner in a brake-repair business—but again, he "was afraid." When I asked how his friend made out, he hung his head a little and acknowledged that he now had three such shops and all were doing well. He had let his natural fears close the door of opportunity and now he was blaming God.

It is this kind of fear that keeps Phlegmatics from being used in their church. I'm convinced that many would like to teach, sing in the choir, or learn to share their faith, but fear stifles them. One of the strengths of the Holy Spirit is faith, which dissolves our fears. A positive result of reading and studying the Word of God is a growing faith. Most people are fearful of failure, but those who succeed in effectively serving God replace their fears with faith.

Conclusion

I have found it well worth the time to try motivating Phlegmatics to work in the church. They make good board members and policy makers as well as excellent Sunday school teachers and department superintendents. Once committed, they become dependable workers for many years. The difficult task is to get them to agree to an assignment in the first place. That is why, like all the other temperaments, they need to "walk in [be controlled by] the Spirit" (Gal. 5:16). I have seen fear-inhibited, stubborn, and selfish Phlegmatics become confident sharers of their faith, cooperative with others, and generous activists—with God's help. They don't become extroverts, but they do become more outgoing. And the interesting thing is that they like their new selves.

Abraham the Phlegmatic makes a good scriptural illustration. Fearful by nature (he tried to palm off his wife twice to save his own neck), he became one of the most unselfish men of faith in all of the Bible. When Hebrews 11 says of him, "Abraham *believed* God and it was counted to him as righteousness," it is saying his greatest weakness—fear—had been overcome and replaced with what became his greatest strength—faith.

Temperament Influences Everything You Do

Now that we have examined the four basic temperaments in detail, you can understand why I insist that no more significant influence naturally motivates your actions and reactions. Would you believe that even your driving habits are inspired by your temperament?

Temperament and Driving Skills

Sanguines are erratic drivers. Sometimes they speed, then for no apparent reason lose interest in driving fast and slow down. Riding in the backseat of a Sanguine's car can be downright dangerous. He is so people-oriented that he wants to look you in the face when talking—even while driving. And since he is a supertalker, he spends very little time watching where he is going when you are in the backseat.

Cholerics are daring speed demons who dart in and out of traffic constantly. They always try to get more accomplished in a given period of time than is humanly possible and attempt to make up time by driving furiously between appointments. Strangely enough they rarely get tickets—not because they don't deserve them, but because they are crafty enough to keep one eye on the rearview mirror to watch for the local "black and white."

Melancholy motorists never leave home without preparing for the trip well in advance. They study the map and know the best route from *A* to *Z*. Of all the temperaments, they are the most likely to keep a complete log of their driving history, including gas and oil consumption and car repairs. Legalists by nature, they rarely speed and may even drive one mile per hour under the speed limit. If they get a ticket, it is usually for refusing to yield the left lane to faster-moving traffic. At this point Martin Melancholy's reaction is one of great indignation. After all, wasn't he observing the speed limit?

Phil Phlegmatic is the slowest driver of all. The last one to leave an intersection, he rarely changes lanes and is an indecisive danger when joining the flow of freeway traffic from an entrance ramp. He invariably stops when he should be moving with the flow of traffic. He is a pokey Sunday driver seven days a week. He gets few tickets and rarely has accidents, but he can be a road hazard.

Temperament and Yard Care

As incredible as it may seem, you can discern a lot about a man's temperament by the way he does the yard work around his home. Sparky Sanguine gets up early Saturday morning to fix his yard. With great gusto he lines up all his tools (he has every gadget known to man because he totally lacks sales resistance) and prepares to cut, trim, shear, and prune. But within thirty minutes his wife can't hear a sound outside. Looking down the street, she observes him chatting joyfully with a neighbor. Before the day is over, he orders his son to "put my tools away" and decides to fix the yard next week. Sparky is clearly one of the world's great procrastinators.

Rocky Choleric hates yard work, and therefore when he does it at all, it is with a vengeance. He is not mechanical by nature and detests repairs or pruning because, quite frankly, he is not very good at it. When he does take on the yard, he works at a frenzied pace in order to get the job done, but neatness is not his hallmark. In fact, the family of a Choleric should *never* let him prune bushes, trees, or hedges, for he has only one idea in mind: "If you have to do it, you might as well do it once for the whole year!" One can usually spot the Choleric's yard while driving through the neighborhood. Just look for miniature hedges and dwarf trees.

Martin Melancholy has a natural aptitude for growing things and usually maintains the best yard in the neighborhood. He is the one who talks to and babies his plants, and on almost any weekend you will find him on hands and knees manicuring his lawns and hedges.

The Phlegmatic's lawn usually suggests that its owner is still in the house late Saturday morning, sipping his third cup of coffee—because he is. Capable of superior lawn care, Phil will scrupulously attend to "the old plantation" because his desire to rest is overcome by his drive to do the accepted thing.

Temperament and Pro Football Players

In talking to some of the San Diego Chargers football players after their weekly Bible study in our home one night, I was told that a man's temperament usually influences the position he plays on the team. (They took for granted that size, weight, and skills were likewise important factors.) They pointed out that quarterbacks who were good ball handlers and field generals were predominantly Cholerics. Pinpoint passers who were only so-so leaders were Melancholies, but quarterbacks serving as both strong leaders and excellent passers were Choleric-Melancholies. Offensive linemen, whose primary job is to protect the passer at any cost and open holes for the running backs, must be predominantly Melancholies—for only a Melancholy would be that self-sacrificing. Wide receivers and running backs are usually Melancholies or Phlegmatics. They have to be perfectionists to run their patterns effectively, preserve self-discipline, and maintain the enormous dedication their positions require. Fullbacks are often Cholerics, as are linebackers (though many are Sanguines or Choleric-Sanguines), because they love body contact. Cornerbacks are often Choleric-Melancholies; safeties are prone to be outspoken Sanguines, Cholerics, or a combination, because extroverts are usually better at instant reactions to others' actions—traits necessary in good defensive players. The special team players could be almost any temperament—they are just trying desperately to make the team.

These informal observations concerning a player's temperament were basically confirmed by the Chargers' former team psychiatrist in a book. He had observed that he could often tell a man's position by the way he kept his locker. The self-sacrificing offensive linemen, wide receivers, and Phlegmatic or Melancholy running backs usually kept neat lockers. The defensive players' lockers often looked like an explosion in a mattress factory.

Temperament and Eating Habits

I can tell a lot about a man's temperament by his eating habits. Sanguines eat everything in sight—and usually look it. Incidentally, in a restaurant they almost never look at a menu until the waitress arrives. They so enjoy talking that they forget about the bill of fare until she asks, "Are you ready to order, sir?" Cholerics are stereotyped eaters—their menu seldom varies from one day to the next, and when it arrives, they bolt it down in big chunks, often talking while chewing their food. Frequently they are the first ones finished. Melancholies are picky eaters; it takes them forever to make up their minds about what to order, but once it arrives they savor every bite. Phlegmatics are the most deliberate eaters of all and are invariably the last ones through eating. That is the main reason they rarely gain weight. All weight specialists warn obese patients to eat slowly, for it takes twenty minutes for food passing into the mouth to shut off hunger pangs. Consequently, the Phlegmatic and the Melancholy often lose their appetites before finishing the entire meal. Not so the Cholerics and Sanguines. They have usually completed the meal in seven minutes and want more because their hunger pangs haven't been satisfied yet—then after the meal they endure that overstuffed feeling.

There are many other areas in which temperament influences your behavior—the clothes you wear, the friends you choose, your work and study habits, your hobbies, and just about everything you do. Thus, you had better determine your temperament and consistently direct it into the best lifestyle for you and your family. Otherwise your temperament will subconsciously direct you. No man can maximize his strengths and minimize his weaknesses by himself. He needs that personal relationship to God that is only possible through his Son, Jesus Christ, and through the indwelling power of his Holy Spirit.

6

The Twelve Blends of Temperament

One of the chief objections to the theory of the four temperaments as advocated by the ancients is that everyone has to be totally representative of only one temperament. As I have said in my previous books on temperament, that just is not true. We are all a blend of at least two temperaments; one predominates, the other is secondary. To my knowledge, nothing had ever been written to demonstrate these blends until I wrote on this subject in the first edition of this book. Twenty years later I am even more convinced that we all are a blend of at least two, and some few people seem to possess three temperaments, one that predominates and two that are secondary.

In an attempt to make the temperament theory more practical and true to life, we shall briefly examine the twelve possible blends of temperament. In all probability, it will be easier for you to identify yourself in one of the blends than in only one of the four basics.

One salient factor should be kept in mind when considering blends—not all are of the same degree. For example, a man who is 60 percent Sanguine/40 percent Choleric will

124

be somewhat different from the man who is 80 percent Sanguine/20 percent Choleric. Consequently, some variables will exist even within these blends. For clarity's sake, I will not attempt to break the temperaments down into more than the twelve blends but shall use 60 percent for the predominant temperament and 40 percent for the secondary temperament. The reader will have to make any further realignment of proportions for himself.

The best way I know to illustrate the blends of temperament based on the chart at the beginning of chapter 5 is by using a figure eight, with the top circle representing the predominant temperament (worth 60 percent), and the bottom portion depicting the secondary temperament (worth 40 percent). As you can see by the chart, each of the four basic temperaments has ten strengths and ten weaknesses. By using a figure eight with a large top circle and a smaller bottom one, we can adequately reflect the ten predominant strengths and ten secondary strengths as well as their influences on a person's behavior. The same, of course, follows for the weaknesses. Essentially, then, each person is capable of possessing twenty strengths and twenty weaknesses to one degree or another. Some of them, as we shall see, cancel each other out, some reinforce each other, and some accentuate and compound others, accounting for the varieties of behavior, prejudices, and natural skills of people with the same predominant temperament but with different secondary temperaments. This will become clearer as you study the following twelve blends of temperament.

The SanChlor

The strongest extrovert of all the blends of temperaments is the SanChlor, for the two temperaments that make up his nature are both extroverts. The happy charisma of the Sanguine makes him a people-oriented, enthusiastic, salesman type, but the Choleric side of his nature will provide him the necessary resolution and character traits that will fashion a somewhat more organized and productive individual than if he were pure Sanguine. Vocationally, this man often starts out in sales or promotion and ends up as sales manager of the company. Almost any people-oriented field is open to him, but to sustain his interest it must offer variety, activity, and excitement. He is invariably a sports enthusiast. Ordinarily, such an individual is financially successful in life if properly trained and motivated and loved by his family, and when not controlled by his weaknesses. His financial success is usually tied to his ability (or training) to learn how to discipline his spending. Good salespeople are often vulnerable to other salesmen. They have no sales resistance and the more they make, the more they spend. Consequently, they can make several fortunes in a lifetime—and lose them all.

The potential weaknesses of a SANCHLOR are usually apparent to everyone because he is such an external person. He customarily talks too much, thus exposing himself and his weaknesses for all to see. He is highly opinionated. Consequently, he expresses himself loudly even before he knows all the facts. No one has more mouth trouble! We were amused when a nationally known SANCHLOR evangelist visited our city and was dubbed by the newspaper as "the fastest lip in the West." His giant ego so dominated his conversation that he often destroyed the good first impression he made and did not wear well. If he sensed that people resisted him, he tended to come on even stronger and make matters worse. I was not surprised to see him blow his ministry by overspending and eventually committing adultery.

If the SANCHLOR is the life of the party, he is lovable, but if he feels threatened or insecure, he can become obnoxious. His leading emotional problem will be anger, which can catapult him into action at the slightest provocation. Ego is a strong factor in his driving activity. The SANCHLOR can be complimentary when it suits his purpose, but if you cross him, he may cut you down. Since he combines the easy forgetfulness of the Sanguine and the jesuit casuistry of the Choleric, he may not have an active conscience. Consequently, he tends to justify his actions, often rationalizing that the law applies to everyone else. This man, like any other temperament, needs to be filled with the Holy Spirit and the Word of God daily!

Simon Peter, the self-appointed leader of the twelve apostles, is a classic example of a New Testament SANCHLOR. He obviously had mouth trouble, demonstrating this repeatedly by speaking up before anyone else could. He talked more in the gospels than all the others put together—and most of what he said was wrong. He was egotistical, weak-willed, and carnal throughout the gospels. In Acts, however, he was a remarkably transformed man, resolute, effective, and productive. What made the difference? He had become filled with the Spirit.

The SANMEL

SANMELS are highly emotional people who fluctuate drastically. They can laugh hysterically one minute and burst into tears the next. It is almost impossible for them to hear a sad tale, observe the tragic plight of another person, or listen to melancholy music without weeping profusely. They genuinely feel the griefs of others. SANMEL doctors, for instance, always display the best bedside manner. Ordinarily they make fantastic instructors, teachers, and col-

lege professors—and are easily the most popular instructors on campus. Almost any field is open to them, especially
public speaking, acting, music, and the fine arts. However,
SANMELS reflect an uninhibited perfectionism that often
alienates them from others because they verbalize their
criticisms. They are usually people-oriented individuals
who have sufficient substance to make a contribution to
other lives—if their egos and arrogance don't make them
so obnoxious that others become hostile to them.

One of the crucial weaknesses of this temperament
blend prevails in his thought life. Both Sanguines and
Melancholies are dreamers, and thus if the Melancholy
part of his nature suggests a negative train of thought, it
can nullify a SANMEL's potential. It is easy for him to get
down on himself. In addition, this man, more than most
others, will have both an anger problem and a tendency
toward fear. Both temperaments in his makeup are prone
to insecurity; not uncommonly, the SANMEL is afraid to utilize his potential. Such a person should always work with
people. Being admired by others is so important to him
that it will drive him to a consistent level of performance.
Of all Sanguine public speakers, the SANMEL will be most
accurate in his statistics and organized in his presentation. He has a great ability to commune with God, and if
he walks in the Spirit, he will make an effective servant of
Christ.

King David is a classic illustration of the SANMEL temperament. An extremely likable man who attracted both
men and women (charisma), he was colorful, dramatic,
emotional, and weak-willed. He could play a harp and sing,
he clearly demonstrated a poetic instinct in his psalms, and
he made decisions on impulse. Unfortunately, like many
SANMELS, he fouled up his life by a series of disastrous and
costly mistakes before he gained enough self-discipline to
finish out his destiny. Not all SANMELS, of course, are able
to pick up the pieces of their lives and start over, as David
did. It is far better for them to walk in the Spirit daily and
avoid such mistakes.

The SanPhleg

The easiest person to like is a SanPhleg. The overpowering and obnoxious tendencies of a Sanguine are offset by the gracious, easygoing Phlegmatic, so the charisma possessed by all Sanguines makes him a delightful associate. SanPhlegs are extremely happy people whose carefree spirit and good humor make them lighthearted entertainers sought after by others. Helping people is their regular business, along with sales of various kinds. They are the least extroverted of any of the Sanguines and are often regulated by their environment and circumstances rather than being self-motivated. SanPhlegs are naturally good family men and preserve the love of their children—and everyone else for that matter. They would not purposely hurt anyone.

The SanPhleg's greatest weaknesses are lack of motivation and discipline. He would rather socialize than work, and he tends to take life too casually. His employer often has mixed emotions—he loves Mr. SanPhleg but wishes he would be more industrious. As an executive remarked about one, "He is the nicest guy I ever fired." He rarely gets upset over anything and tends to find the bright side of everything. He is the one person most likely to tell his wife with a smile, "Look at this pink slip. I got fired today!" He usually has an endless repertoire of jokes and delights in making others laugh, often when the occasion calls for seriousness. When Jesus Christ becomes the chief object of his love, he is transformed into a more resolute, purposeful, and productive person.

The first-century evangelist Apollos is about as close as we can come to a New Testament illustration of the SanPhleg. A skilled orator who succeeded Paul and other early church founders, he did the work of stirring the churches with his Spirit-filled preaching and teaching. Loved by all, followed devotedly by some, this pleasant and dedicated man apparently traveled a great deal but did not establish new works.

The CHLORSAN

The second strongest extrovert among the blends of temperaments will be the reverse of the first—the CHLORSAN. This man's life is given over completely to activity. Most of his efforts are productive and purposeful, but watch his recreation—it is so activity-prone that it borders on being violent. He is a natural promoter and salesman with enough charisma to get along well with others. Certainly the best motivator of people and one who thrives on a challenge, he is almost fearless and exhibits boundless energy. His wife will often comment, "He has only two speeds: wide open and stop." Mr. CHLORSAN is the courtroom attorney who can charm the coldest-hearted judge and jury, the fund-raiser who can get people to contribute what they intended to save, the man who never goes anywhere unnoticed, the preacher who combines both practical Bible teaching and church administration, and the politician who talks his state into changing its constitution so he can represent them one more time. He is a convincing debater; what he lacks in facts or argument he makes up in bluff or bravado. As a teacher, he is an excellent communicator, particularly in the social sciences; rarely is he drawn to math, science, or the abstract. Whatever his professional occupation, his brain is always in motion.

The weaknesses of this man, the chief of which is hostility, are as broad as his talents. He combines the quick, explosive anger of the Sanguine (without the forgiveness) and the long-burning resentment of the Choleric. He is the one personality type who not only gets ulcers himself, but gives them to others. Impatient with those who do not share his motivation and energy, he prides himself on being brutally frank (some call it sarcastically frank). It is difficult for him to concentrate on one thing very long, which is why he often enlists others to finish what he has started. He is opinionated, prejudiced, impetuous, and inclined doggedly to finish a project he probably should not have started in the first place. If not controlled by God, he is apt to justify anything he does and rarely hesitates to manipulate or walk over other people to accomplish his ends. Most CHLORSANs get so engrossed in their work that they neglect wife and family, even lashing out at them if they complain. A wife married to a CHLORSAN becomes an emotionally shell-shocked woman who feels unneeded and unloved. She usually admires him, fears him, and is resentful toward him. When the children grow up, she may leave him because he has made her a nonperson. Once he comprehends the importance of his love and approval to his family, however, he can transform his entire household.

James, the author of the biblical book that bears his name, could well have been a CHLORSAN—at least his book sounds like it. The main thrust of the book declares that "faith without works is dead!"—a favored concept by work-loving Cholerics. He used the practical and logical reasoning of a Choleric, yet was obviously a highly esteemed man of God. One human weakness he discussed—the fire of the tongue and how no man can control it (James 3)—relates directly to this temperament's most vulnerable characteristic, for we all know that CHLORSANs feature a razor-sharp, active tongue. His victory and evident productiveness in the cause of Christ is a significant example to any thoughtful CHLORSAN.

The CHLORMEL

The 60 percent Choleric/40 percent Melancholy is an extremely industrious and capable person. The optimism and practicality of the Choleric overcomes the tendency toward moodiness of the Melancholy, making the CHLORMEL both goal-oriented and detailed. Possessing a quick, analytical mind, such a man usually does well in school. Being decisive, he develops into a thorough leader, the kind whom one can always count on to do an extraordinary job. This man is the type of lawyer you would engage as a defense attorney. He is an excellent debater. In fact, never take him on in a debate unless you are assured of your facts, for he will make mincemeat of you, combining verbal aggressiveness and attendance to detail. This man is extremely competitive and forceful in all that he does. His battle plan is always the same: "Go for the jugular vein!" He is a dogged researcher and is usually successful, no matter what kind of business he pursues. The brilliant chief surgeon of a great California hospital, a CHLORMEL, is also an extremely capable Bible teacher in his church. I know architects, plant superintendents, politicians, football coaches, preachers, businessmen, tradesmen (though they usually end up as foremen or bosses), and leaders in many fields who are CHLORMELS. This temperament probably makes the best natural leader. General George S. Patton, the great commander of the U.S. Third Army in World War II who drove the German forces back to Berlin, was probably a CHLORMEL.

Equally as great as his strengths are his weaknesses. He is apt to be autocratic, a dictator type who inspires admiration and hate simultaneously. As an opinionated man, he loves an argument, enjoys the role of devil's advocate, and will even argue against his own position just to argue. He is usually a quick-witted talker whose sarcasm can devastate others. In fact, it is not uncommon for him to keep right on jabbing, even after his victim is dead. He is a natural-born crusader whose work habits are irregular and long. Many of the leaders of activist organizations are CHLORMELS, their philosophy of life determining which side they are on.

A CHLORMEL harbors considerable hostility and resentment, and unless he enjoys a good love relationship with his parents, he will find interpersonal relationships difficult, particularly with his family. No man is more apt to be an overly strict disciplinarian than the CHLORMEL father. He combines the hard-to-please tendency of the Choleric and the perfectionism of the Melancholy. One such father, a supersuccessful life-insurance agent, ordered his fifteen-year-old son to spend all daylight hours in his room for an entire summer. Needless to say, that dad "provoked his son to wrath" and ultimately drove him away from the family and God. Such a man commonly suffers from bleeding ulcers without an organic cause, colitis, and high blood pressure; he is a prime candidate for a heart attack after fifty. When controlled by the Holy Spirit, however, his entire emotional life is transformed and he makes an outstanding Christian.

There is little doubt in my mind that the apostle Paul was a CHLORMEL. Before his conversion he was hostile and cruel, for the Scripture teaches that he spent his time persecuting and jailing Christians. Even after his conversion, his strong-willed determination turned to unreasonable bullheadedness, as when he went up to Jerusalem against the will and warning of God. His writings and ministry demonstrate the combination of the practical-analytical reasoning and self-sacrificing but extremely driving nature of a CHLORMEL. He is a good example of God's transforming power in the life of a CHLORMEL who is completely dedicated to his will.

The CHLORPHLEG

The most subdued of all the extrovertish temperaments is the CHLORPHLEG, a happy blend of the quick, active, and

hot with the calm, cool, and
unexcited. He is not as apt to
rush into things as quickly as
other extroverts because he
is more deliberate and subdued. He is extremely capable in
the long run, although he does
not particularly impress you that
way at first. He is an organized person who combines planning activities and hard work. People usually
enjoy working with and for him
because he knows where he is
going and has charted his course,
yet he is not unduly severe with
people. He has the ability to help
others make the best use of their skills and rarely offends
people or makes them feel used. He often gets more accomplished than any other temperament because he has no
inclination to do it all himself and invariably thinks in terms
of enlisting others in his work. His motto reads "Why do the
work of ten men when you can get ten men to do the work?"

A CHLORPHLEG minister who organized one of my Family
Life Seminars recently exemplified this temperament when
it became necessary, because of a larger attendance than
we had expected, to move hundreds of books to another
place. Instead of furiously carrying them all downstairs himself, he looked the crowd over and quietly collected ten
people to help him. The whole process took four minutes,
and he carried only one load of books. The CHLORPHLEG's
slogan on organization states "Anything that needs to be
done can be done better if it's organized." These men are
usually good husbands and fathers as well as excellent
administrators in almost any field.

In spite of his obvious capabilities, the CHLORPHLEG is not
without a notable set of weaknesses. Although not as
addicted to the quick anger of some temperaments, he is
known to harbor resentment and bitterness. Some of the
cutting edge of the Choleric's sarcasm is here offset by the
gracious spirit of the Phlegmatic, so instead of uttering cut-

ting and cruel remarks, his barbs are more apt to emerge as cleverly disguised humor. One is never quite sure whether he is kidding or ridiculing, depending on his mood. No one can be more bullheadedly stubborn than a CHLOR-PHLEG, and it is difficult for him to change his mind once it is committed. Repentance or the acknowledgment of a mistake is not at all easy for him. Consequently, he will be more apt to make it up to those he has wronged without really facing his mistake. The worrisome traits of the Phlegmatic side of his nature may so curtail his adventurous tendencies that he never quite measures up to his capabilities.

Titus, the spiritual son of the apostle Paul and leader of the hundred or so churches on the Isle of Crete, may well have been a CHLORPHLEG. When filled with the Spirit, he was the kind of man on whom Paul could depend to faithfully teach the Word to the churches and administrate them capably for the glory of God. The book Paul wrote to him makes ideal reading for any teacher, particularly a CHLORPHLEG.

The MELSAN

Now we turn to the predominantly introvertish temperaments. Each will look somewhat similar to one we have already examined, except that the two temperaments that make up their nature will be reversed in intensity. Such variation accounts for the exciting individuality in human beings. Mr. MELSAN is usually a gifted person, fully capable of being a performing arts musician who can steal the heart of an audience. As an artist, he not only draws or paints beautifully but can also sell his own work—if he's in the right mood. Industry uses such a man in production control and cost analysis; often he can work his way up to a supervisory position. It is not uncommon to encounter him in the field of education, for he makes a good scholar and probably the best of all classroom teachers, particularly on the high school and college levels. The Melancholy in him will ferret out little-known facts and be exacting in the use of events and detail, while the Sanguine will enable him to communicate well with students. He usually majors in the social sciences, theology, philosophy, humanities, law, or medicine. If he goes into medicine or the health care industry, he will likely become a specialist with a good bedside manner.

Sometimes the MELSAN will go into sales, but it will usually be low-pressure selling that calls for exacting detail and the presentation of many facts, as in computers, calculators, cash registers, textbooks, and so on. He also makes a good lawyer, dentist, or doctor. In fact, almost anything in the medical field is open to him. It may come as a surprise to you, but many great actors, opera stars, and country-western singers are MELSANS. Give one a guitar and he can usually delight an audience for hours. He is a delightful emcee, and if he enters into the ministry, he will become a good preacher because he will study thoroughly to offer a substantive message in an interesting style. As a minister, he usually wears well with his people. Almost any craft or trade welcomes this man. He is often a loyal husband and devoted father if he learns to accept people and not be too critical of them. Although extremely capable, he usually works for someone else and rarely is venturesome enough to launch out in his own business or found an organization.

Mr. MELSAN shows an interesting combination of mood swings. Be sure of this: He is an emotional creature! When circumstances are pleasing to him, he can reflect a fantastically happy mood. But if things work out badly or he is rejected, insulted, or injured, he drops into such a mood that his lesser Sanguine nature drowns in the resultant sea of self-pity. Like any predominant Melancholy, he must guard his thinking process or he will destroy himself. He is easily moved to tears and feels everything deeply, but he can be unreasonably critical and hard on others. He tends to be rigid and usually will not cooperate unless things go his way, which is often idealistic and impractical. As a college student he gets superior grades but may take five or six years to finish because he changes his major so many times. It is not unlike him to abandon his education, which makes it difficult for him to measure up to his potential. He is often a fearful, insecure man with a poor self-image that limits him unnecessarily. These people are much more capable than they realize, but they internalize so much that others often do not recognize their potential. This temperament blend is responsible for most of the folk tunes and ballads of our day. Listen carefully and you will often detect a melancholic lament, mournful wail, or ballad of doom by the singer. If he has undergone a tragic experience or been rejected in love, watch out! Before he finishes, the tune will lower your mood to match his. As a counselor with a yen to help Melancholies experience upbeat emotions a majority of the time, I know what the power of God can do for them if they learn the habit of thanksgiving thinking (1 Thess. 5:18); it can transform their lives.

Many of the prophets were MELSANS—John the Baptist, Elijah, Jeremiah, and others. They had a tremendous capacity to commune with God; they were self-sacrificing people-helpers who had enough charisma to attract a following; they tended to be legalistic in their teachings and calls to repentance; they exhibited a flair for the dramatic; and they willingly died for their principles. Even some of these godly men had problems with depression.

The MELCHLOR

The mood swings of the Melancholy are usually stabilized by the MELCHLOR's self-will and determination. There is almost nothing vocationally that this man cannot do well. He is both a perfectionist and a driver. He makes an excellent attorney, particularly in fields that demand research and accuracy, such as corporate law, securities, or taxes. And because he prepares twice as hard for a case as anyone else, he seldom loses. As a doctor, he is familiar with the last word in medicine—and usually lets you know that he knows. He possesses strong leadership capabilities, enjoys being chairman of the board, and never comes to a meeting unprepared. He is more apt to be a family dentist than a specialist but may give up dentistry after fifteen to twenty years to go into something else. I have noticed that many airline captains are MELCHLORs, mixing precision with decisiveness and determination. As an educator, he often leaves the classroom for administration. He could become an executive vice president of practically any well-organized business and improve it. Almost any craft, construction, or educational level is open to him. Unlike the MELSAN, he may found his own institution or business and run it capably—not with noise and color but with efficiency. Many a great orchestra leader and choral conductor is a MELCHLOR. He often goes into politics, as evidenced by the fact that many of our founding fathers could well have been MELCHLORs, and a variety of athletic fields attract him. Many superstars (particularly baseball pitchers), some above-average quarterbacks, and a number of running backs are of this mixture of temperaments. Numerous mission boards, colleges, and Christian organizations were founded by Spirit-dedicated MELCHLORs.

The natural weaknesses of MELCHLORs reveal themselves in the mind, emotions, and mouth. They are extremely difficult people to please, rarely satisfying even themselves. Once they start thinking negatively about something or someone (including themselves), they can be intolerable to live with. Their mood follows their thought process. Although they do not retain a depressed mood as long as the other two blends of the Melancholy, they can lapse into it more quickly.

The two basic temperaments haunted by self-persecution, hostility, and criticism are the Melancholy and the Choleric. Put those together in a MELCHLOR and look for him under the pile as soon as things go wrong. His favorite prayer is "Lord, why me?" It is not uncommon for him to get angry at God as well as his fellowman, and if such thoughts persist long enough, he may become manic-depressive. In extreme cases, he can become sadistic. When confronted with his vile thinking pattern and angry, bitter spirit, he can be expected to explode.

His penchant for detailed analysis and perfection tends to make him a nitpicker who drives others up the wall. Unless he is filled with God's Spirit or can maintain a positive frame of mind, he is not enjoyable company for long periods of time. No one is more painfully aware of this, of course, than his wife and children. He not only emotes disapproval, but he also feels compelled to castigate them verbally for their failures and to correct their mistakes—in public as well as in private. He usually strips his wife of all psychological self-protection by his spirit and words of condemnation and criticism until she feels dehumanized. Unless his children are perfectionists, he treats them the same way. He finds it difficult to be aroused sexually when in bed with his wife unless her housekeeping has passed his "white-glove inspection." A MELCHLOR has been known to withhold sex from his wife for months because she didn't please him in the way she cooked, cleaned house, or handled the money. His attitude is "That should teach her." This man, by nature, desperately needs the love of God in his heart, and his family needs him to share it with them.

Many of the great men of the Bible show signs of a MELCHLOR temperament. Two that come to mind are (1) Paul's tireless traveling companion, Dr. Luke, the painstaking scholar who carefully researched the life of Christ and left the church the most detailed account of our Lord's life, as well as the only record of the spread of the early church, and (2) Moses, the great leader of Israel. Like many MELCHLORS, the latter never gained victory over his hostility and bitterness. Consequently, he died before his time. Like Moses, who wasted forty years on the back side of the desert harboring bitterness and animosity before surrendering his life to God, many a MELCHLOR never lives up to his amazing potential because of the spirit of anger and revenge. Learning to "walk in the Spirit" and not in his MELCHLOR flesh can literally transform his life.

The MELPHLEG

The greatest scholars the world has ever known have been MELPHLEGS. They are not nearly as prone to hostility as the two previous Melancholies and usually get along well with others. These gifted introverts combine the analytical perfectionism of the Melancholy with the organized efficiency of the Phlegmatic. They are usually good-natured humanitarians who prefer a quiet solitary environment for study and research to the endless round of activities sought by the more extrovertish temperaments. MELPHLEGS are usually excellent spellers and good mathematicians. In addition to higher education, they excel in medicine, pharmacy, dentistry, architecture, decorating, literature, theology, and many other cerebral fields. They are highly respected writers, philosophers, and scientists, masters in the crafts, construction, music, and art. Extremely detail conscious and accurate, they make good accountants and bookkeepers. If they enter medicine or dentistry, it is not uncommon for them to become specialists.

During the past few years, my family dentist has sent me several times to a dental clinic for root-canal work. All these dentists are specialists and, interestingly enough, all are MELPHLEGS. These gifted people have greatly benefited humanity. Most of the world's significant inventions and medical discoveries have been made by MELPHLEGS. One such individual whom I know well is so gifted that I have often said, "He is the only man I know who is incapable of incompetence."

Despite his abilities, the MELPHLEG, like the rest of us, has his own potential weaknesses. Unless controlled by God, he easily becomes discouraged and develops a negative thinking pattern. But once he realizes it is a sin to develop the spirit of criticism and learns to rejoice evermore, his entire outlook on life can be transformed. Ordinarily a quiet person, he is capable of inner angers and hostility caused by his tendency to be revengeful. If he indulges it long enough, he can even be vindictive.

I know two brilliant MELPHLEGS with a number of similarities. Both are the best in their fields, highly competent and well paid. Both are family men and active Christians, but there the comparison ends. One is loved and admired by his family and many friends. He is a self-taught Bible scholar and one of the greatest men I know. The other man is not respected by his family, antisocial, disliked by others, and miserable. The difference? The second man became bitter years ago, and today it influences his entire life; in fact, it even shows on his face.

MELPHLEGS are unusually vulnerable to fear, anxiety, and a negative self-image. It has always amazed me that the people with the greatest talents and capabilities are often victimized by genuine feelings of poor self-worth.

In addition to enduring mood swings, they are so stubborn and rigid that they too easily become implacable and uncooperative. Their strong tendency to be conscientious allows them to let others pressure them into making commitments that drain their energy and creativity. When filled with God's Spirit, these people are loved and admired by their families because their personal self-discipline and dedication are exemplary in the home, even though humanitarian concerns may cause them to neglect their families. Unless they learn to pace themselves and enjoy diversions that help them relax, they often become early mortality statistics.

The most likely MELPHLEG in the Bible is the beloved apostle John. He obviously had a sensitive nature, for as a youth he laid his head on Jesus' breast at the Lord's Supper. On one occasion he became so angry at some people that he asked the Lord Jesus to call fire from heaven down on them. Yet at the crucifixion he was the lone disciple who devotedly stood at the cross. As Jesus died, John was the one to whom he entrusted his mother. Later the disciple became a great church leader and left us five books in the New Testament, two of which, the Gospel of John and the Book of Revelation, particularly glorify Jesus Christ.

The PHLEGSAN

The easiest of the twelve temperament blends to get along with over a protracted period of time is the PHLEGSAN. He is congenial, happy, cooperative, thoughtful, people-oriented, diplomatic, dependable, fun loving, and humorous. A favorite with children and adults, he never displays an abrasive personality. Rarely does he take up a career in sales, although he could do it well if he represented a good firm where high-pressure selling was not required. He is often found in education and also makes an excellent administrator, college registrar, accountant, mechanic, funeral director, working scientist, engineer, statistician, radio announcer, counselor, visitation minister, veterinarian, farmer, bricklayer, or construction worker. He is usually a good family man who enjoys a quiet life and loves his wife and children. Ordinarily he deports himself honorably and becomes a favorite in the neighborhood. If he is a Christian and attends a church where the pastor is a good motivator, he probably takes an active role in his church.

The weaknesses of a PHLEGSAN are as gentle as his personality—unless you have to live with him all the time. Since he inherited the lack of motivation of a Phlegmatic and the lack of discipline of a Sanguine, it is not uncommon for the PHLEGSAN to fall far short of his true capabilities. He often quits school, passes up good opportunities, and avoids anything that involves "too much effort." He tends to putter around, enjoys solitude, and doesn't seem to mind that the years pass him by and he doesn't go anywhere. Since opposites tend to attract each other in marriage, a PHLEGSAN woman will often marry an aggressive man who carries her through life. When the man is a PHLEGSAN, it's a different ball game. A wife finds it difficult to carry her husband vocationally, and his passive ways often become a source of irritation to her. The PHLEGSAN's wife buys him every new self-improvement book that hits the market, but he falls asleep reading them. The most common question I am asked at my Family Life Seminars is "How does a Choleric wife motivate a Phlegmatic husband?" One Choleric woman's answer was, "When you get him up, keep him moving."

Fear is another problem that accentuates his unrealistic feelings of insecurity. With just 10 percent more faith he could be transformed from his timidity and self-defeating anxieties, but he prefers to build a self-protective shell around himself and selfishly avoid the kind of involvement or commitment to activity that he needs and that would be a rich blessing to his partner and children. I have tremendous respect for the potential of these happy, contented men, but they must co-operate by letting God motivate them to unselfish activity.

The man in the Scripture that reminds me most of the PHLEGSAN is gentle, faithful, good-natured Timothy, the favorite spiritual son of the apostle Paul. He was dependable and steady but timid and fearful. Repeatedly, Paul had to urge him to be more aggressive and to "do the work of an evangelist" (2 Tim. 4:5).

The PHLEGCHLOR

The most active of all Phlegmatics is the PHLEGCHLOR, but it must be remembered that since he is predominantly a

Phlegmatic, he will never be a ball of fire. Like his brother Phlegmatics, he is easy to get along with and may become an excellent group leader, foreman, executive vice president, accountant, educator, planner, and laborer in almost any area of construction. The Phlegmatic has the potential to become a good counselor, for he is an excellent listener, does not interrupt the client with stories about himself, and is genuinely interested in other people. Although the PHLEGCHLOR rarely offers his services to others, when they come to his organized office where he exercises control, he is professional. His advice will be practical, helpful, and if he is a Bible-taught Christian, quite trustworthy. He has the patience of Job and often is able to help those who have not found relief with other counselors. His gentle spirit never makes people feel threatened. He always does the right thing, but rarely goes beyond the norm. If his wife can make the adjustment  to his passive lifestyle and reluctance to take the lead in the home, particularly in the discipline of their children, they can enjoy a happy marriage.

The weaknesses of the PHLEGCHLOR are not readily apparent but gradually come to the surface, especially in the home. In addition to the lack of motivation and the fear problems of the other Phlegmatics, he can be determinedly stubborn and unyielding. He doesn't blow up at others but simply refuses to give in or cooperate. He is not a fighter by nature but often lets his inner anger and stubbornness reflect itself in silence. One such man with a fast-talking wife said, "I've finally learned how to handle that woman!" When I asked, "How?" he replied, "Silence! Last week I didn't talk to her for five days—she can't stand it!" I warned him that he had just chosen the well-paved boulevard to ulcers. Little did I realize what a prophet I was, for he was rushed to the hospital twenty-eight days later with bleeding ulcers.

The PHLEGCHLOR often retreats to his workshop alone or nightly immerses his mind in TV. The older he gets, the more he selfishly indulges his sedentary tendency and becomes increasingly passive. Although he will probably live a long and peaceful life, if he indulges these passive feelings, it is a boring life—not only for him but also for his family. He needs to give himself to the concerns and needs of his family. This is one of the few types that should take on more than they think they can do, for they work well under pressure and are externally motivated.

No man in the Bible epitomizes the PHLEGCHLOR better than Abraham in the Old Testament. Fear characterized everything he did in the early days. For instance, he was reluctant to leave the security of the pagan city of Ur when God first called him; he even denied his wife on two occasions and tried to palm her off as his sister because of fear. Finally, he surrendered completely to God and grew in his Spirit. Accordingly, his greatest weakness became his greatest strength. Today, instead of being known as fearful Abraham, he has the reputation of being "the man who believed God and it was counted unto him for righteousness."

The PHLEGMEL

Of all the temperament blends, the PHLEGMEL is the most gracious, gentle, and quiet. He is rarely angry or hostile and almost never says anything for which he must apologize (mainly because he rarely says much). He never embarrasses himself or others, always does the proper thing, dresses simply, is dependable and exact. He tends to exhibit the natural gifts of mercy and help, and he is neat and organized in his working habits. He does well in photography, printing, inventory, analysis, layout, advertising, mechanics, education, pharmacy, dentistry, finish carpentry (almost never piecework or production—he is a plodder), glassblowing, wallpaper hanging, painting, or anything that involves intricate detail and great patience. Like any Phlegmatic, he is handy around the house and as energy permits will keep his home in good repair. If he has a wife who recognizes his tendencies toward passivity (but tactfully waits for him to take the lead in their home and for biblical reasons labors at submission), they will have a good family life and marriage. If she resents his reticence to lead and be aggressive, however, she may become discontented and foment marital strife. Unless taught properly in his church, he may neglect the discipline necessary to help prepare his children for a productive, self-disciplined life. Although he seldom admits it, a passive father who lets his children grow up sassing and disobeying him and their mother is just as guilty of "provoking his children to wrath" as the angry tyrant whose unreasonable discipline makes them bitter.

The other weaknesses of this man revolve around fear, selfishness, negativism, criticism, and lack of self-image. Recently a good-looking young painter acknowledged at one of our Family Life Seminars that my wife's talk on fear really spoke to him, and for the first time he was willing to face the fact that fear was a sin. Her presentation made him acutely aware of his reluctance to take advantage of a tremendous business opportunity that confronted him. As he talked, I could tell that here was a superbly qualified and dedicated PHLEGMEL who had been selling himself short. Someone has said, "There are two kinds of thinkers—those who think they can and those who think they can't—and they are both right." Once a PHLEGMEL realizes that only his fears and negative feelings about himself keep him from succeeding, he is able to come out of his shell and become an effective man, husband, and father. Most PHLEGMELs have an obsession against involvement. They are so afraid of overextending themselves or getting overinvolved that they automatically refuse almost any kind of affiliation. I have never seen a PHLEGMEL overinvolved in anything—except in keeping from getting overinvolved. He must recognize that since he is not internally motivated, he definitely needs to accept more responsibility than he thinks he can fulfill, for that external stimulation will motivate him to greater achievement. All Phlegmatics work well under pressure, but it must come from outside. In addition to cultivating his spiritual life, this man should give special thought to taking vitamins and keeping his body toned through physical exercise, which can give him a whole new lease on life. His greatest source of motivation, of course, will be the power of the Holy Spirit.

Barnabas, the godly saint of the first-century church who accompanied the apostle Paul on his first missionary journey, was in all probability a PHLEGMEL. He was the man who gave half his goods to the early church to feed the poor, the man who contended with Paul over providing John Mark, his nephew, with another chance to serve God by accompanying them on the second missionary journey. Although the contention became so sharp that Barnabas took his nephew and they proceeded on their journey alone, Paul later commended Mark, saying, "for he is profitable to me for the ministry" (2 Tim. 4:11 KJV). Today we have the Gospel of Mark because faithful, dedicated, and gentle Barnabas was willing to help him over a hard place in his life. PHLEGMELs respond to the needs of others if they will just let themselves move out into the stream of life and work with people where they are.

Additional Variables to Consider

With twelve temperament blends to choose from, it should be easier for you to identify with one of them than it was when presented with only the four basic temperaments. But don't be discouraged if you find that you don't quite fit into any one of these twelve either. No two human beings are exactly alike. Consequently, other variables could alter the picture sufficiently so that you will not fit any model precisely. Consider the following:

1. Your percentages may be different than the 60/40 I arbitrarily chose. I think you will agree that it would

be nearly impossible to detail all the conceivable mixtures of temperaments. I leave that to the reader. For example, a 60/40 MELCHLOR will be significantly different from an 80/20 MELCHLOR. Or consider the disparity between a 55/45 SANPHLEG and an 85/15 SANPHLEG. Only detailed scientific testing can establish an accurate diagnosis, and although I am currently working on this possibility with computer specialists, we are far from completing our studies. Currently, my temperament test is based on diagnosing only two temperaments.

2. Different backgrounds and childhood training alter the expressions of identical temperament blends. For example, a SANPHLEG raised by loving but firm parents will be much more disciplined than one raised by permissive parents. A MELPHLEG brought up by cruel, hateful parents will be drastically different from one raised by tender, understanding parents. Both will share the same strengths and talents, but one may be overcome by hostility, depression, and self-persecution so that he will never use his strengths. Although upbringing wields a powerful influence on the child, it is all but impossible to assess a wide variety of backgrounds in such a temperament analysis as this. I can only suggest that if you cannot identify your temperament blend readily, consider this variable.

3. You may not be objective when looking at yourself. Therefore, you may wish to discuss your temperament with loved ones and friends. All of us tend to view ourselves through rose-colored glasses. To paraphrase the yearning of the poet Robert Burns, "Oh, to see ourselves as others see us."

4. Education and IQ will often influence the appraisal of a person's temperament. For example, a MELSAN with a high IQ will appear somewhat different from one who is average or lower in intelligence. An uneducated person takes longer to mature than an educated man, as a rule, because it may take much longer to excel at something and thus "find himself." By "educated" I

include the trades. It is not uncommon for a man who learns a skill (such as plastering, plumbing, and so on) to be more outgoing, confident, and expressive than he would be otherwise. Even so, if you carefully study the strengths and weaknesses of people of a particular temperament blend, you will find, in spite of their IQ, educational, or experience levels, that they will be basically similar in their strengths and weaknesses.

5. Health and metabolism are important. A CHLORPHLEG in top physical condition will be more aggressive than one with a faulty thyroid gland or other physical ailment. A nervous PHLEGMEL will also be more active than one who is suffering from low blood pressure. Recently I worked with a hyperactive SANCHLOR minister who is a charming, superaggressive charger who made me tired just being around him. He was too powerful even to be a SANCHLOR. It didn't come as a surprise to learn that he had high blood pressure, which often produces the "hyper" dimension to any temperament.

6. Three temperaments are often represented in one individual. Although there have been no scientific studies to confirm it, there is always the possibility that a person could be predominantly one temperament with two secondary temperaments. More people think that of themselves than I have actually observed as being true. The reason they make such a diagnosis is that either they don't thoroughly understand the characteristics of the four basic temperaments or they are not really objective about themselves. Even though I have not met anyone whom I felt certain was really three temperaments, it certainly is a possibility.

7. Motivation is the name of the game! "Keep your heart with all diligence, for out of it spring the issues of life" (Prov. 4:23). If a person is properly motivated, it will have a marked impact on his behavior regardless of his temperament blend. That is why I have written this book—so men who are improperly motivated at present will experience the power of God to com-

pletely transform their behavior. I have heard testimonies that it has happened to thousands as a result of reading my other books on temperament or attending my lectures on the subject. I trust God will use this book with its greater detail and suggestions for an even greater number of people.

8. The Spirit-controlled life is a behavior modifier. Mature Christians whose temperament has been modified by the Holy Spirit often find it difficult to analyze their temperamental makeup because they make the mistake of examining the temperament theory in light of their present behavior. Temperament is based on the natural man; there is nothing spiritual about it. That is why we find it so much easier to diagnose and classify an unsaved person or a carnal Christian than a dedicated, mature Christian. Because such a person has already had many of his natural weaknesses strengthened, it is difficult to assess his temperament. He should either concentrate only on his strengths or consider his behavior before he became a Spirit-controlled believer.

Temperament Theory—A Useful Tool

The temperament theory is not the final answer to human behavior, and for these and other reasons it may not prove satisfactory to everyone. But of all behavior theories ever devised, it has served as the most helpful explanation. Additional factors could be included to explain some of the other differences in people, but these will suffice. If you keep them in mind, you will probably find that you and those you try to help in life fall into one of the twelve blends we have studied. (If you are interested in a thorough evaluation of your personal primary and secondary temperaments, see the end of this book for information about ordering the LaHaye Temperament Analysis.) Now a question arises: What can be done about it? The answer will be found in the next chapter.

7

How to Overcome Your Weaknesses

What is the best temperament blend?" Although I have been asked that question repeatedly, I can find no valid answer, for all temperament blends embody strengths and assets that contribute to humanity. Unfortunately, they each also have their weaknesses, and that is where the problem arises. If all we had were strengths and talents, then our culture and vocation would determine the ideal blend. For example, if a business needs an accountant, they don't want a strong Sanguine or Choleric. People with these temperaments might make the company successful but would find it all but impossible to balance the books. Certain temperaments are better for certain tasks. The problem, however, is that because we all have inherited a fallen nature, no temperament blend is without its own set of weaknesses. When an individual indulges these, he nullifies or, at best, limits his strengths. It also seems that the more prominent a person's strengths, the more dangerous his potential weaknesses.

Success for each individual, then, seems to depend on two factors: (1) finding the appropriate objective for your strengths so you can seek the best training available within your means to pursue that field, and (2) overcoming the weaknesses of your temperament before they cripple the expression of your strengths. Many people with good education and opportunities fail in life because they never gain victory over their weaknesses. That is what this chapter is all about.

Occasionally I find someone who rejects his temperament and wastes his time wishing he were other than he is. Recently a SanMel wrote to me after studying my analysis of his temperament. He didn't disagree with any of it, but he didn't like it. He wanted me to send him one that showed him a ChlorSan. Spending time wishing to be something else is an exercise in futility. You are what you are! You can sharpen your talents and improve and train them, but you will never acquire more than those with which you were born. Fortunately, every normal person has sufficient raw material to live an effective, productive, and happy life. But he can't do it without God's help! That is one of the reasons Christ came, for he said, "I have come that [you] may have life, and that [you] may have it more abundantly" (John 10:10). That abundant life, which is well within the grasp of every human being, enables any person to make full use of his capabilities.

Did you notice something special in the previous chapter? I hope you recognized that the Bible demonstrates God has used someone with each of the twelve temperament blends. After all, he is "no respecter of persons" (see Acts 10:34 KJV), so naturally he uses all types of people. If we took the time, however, we could explore the Bible and also illustrate a person of each temperament blend whom he did *not* use. What makes the difference? One surrendered himself to God for cleansing from sin and a strengthening of his weaknesses; the other did not. It's just that simple.

Are You Different?

One of my basic assumptions is that when a natural human being accepts Jesus Christ as his Savior, he ought to be different. Or stated another way, when a normal human being receives the supernatural power of Christ, he ought to change. How will that modification be revealed? In the strengthening of the person's weaknesses. That is what Paul meant in Galatians 5:16 when he commanded, "Walk [live] in the Spirit, and you shall not fulfill the lust of the flesh." In other words, when the power of Christ controls your life, you will be dominated not by your weaknesses but by his Spirit, who will provide sufficient strength to compensate for them. Galatians 5:22–23 lists the nine strengths of the Spirit that all believers need to appropriate: "Love, joy, peace, longsuffering, kindness, goodness, faithfulness, gentleness, self-control."

The most important discovery I have ever made for helping people is that among the fruit of the Spirit is a strength for every human weakness. Although it may seem an oversimplification to declare to someone who is oppressed by his weakness, "You need to be filled with the Spirit," it is nevertheless true! To be specific, he must be controlled by the Spirit instead of his own natural weaknesses, for God provides exactly the strength one requires to overcome rather than *be* overcome.

To prove my point, I have compiled a list of all forty natural weaknesses of the four basic temperaments and examined them in light of the strengths of the Spirit. At least one strength, and in most cases two or three strengths, of the Holy Spirit will overcome each weakness. To verify this fact to yourself, I would urge you to diagnose your temperament, then list on a sheet of paper the ten weaknesses of your primary temperament followed by the ten weaknesses of your secondary temperament. Some of your weaknesses will be strengthened by the opposite temperament, so you may not actually record all twenty weaknesses. Circle the ten from the list of twenty that you consider your greatest weaknesses, then beside them list one or more strengths of the Spirit for each weakness. In this way, you will graphically expose the ten areas you should work on first. By the time you have gained victory over these weaknesses, you will probably discover that you have automatically attended to the others.

How to Be Strengthened by the Holy Spirit

When I learned to fly, my instructor first taught me the Four Cs of Emergency Procedure.

1. *Climb.* The higher you climb, the safer you are and the more options you acquire.
2. *Call.* Radio the local flight service, radar controller, or "May Day."
3. *Confess.* Admit you are in trouble and describe it briefly.
4. *Comply.* Do exactly what he tells you.

The Federal Aviation Administration has spent millions of man-hours and dollars on developing these procedures in an attempt to make flying safe. Any well-trained pilot can navigate a good plane safely when everything is working and nothing unusual occurs. In fact, it is statistically safer than driving a car. But sooner or later every pilot will encounter emergency or near-emergency conditions, at which time he had better know the Four Cs of Emergency Procedure and follow them carefully. The life of many a pilot and passenger has been saved by using these principles.

The same is true spiritually. God has established a simple method for coping with the emergency conditions of life that occur because of our mistakes and sins or, in some cases, the uncertain circumstances of life over which we have no control. He labels his program "Walk in the Spirit" or "Be filled with the Spirit." In either case, the results will be the same—you will strengthen your weaknesses.

The Four Cs for Overcoming Weaknesses

Therefore do not be unwise, but understand what the will of the Lord is. And do not be drunk with wine, in which is dissipation; but be filled [controlled] with the Spirit.

Ephesians 5:17–18

> This I say then: Walk in the Spirit, and you shall not fulfill the lust of the flesh.
>
> Galatians 5:16

Of all the commands in the Bible, these two passages most explicitly direct us to be controlled by the Holy Spirit. Every Christian would be wise to concentrate on implementing these commands in his everyday life, for in so doing he will automatically overcome his weaknesses. But how do you do it? One of the reasons I believe my books *Spirit-Controlled Temperament, Transformed Temperaments*, and *Why You Act the Way You Do* were so well received is that I offered a practical, workable method for being controlled by the Holy Spirit—a subject that most speakers and writers on the Spirit-filled life tend to ignore. Without repeating what I have said in my previous books, and in an attempt even to simplify the techniques given there, I would have you consider the Four *C*s for Overcoming Weaknesses.

1. Confess

The confession of sin is always the proper starting place whenever a person desires a closer walk with God. The psalmist has said, "If I regard iniquity [sin] in my heart, the Lord will not hear me [when I pray]" (Ps. 66:18). If you cling to sin in your life, you will be conscious of it, for the Holy Spirit always convicts his children of their transgressions (see John 16:8). He will not be nebulous either, but will point out the specific sin with which he is displeased—for example, hate, jealousy, covetousness, fear, lust, selfishness, or disobedience (see Gal. 5:19–21).

The clearest verse in the Bible on forgiveness is 1 John 1:9: "If we confess our sins, He is faithful and just to forgive us our sins and to cleanse us from all unrighteousness." This verse assures us of immediate cleansing and forgiveness, but the word *confess* is often mistaken to mean just admitting with our mouth that an evil habit is sin. That is not true! *Confess* literally means to agree with God that something is sin. In other words, we are in accord with a holy, righteous God that a particular practice or habit is

an ugly sin and should have no place in our lives. Such confession does not include the carnal practice of divulging
to God a sin that we have no intention of discontinuing.
The whole purpose of confession is to acknowledge that
what he has convicted us of is contrary to his will for our
lives and should be eliminated, just as the Lord told the
woman caught in adultery, "Go and sin no more!" That kind
of confession is always greeted with forgiveness and
cleansing.

You can be forgiven of a sin if you commit it again, of
course, for God knows your frailties and weaknesses. At
the moment of confession, however, your attitude of heart
is to acknowledge both the sin's repugnance and your
intent to expunge it from your life with God's help. After
all, he knows the power of habit in your life and recognizes that a significant change will take time. But if your
intent is to not eliminate it, your confession becomes a
mockery.

What about the person who is convicted of a sin or
habit he is unwilling to face or discard from his life? He
can forget walking in the Spirit (and the blessing of God)!
It is impossible to experience the control of the Spirit and
simultaneously practice sin. Unless you sincerely desire
to obey God in everything, you will never walk in the
Spirit.

Consider one further aspect of confession. Once you
have confessed a sin, forget it! Don't let Satan use your
overactive guilt complexes to keep beating you down after
you have confessed in the name of Jesus Christ. Recently
a young minister complained that he was assailed by guilt
feelings for his sexual promiscuity before marriage. He
had been faithful to his wife of seven years but was still
plagued by his guilt. When I asked the obvious, "Have you
confessed that sin?" he replied, "Hundreds of times." I then
instructed him, "Never again confess that sin. Once is
enough!" "What should I do when it comes to mind?" he
asked. I assured him that he need only to thank God by
faith for his forgiveness; gradually his guilt would cease
to bother him.

2. Communicate

Just as the instrument pilot flying through the fog is dependent on two-way communication with the radar controller to be guided to safety, so the Christian needs to converse with God and hear his voice regularly. At times during radar contact (the controller knows where you are by watching your blip on his radarscope), you don't hear from him for long periods. But as in life, when an emergency arises or while facing numerous decisions preparatory to landing, the pilot maintains constant radio contact, both parties talking and listening. God's children likewise need to hear from him through the Bible, and he wants you to talk to him in prayer. There is no possible way a Christian can "walk in the control of the Spirit" until he develops that two-way communication with God.

Of the two methods of communication, the more important involves daily reading of the Word of God. Though I am aware that some "prayer warriors" will challenge me, I am convinced that it is more important for us to hear from God than for God to hear from us. Certainly we are not going to tell him anything he doesn't know, but reading his Word regularly will flood the searchlight of his truth upon the pathway of life along which we walk. I believe it is imperative that we set aside time for reading God's Word; otherwise it is impossible to walk in the Spirit. Just as the drunk depicted in Ephesians 5:18 must keep drinking alcohol or he will sober up, so we must drink in the Word of God or inevitably we will depart from his will. Remember, walking in the Spirit means walking in the *control* of the Spirit. It is impossible for a man to walk in the control of the Holy Spirit unless he knows God's will, which is communicated to us through the Scriptures. Men and women who do not read and study the Bible regularly are just kidding themselves if they think they are walking in the Spirit. They are so uninformed about the Word of God that they don't even realize when they are disobedient to him. That is one reason so many Christians never grow spiritually—they never feed their spiritual lives. It also explains why many others never seem to know the will of God for their lives, for he has given us his Bible to clarify his will. To find his will, we must read it daily.

The San Diego Chargers football players who attended our weekly Bible study inspired me to write a book to help them read and study the Bible for themselves. I developed a simple program to make this quiet time highly practical and helpful and to guide them into other studies. For that reason, I included copies of their study charts as samples.[2]

The book proved helpful to those men, several of whom were young Christians. It has sold over six hundred thousand copies and many of its readers have testified that it has encouraged them to be consistent in a daily reading of God's Word for the first time in their lives. In the book, I offer a foolproof method for guaranteeing the consistency that every sincere Christian desires.

Everyone I have counseled who was being overcome by his weaknesses failed to maintain a regular reading of God's Word. As you work on the elimination of your ten major weaknesses, you will find that daily reading and studying of the Word of God will fortify your spirit and accentuate the power within you so that you can overcome them.

One night during a Chargers' Bible study on the two natures in the heart of the Christian, one of the players asked, "Which nature, the old or the new, will control my life?" Before I had time to answer, the safety on the team perceptively replied, "The one you feed the most!" It could not have been stated better. Just as you must eat right to build up your body, so you must nourish the inner man with spiritual sustenance. That is why Peter declared, "As newborn babes, desire the pure milk of the word, that you may grow thereby" (1 Peter 2:2). That kind of spiritual growth will help you overcome your weaknesses and walk in the Spirit.

The other half of communication necessary to walk in the Spirit is prayer. No facet of your life can be exempt from prayer. Paul, the CHLORMEL activist, instructed us to "pray without ceasing" (1 Thess. 5:17). That is, communicate with God as you move through every experience of life. This is an excellent habit to develop, for it makes you sensitive to his leading. Whenever I fly only by instruments I am in constant touch with the radar controller. We aren't talking every minute, but my radios are on and I am alert to his slightest command. If I want to change direction or altitude, or if I wish to check the weather ahead, I press my mike button and communicate with him. The Spirit-controlled life is like that. As we walk in the Spirit, we remain in constant touch with our heavenly Father, apprising him of both big and small decisions.

Some Christians only talk to their heavenly Father when faced with "big decisions." Not me! I take literally the psalmist's words—"In all your ways acknowledge him." Consequently, I like to check with him on everything. Just the other day I was hurriedly packing to get to the airport on time to go to a seminar, and I was missing a whole set of my overhead transparencies for one of my messages. After looking frantically for ten minutes, I paused and asked the Lord to help. Within two minutes I found them (where I doubt I would have ever looked) and was on board the airplane just before they closed the door.

The secret to good instrument flying is planning. A good pilot does not wait until he is confronted with a perilous situation to start making decisions. The same is true in life. Plan ahead, check your decisions by the Bible just as a pilot checks his flying charts, and then discuss them in prayer with the heavenly Father far enough in advance so that you will not have to act under the pressure of emergencies. Too many Christians stagger from crisis to crisis, most of which could have been avoided by steadfast reading of God's Word and by prayer. That two-way communication is essential to walking in the Spirit!

3. Commit

The hardest part of instrument flying for me at first was committing myself completely to the instruments. When I lost visual contact with the ground, my instincts invariably contradicted the instruments so that I could actually fly upside down when I thought I was right side up. The horizon indicator is an extremely reliable instrument that shows where you are in relation to the horizon, but it usually indicates the reverse of your instincts. To ignore those instincts—and commit myself to that indicator—was difficult for me to learn.

A 100 percent commitment to the Holy Spirit is extremely difficult for most Christians, particularly strong-willed and analytical types. A 90 to 97 percent commitment is probably the primary reason many sincere Christians do not walk in the Spirit. They fail to understand that God requires 100 percent commitment to him. This shouldn't come as such a surprise, for he commands total surrender frequently throughout the Scriptures. In Colossians 2:6 he says through Paul, "As you have therefore received Christ Jesus the Lord, so walk in Him." How did you receive Christ? Was it *your* works plus *his* grace that saved you? Absolutely not! It was a total commitment of your sin and worthlessness to the Christ of the cross that redeemed you—not faith in Christ and Buddha or Christ and your education, but total faith in Christ alone. The same is true of walking by faith through life. Anything short of that 100 percent commitment is unbelief, a sin that quenches the work of the Holy Spirit.

Two verses spell out total commitment or surrender:

Do not present your members as instruments of unrighteousness to sin, but present yourselves to God as being alive from the dead, and your members as instruments of righteousness to God.
Romans 6:13

I beseech you therefore, brethren, by the mercies of God, that you present your bodies a living sacrifice, holy, acceptable to God, which is your reasonable service.
Romans 12:1

There is something you should understand. God wants your body! He created you. He saved you through the gift of his Son, and he wants you to surrender the control of your life to him. He will not coerce you, but you will never find real happiness until you totally surrender everything in your life to him. That means your talents, education, ambition, vocation, children, relationship to your partner, church, hobbies, even your sins and weaknesses. A 97 percent commitment to aeronautical instruments leaves ample margin for error to make any pilot a casualty—just as a 97 percent commitment of one's life to God continues to destroy the effectiveness of most Christians' lives today. No pet habit, sin, desire, or rebellion can be worth a second-rate life of powerlessness. Sure, you will go to heaven when you die, but a non-Spirit-controlled life is a far cry from the abundant life of fulfillment that Jesus Christ promises his children in John 10:10, and it is no formula for overcoming your weaknesses.

After a seminar in Memphis, a sharp-looking young man handed me a tract he had written with the picture of an old restored car on the cover. It seems that the old car had been the 3 percent of his life that was uncommitted to God, and consequently he had lived a mediocre Christian life. Only when he surrendered that 3 percent did he experience the Holy Spirit's filling and power. Everyone has his "thing" ("the sin which so easily ensnares us" of Heb. 12:1). The following include some of the distractions that men have labeled as their "things": bitterness at a parent, wife, boss, or even God; lust; alcohol or cigarettes; jealousy; gossip; ambition; pride; dishonesty; cheating on income tax; hobbies; athletics; and motorcycles. Can you add to the list?

God doesn't always take the 3 percent away from us unless it is sin. Sometimes he gives it back with abundance after we commit it to him. As a pilot I can identify with the U.S. Air Force pilot after World War II who found it difficult to surrender his life to Christ for the ministry because he was afraid he would probably never fly again. But by faith he finally surrendered his life, including his flying, and went off to college. Shortly after arriving on campus, he discovered a desperate need for a flight instructor in the missionary aviation program. Since he had an instructor's rating, he offered his services and was hired. He worked his way through college that way, and then God led him into missionary aviation, a ministry he enjoyed for twenty-five years. But his life of fulfillment and joy would never have been realized had he not made that full surrender of the 3 percent of his life that God wanted. Reader, it is the same with you.

Many Christians fear that if they surrender 100 percent of themselves to Christ, he will make them do something they don't want to do. I've known of some that even expected him to take every ounce of joy from them. That is nonsense! Such fear stems from an inadequate view of God and his love for us. You should get one thing very clear right now: God is for you, not against you. Romans 8:31–32, which makes that crystal clear, inquires, "What then shall we say to these things? If God is for us, who can be against us? He who did not spare His own Son, but delivered Him up for us all, how shall He not with Him also freely give us all things?"

Bill Bright cleared this point up for me years ago with his classic story comparing the human father-son relationship to the heavenly Father-son kinship. (We know this is a legitimate comparison because our Lord himself used it in Luke 11:13.) Bright asked, "If your son greeted you at the door, threw his arms around you, and said, 'Daddy, I love you and I'll do anything you want me to,' would you respond, 'Great! Now I've got you where I want you. I'll sell all your toys and shove you in the closet for the next week'?" Of course not. You would be so moved by his love that you would heap blessings upon him. God responds to us just this way but on a divine level. I have never seen God take anything away from an individual if it was not for his good. And when he does take something, he always replaces it with something better.

Have you ever formally committed your life to Christ? If you have not, or are unsure, I would suggest the following procedure, which has been a help to many people. Find a solitary place where you will not be disturbed for a few minutes and visualize in prayer an altar such as they used in

Bible times. Then on the basis of Romans 12:1, picture yourself lying on that altar *fully* committed to God. Place upon that altar the biggest thing in your life. I have prayed with a professional ball player whose thing was a baseball glove. Until he visually pulled it up onto the altar, he wasn't fully committed to Christ. Another was a professional musician who had to surrender his trumpet. I have seen lawyers, doctors, and many others surrender professions, stocks, cars, boats, cigarettes, alcohol—you name it, for things come in all sizes and shapes. Of one thing I am certain—every Christian should fully commit himself and all that he is or has to the Lord Jesus Christ. Only then will he be filled with or controlled by the Holy Spirit.

God guarantees that the best bargain you will ever make in life is to give yourself 100 percent to him. Surprisingly, many Christians don't live as though they believe that. It seems they think they have to help God by holding back something for their own use. That has not been my experience, or that of the hundreds of people I have challenged to give themselves completely to God. Our Lord said, "Seek first the kingdom of God and His righteousness, and all these things shall be added to you" (Matt. 6:33). The best way to get maximum mileage out of your life is to commit it totally to him to do with it whatever he sees fit. He is for you—we have seen that. Inasmuch as he knows what is best for your future, you can count on him to make the best decisions for your life. Our Father operates on principles and promises. One of those is "Give and it shall be given." As you give him control of your life, he will be a blessing to far more people than if you kept it for yourself. I made that decision over forty years ago, and I can say I have no regrets. Giving my life to God was the best bargain I ever made. God is no man's debtor. He always does "exceedingly abundantly above all that we ask or think."

4. Comply

Once an instrument pilot commits himself to his instruments and the radar-control operator, he must comply with the directions he receives, for otherwise he is no longer "committed" to them and will go out of control. It is the same with a Christian. To maintain our commitment to God, we must obey what the Holy Spirit tells us, starting with the Bible. If a committed Christian obeys the Scripture, he will submit to the Spirit and not to the shackles of self-will. Whatever the Bible says, he will do it by faith.

One young Christian did not wish to follow the Lord in baptism, even though he had committed himself to Christ. Rather than get involved with his traditions and prejudices, I asked him to read Matthew 28:18–20 and then inquired, "What does Jesus say about baptism there?" He studied it for a moment and replied, "He commanded his disciples to teach and baptize and instruct others to do the same." "How does that apply to you today?" He grinned sheepishly and said, "I guess he is indirectly commanding me to be baptized." He was baptized two weeks later.

When you find such instructions in the Bible, your attitude should always be "I am going to comply with whatever God says to do." One husband I counseled claimed to be filled with the Spirit but had no love for his wife. He insisted, "I am absolutely dead toward her." When I turned to Ephesians 5:18 and showed him that he must be filled continually with the Spirit, he responded, "I am, most of the time." I countered kindly, "Friend, you are kidding yourself! Just seven verses later God says, 'Husbands, love your wives, even as Christ also loved the church'" (Eph. 5:25). "That's impossible," he moaned. "No," I replied, "God never commands us to do anything he won't enable us to do." Then I pointed to another passage in the Bible he was violating. "In everything give thanks; for this is the will of God in Christ Jesus for you" (1 Thess. 5:18). As long as he griped and found fault with his wife mentally and verbally, he was killing his love for her. Not until he stopped disobeying God in his mind and complied with God's commands—by thinking positively about her and thanking God for her—would his love for her return. No one can violate God's principles and enjoy the benefits of the Spirit-controlled life.

There is more talk about and concern for the Spirit-filled life today than in the past seventy-five or more years. That is the reason for so many radiant, joyful Christians in our churches and for such large numbers of people (according to the latest Gallup poll) turning to Christ. In addition, we must recognize that secular humanism has produced a despair in the hearts of people who can find no other source of consolation than Jesus. Back in the seventies, *Newsweek* magazine shocked the secular media by acknowledging what they called the phenomenon of that decade, which they dubbed a "religious renewal." They even labeled 1971 the year of the evangelical. Since then they have begrudgingly acknowledged the enormous growth in the population of Christians. Little do they realize there is even now a sincere movement of the Spirit of God that is awakening in Christians a new desire to serve him and to walk in the Spirit. Many are excited about "being led of the Spirit," "anointed by the Spirit," or "guided by the Spirit." And it is true; God the Holy Spirit will chart our course, but be certain of one important precept: he will never lead us to violate the Bible's teachings! Otherwise he would be the "author of confusion," which is contrary to his nature and judged as impossible in the Scriptures. The Holy Spirit wrote the Bible—through prophets and holy men of old (2 Peter 1:21)—so his leading today will always be in agreement with the Scriptures. That is another reason you should be careful to read the Word of God daily; otherwise you will have nothing to test that voice within you. Whenever the voice directs you to satisfy a principle that is in agreement with the Word of God, comply with it. But if it contradicts the Scripture, reject it. Clearly the inner guidance that people receive today is not exclusively of the Holy Spirit. Make sure yours is. "Let the peace of God rule in your hearts, to which also you were called in one body; and be thankful" (Col. 3:15).

The Proof Is in the Pudding

You may be asking, "How can I tell when I'm controlled by or filled with the Spirit?" The answer is simple—examine your actions. Jesus said, "Therefore by their fruits you will know them" (Matt. 7:20). In other words, what you do reveals what you are. That is certainly clear from those two great passages in the Scriptures that command us to be filled with the Spirit (Eph. 5:18) and walk in the control of the Spirit instead of the flesh (Gal. 5:16). The deeds of the Spirit and of the flesh are distinctly rendered in these passages. Examine the chart below and use it to test your actions, in order to determine which "spirit" is controlling you. Be sure of this: Your spiritual nature will never lead you to sin. Your flesh nature is fully capable of sparking any number of the eighteen works of the flesh, plus many more.

The Deeds of the Flesh Galatians 5:19–21	The Deeds of the Spirit Ephesians 5:13–6:9 Galatians 5:22–23
Sexual Sins Adultery, uncleanness, fornication, licentiousness	*Love* Husbands, love your wives . . . as Christ loved the church . . . [and] as [you do your] own bodies. (Eph. 5:25, 28)
Religious sins Sorcery, witchcraft, heresies, idolatry	*Joy* Song in your heart (Eph. 5:19) Thanksgiving spirit (Eph. 5:20)
Emotion sins (sins of the mind) Hatred, envyings, strife, wrath, jealousy, divisiveness, heresies	*Peace* Submitting yourselves to one another; wives yielding to their husbands as to the Lord (Eph. 5:21–22)
Overt sins Murders, drunkenness, revelries	*Longsuffering* *Gentleness* *Goodness* *Faithfulness* } (Gal. 5:22–23) *Kindness* *Self-Control*

The Deeds of the Flesh	The Deeds of the Spirit
	Obedience
	"Children, obey your parents." (Eph. 6:1)
	"Fathers, do not provoke your children to wrath, but bring them up in the training and admonition of the Lord. (Eph. 6:4) *You will never find a Spirit-controlled father who neglects the raising of his children, regardless of his temperament.*
	Employees, be obedient to your employers; serve them with a joyful heart, doing the will of God. (Eph. 6:5) *Spirit-controlled employees put in a full day's work.*
	Employer, don't threaten them, for the Lord is over you, too. (Eph. 6:9)
	Respect all men

When you are not controlled by the Spirit, resort to the Four *C*s for Overcoming Weaknesses.

1. *Confess* the action as a sin.
2. *Communicate* to God that it is a sin.
3. *Commit* yourself again to God.
4. *Comply* by bringing your thoughts, feelings, and actions into conformity to his Word and will.

Shortly after passing my instrument rating, I had to fly to the Orange County Airport for a speaking engagement. The weather service reported overcast conditions and a 1,800-foot ceiling, so I took off into the fog, not realizing that the cloud cover had lowered to 900 feet above the ground (quite safe for professionals, but not for greenhorns). When prepared for landing, I was not surprised when the controller vectored me north and east of the airport and at 170 degrees cleared me for the approach. I knew the runway heading was 190 degrees, so I banked right 20 degrees and lined up properly. At an altitude of 3,000 feet, I started to descend slowly through the fog. By the time my altimeter showed 1,200 feet I still couldn't see beyond the windshield, and when I arrived at the missed approach point, I called the controller and climbed back up to 3,000 feet, preparing to go around again. Would you believe I did that twice? Finally, I held a brief dialogue with myself (as the beads of cold perspiration dropped off my chin into my lap). "LaHaye, if you are going to get this bird on the ground, you had better follow your instructor's advice, 'Never down, never in.'" I was cleared for 780 feet above the ground but was "too chicken" to descend that low. The third time, I started my descent immediately after passing the final approach fix while lined up again on 190. When I passed through the 1,200-foot level, my hands were clammy, but I put my trust in those instruments (and the Lord), continuing my descent through 1,100 feet, then 1,000 feet, and finally at 900 feet I broke through the clouds. Was that ground a welcome sight! But I still couldn't locate the airport, glancing both left and right. The DME showed 3.6 miles when the controller asked, "Do you have the airport in sight?"—"Negative!" He responded, "It's at twelve o'clock." I looked straight ahead and there it was—right where it was supposed to be. My instruments had been accurate all along.

At times you will have to navigate through the fog of life with only the Word of God and the indwelling Spirit of God to guide you. Friend, that is enough. When you cannot see the next day or the next dollar, trust God, his Word, and the Holy Spirit. He never fails, and his way is always best.

You may wonder at times if writers practice what they preach. I am writing these words at a hotel in Caracas, Venezuela, waiting to begin the second of fifty Family Life Seminars for missionaries in population centers around the world. For almost two years my wife and I prayed about conducting these two-day programs, with an extra day available for counseling as needed, free of charge for missionaries. Our church granted us a sabbatical leave of absence for one year in view of our twenty years of service there. Today I am four thousand miles from home, leaving behind a growing church that *Christian Life* magazine listed as fortieth in size nationally, a booming Christian high school, a seven-year-old flourishing Christian Heritage College, the Institute for Creation Research, the San Diego Community Christian School System (our brand-new endeavor) and, of course, Family Life Seminars. This latter ministry is totally dependent on our activities, yet it will accrue no income from seminars for one year. Those ministries comprise my vocational life, for I have invested my lifeblood in them. Now I have completely entrusted them to God, confident that we are doing the will of God today and that under the capable leadership of our associates, these ministries will continue to flourish without us. By faith we expect each of them to be better off spiritually, numerically, and financially next year when we return.

Periodically, of course, I am impelled to rehearse the promises of God in his Word just to strengthen my flagging faith. I even have to recall occasionally the Holy Spirit's leading just to reassure myself that he has directed us. In other words, being fully committed to my instruments (the Word of God) and complying with the guidance of his Holy Spirit (similar to the radar controller), I fully expect to make a safe landing.

You can expect similar results if you are willing to use this formula. In every detail of life, avail yourself of the strengths of the Holy Spirit for the temperament modification you need to strengthen your weaknesses.

Temperament and Your Spiritual Gift

Much is said today in our churches about spiritual gifts, some of it clear and some confusing. But we may accept such discussions as indications that many of God's people are interested in committing themselves to the Lord and want him to use their lives.

I don't think we receive new gifts when filled with the Spirit, other than the nine strengths of the Spirit listed in Galatians 5:22–23. It is these strengths, when your life is committed to God, that enable you to overcome your weaknesses and allow him to use your life. It may seem like you have new gifts, but what really happens is the Holy Spirit strengthens you to overcome your weaknesses so your natural talents can be used by God. I would speculate that right now you possess all the talents and basic gifts that God intended for you. In fact, you received them at conception in the form of your temperament and IQ. They can be influenced by childhood training, experiences, education, practice, and *most of all* the motivation of the Holy Spirit. You will, however, be empowered to make maximum use of those basic attributes because the Holy Spirit ensures strength to negate your weaknesses.

You may ask, "Where does the spiritual gift part come in?" Consider this possibility. God has conferred upon every one of us gifts, talents, and traits through our temperament, "distributing to each one individually as He wills" (1 Cor. 12:11). As I noted in chapter 6 on the twelve blends of temperament, each individual has the potential for at least twenty strengths of varying degrees of intensity, depending on his temperament. But no one will make full use of his talents naturally, because his twenty weaknesses of temperament will hinder or, in some cases, destroy his potential. When a Christian is filled with the Holy Spirit, the manifestation is "given to each one for the profit of all" (1 Cor. 12:7), and he will enjoy a new dimension of power for the overcoming of his weaknesses. Then, instead of being limited by his weaknesses, he will be freed by God for maximum use of his strengths and directed by his Spirit into productivity. I have never seen a Spirit-filled Christian function irrespective of his natural temperament. CHLORSANs don't often write music or paint pictures, and PHLEGSANs aren't apt to start new ventures, but all are vitally and equally usable by God when their weaknesses are overcome by the power of the Holy Spirit.

8

The Influence of Temperament on Manhood

Some years ago I was asked to pray at an athletic awards banquet attended by Earl Faison, the six-foot-seven, three-hundred-pound tackle who for ten years was one of the "fearsome foursome" on the San Diego Chargers' line. As I entered the hotel, Earl, whom I recognized but had never met, was walking toward me. In what must have been a reckless mood, I stopped in the middle of the doorway, placed my hands on my hips and, looking up at him towering one foot above me, announced, "Who said all men are created equal?" For a moment he looked at me fiercely; then, catching my mood, he creased his black face with a big white smile and laughed heartily. (Man, was I relieved!)

All Men Are Different

Anyone who says that all men are created equal is simply not very perceptive. Historically, of course, that expression suggests that in this land of the free and the just all men are created equal *under the law*. That is much different than maintaining that a man with an IQ of 168 is equal to my old platoon sergeant, who lost his stripes because he couldn't score 90 on the test the fourth time he took it.

It would be much more accurate to assert that all men are created different, regardless of what social experimenters would have us believe. I hope that the growing number of sociobiologists who recognize the existence of inborn temperaments will cause others to realize that temperament, sex, intelligence, and physical ability all play an important part in human behavior. Admittedly, childhood training, education, and life experiences are significant, but temperament is by far the most influential single human characteristic. When we amalgamate the various blends of temperament and the ten different characteristics of manhood, we total at least one hundred and twenty combinations. By the time we project other variables such as background, childhood, education, etc., you can understand why there are hundreds of manifestations of manhood. For simplicity's sake and to demonstrate how these differences come about, we shall revert to the four basic temperaments and show how the characteristics of manhood vary in accord with one's primary temperament. The reader will have to make his own adaptation for his particular blend of temperament.

Each of the following drawings is designed to clarify which of the ten natural characteristics predominate in each temperament. They make no provision for childhood training, which can significantly alter a person's behavior. For example, the Sanguine usually inherits little character. But if his parents are aware of that and work on it early in childhood, his character will have a much greater influence on his behavior than if they do not.

Another trait I have kept standard for each temperament is its core, or "selfishness quotient." All temperaments face a natural problem in this area, though each tends to manifest it differently. The only significant influences on selfishness are childhood training and spiritual motivation.

The Sanguine Man

Sparky Sanguine's manhood characteristics show that his personality, emotions, physical attributes, and boyishness predominate. The ruination of many a Sanguine is his charming personality, which somehow extricates him from every jam. Consequently, he spends little time learning self-discipline and character but much time becoming a con artist. Being a good emoter and exuding considerable sensual appeal makes him a charmer of the ladies, which can often lead to his downfall.

All Sanguines should concentrate on their naturally weak areas, especially on becoming better organized and detailed so they can develop into better leaders and thus permit that sparkling personality to work in their favor. They should force themselves to read more, expanding their minds and horizons. A Sanguine's boundless energy should be channeled into meaningful work, and he should refuse to inaugurate a challenging project until he finishes the one to which he is already committed. Consistency in a daily quiet time—reading God's Word and communicating with him in prayer—has transformed many a Sanguine. Just this week I met an overweight Sanguine who had lost ninety-six pounds over the past two years and proudly announced, "I have only fifty-six pounds to go!" His secret? When he learned spiritual discipline, he acquired physical discipline. Let's face it: Discipline is basic. Develop it in one area and you will find it spreading into others. The Sanguine (and every other temperament) will never live up to his potential unless he learns self-discipline. I am convinced there is no such thing as success in any field without self-discipline. That is the Sanguine's greatest need and should be his chief quest with the Holy Spirit.

The Choleric Man

Rocky Choleric's temperament provides him lots of natural character, leadership, productivity, and courage to be a dynamic person. If his parents inculcate moral principles and guidelines early in life, he will develop a strong moral character. If not, he will become a strong but malignant character, and his whole lifetime will be spent as though the end justifies the means. Many of the world's great dictators and gangsters have been Cholerics without moral values.

Rocky would be advised to cultivate his emotions, mind, and boyishness. Actually, the chart is somewhat misleading in giving him a large emotional quality. In actuality, it contains the emotion of anger almost exclusively. If we portrayed his love capabilities, they would be razor-thin. I have determined that the number one quest of a Christian Choleric should be love, the principal need for him and his family. Just recently I was seated at a table with ten others for six meals at a camp. The Choleric was naturally the headman at our table and easily the busiest individual in camp. Though he talked about the Spirit-filled life, I saw little evidence of love. He had allowed the Spirit to lead him in his vocational pursuit or he would not have been there, but I did not observe one kind or gentle action toward his wife or children. He commanded that food be passed rather than saying please, and he showed no personal interest in anyone at the table. Obviously he was a well-intentioned Choleric whose dedication was erroneously making a priority out of working hard for God, rather than soliciting the first fruit of the Spirit—love. Like most capable Cholerics, he has a long way to go.

In addition to love, the Choleric needs to relax in the Spirit, avoid taking himself and life so seriously, and feed that fun-loving boy within. He is dying of malnutrition and disuse. The many other needs of a Choleric have been detailed previously, but one that should be emphasized is the development of his mind. Though an activist, he may never have developed the habit of reading. His mind is always working in practical areas, but he tends to become stereotyped in thought and action unless he reads. This is particularly true of him spiritually. He will never become a strong Spirit-controlled man unless he develops the habit of studying the Word of God regularly.

One of the greatest problems pastors have in our churches is Choleric members (both men and women) who see the church as an ideal opportunity for them to take charge and run it. Most Cholerics think the church is too inefficiently operated and they are God's gift to make it shape up. Few pastors would agree. Before long the congregation polarizes between the pastor, who is called and paid to be the leader, and the self-appointed dictator, who because of his natural leadership ability tries to take over. Eventually a bitter spirit develops and hinders the spiritual purpose of the church.

I remember just such a conflict when I had first arrived in San Diego. I should have been suspicious when I learned that of the two pastors before me one had died of a heart attack and the other had resigned with bleeding ulcers. Two weeks after my arrival a godly prayer warrior told me she prayed for me every day "because to pastor this church you have to have the hide of a rhinoceros." It didn't take long to discover she was right, or the source of the trouble. Fortunately, I had learned early in my ministry to solve problems quickly. I invited the would-be dictator in for a confrontation and made it clear that he may have run the

last two pastors, but I considered it my calling and responsibility to be the spiritual leader of the church, and no organization can function with two heads. He didn't like it much,
but for the sake of his family he backed off, and later we
became friends. Eventually, two of his girls married missionaries and have spent their lives serving the Lord. I have
known of other Cholerics who didn't react in the Spirit and
ended up losing their children to the world.

The Choleric by temperament is a capable and productive human being; consequently, he tends to rely on himself instead of the Spirit of God. He tries to serve the Lord
in the energy of the flesh, often neglecting the spiritual side
of his nature at his peril. But if he keeps in the Word and
prays, God can enrich his life and use him productively. But
he may have a lifetime battle learning to submit to authority in the church.

The Melancholy Man

Martin Melancholy is depicted on the chart as predominantly mind, emotions, productivity, and character. His mental gifts usually become apparent early
in life, and his potential is unlim-
ited unless his tremendous
emotional nature becomes
warped and he develops
the habit of indulging in
revengeful   thoughts,
self-pity, negativism,
pessimism, self-perse-
cution, or criticism.
If taught the art of
"thanksgiving living" as
a small child by his par-
ents, this man can be a
vibrant individual. No one
else is more emotionally responsive to his own thinking, but
he absolutely must maintain a positive and thanksgiving men-

tal attitude. If he does, his creative genius will be consistent, not just the sporadic production of his positive mood, as has usually been the case with the great composers, artists, and others.

Although this man is not usually gifted in leadership, he can learn management techniques and, as his confidence grows, become an effective leader, though usually he avoids such responsibilities because he would rather work alone. He often neglects his physical appearance and body conditioning, but he will be enriched emotionally and mentally as any other man when he keeps himself in shape spiritually and physically. In this day of physical fitness, many a Melancholy has had the assurance of his manhood enhanced by regular jogging, which improves his muscle tone. It is particularly necessary to offset the lethargy that sets in due to our sedentary way of life. His personality is often more underdeveloped than the chart reveals, depending on his childhood training and experiences. Melancholies should use their character, mental gifts, and motivation to help others; they should work at being more outgoing, personable, and interested in others.

Here is a poignant story for every Melancholy. A man came to me deeply disturbed that he was such an introvert. In addition to the spiritual therapy of regular Bible study, I challenged him to overcome his fear of knowing what to say at social gatherings by concentrating on remembering the names of those he met via a kind of memory game. We developed a list of five questions he would ask, using the individual's name each time: (1) "Mr. Jones, do you live in our city?"; (2) "What kind of work are you in, Mr. Jones?"; (3) "Are you new to this group, Mr. Jones?"; (4) "Mr. Jones, are you married?"; and (5) "Do you have children, Mr. Jones?" I love to work with Melancholies, because if they are convinced my advice will work, they usually respond readily. Within a month he returned, quite elated at his progress. Social activities now seemed exciting and interesting to him, for suddenly he was becoming a favorite at parties. Why? He showed an interest in other people. Ask almost any person a few questions about himself and he will talk readily. Let's face it—everyone is interested in himself. I chuckled at his admission: "Even though I memorized all five leading questions, I never asked anyone more than three. By that time we were talking." I could almost have predicted that, but I foresaw that a typical Melancholy had to command five guns in his arsenal before he possessed the courage to go forth to the conversational wars. Melancholies are usually incredibly capable people if they can overcome their unfounded lack of confidence and other groundless fears.

The Phlegmatic Man

Philip Phlegmatic majors in four areas of manhood: strong character, an excellent mind, good-humored boyishness, and emotional control. In addition, he can be a fine leader if the position is forced upon him (or if he is spiritually motivated), and he *can* be productive if his work demands it. But as we have seen, he rarely does more than is expected and never volunteers for anything (though his wife sometimes volunteers his services for him). Although Philip enjoys a stable emotional life, his emotions are apt to accentuate the negative areas of fear, worry, and anxiety rather than love for others. He must reject this imbalance throughout his life or he will seriously limit his potential effectiveness. Naturally, the Christian Phlegmatic gains spiritual power substantially once he learns to be consistent in his devotional habits and spiritual walk. He stops limiting himself through fear because the Word of God makes him a man of faith.

The best illustration I know concerns a man who dropped out of my men's Saturday Bible class four times. The fifth time I started the series, he showed up again. I wondered how long he would last this time, but to my amazement he stuck with the program and gradually became a different man. After growing spiritually, he returned to college, earned a counseling degree, and today is a highly successful personnel director in industry. His vocational life grew in direct proportion to his spiritual life.

Of all the temperaments, Phil Phlegmatic is the most likely to be a personality zero. One good friend provides an extreme example. He will accept church offices if asked but contributes almost nothing. At one important meeting that lasted over an hour, his conversation consisted of four words: *Good evening* and *Good night.* (One time he did raise his hand when a vote was taken.) Such an individual will never be a ball of fire, but he can force himself to become more outgoing. He usually has practical contributions to make but tends to keep them bottled up inside. I have noted that unless he develops a more externalized personality, he will stifle that big fun-loving boy inside—and that's a loss for everyone, particularly for himself. He also needs to take on more activities than he thinks he can do, and because of his dependable nature, he will be kept busier and appreciate himself more in the process.

Philip should also concentrate on physical fitness. His natural body-at-rest-tends-to-stay-at-rest ways make him the last in the office to try jogging and exercise. Unfortunately, he is probably the one who needs it most. It would clean out his respiratory system, add years to his heart, and actually give him more energy, not to mention greater confidence—and he needs all he can get. He is an easy man to live with, but he does need external motivation—and God provides the best in the self-control of the Holy Spirit.

A Note to Wives on Manhood

Stereotypes are always dangerous, particularly when one assesses manhood. Every man is different and must be accepted as such. Many a wife is troubled by the fact that her husband is so different from her father. I was amused by a lady who wrote to the "Dear Abby" column. Apparently her dad was a Mr. Fix-it, and she grew up holding tools for him. Evidently, she also had a mechanical bent of mind and learned to be handy. Unfortunately, her husband was just the opposite. He didn't know a Phillips-head screwdriver from the regular type and didn't care to learn. He even jogged five miles to a gas station one time rather than change a tire. During her eighth month of pregnancy she went to bed utterly exhausted, only to be awakened two hours later by a calamity in the bathroom. Her husband had broken a faucet and water was squirting everywhere. She dressed, found a wrench in the garage, went out to the water main and shut it off (he had no idea where it was). She wailed to Abby that, although she loved her husband and he was a good provider, she simply could not endure this mechanical ignoramus. Abby wisely advised her to accept him as he was, love him, be grateful for him—and hire a handyman to do the repairs.

A thoughtless wife may get annoyed with the less rugged, "unmanly" ways of a husband whose profession does not lend itself to physical labor. But the steeplejack or brick-layer she admires may not be as gentle and loving as her mate. I have met many a rugged man whose crudeness and callous indifference to his wife's need of tenderness made him anything but a matrimonial asset. The second most selfish man I ever counseled was a "superjock" pro football player. I couldn't fault him on masculinity (from outward appearance), but he knew nothing about true manhood. The man who responsibly toils day after day at a job he detests in order to support his family may not feature a robust constitution or physical "animalism," but he is more of a man than the hulking weight lifter who abandons his family to satisfy his own selfish desires.

It is always wrong to assess only one area of a person's life, and it is even worse to compare one individual to another. Since God gave you your man, it is his will that you love and admire only him. You will both be happier if you accept him as he is and trust God to modify any areas that need improvement as your heavenly Father sees fit. As I urged one woman in the counseling room, "Stop saying, 'I wish my husband were more _____,' and start saying, 'I thank God my husband is _____.'" You are the only person in the world who can help your husband feel comfortable in his manhood. Work at it—you'll both be richer for it!

The Motivation for Change

According to sociologists, everyone resists change. That is particularly true if someone else is arbitrarily trying to force some change upon us. Any temperament or manhood modification must come from within.

In the four sample diagrams shown in this chapter, you probably noticed that all were drawn with self on the throne of the will. That is because I was trying to portray the raw material of temperament and manhood as it applies to each of the four temperaments. I assumed that you already recognized that once that throne has been surrendered to Jesus Christ, as described in chapter 3, the individual has brought a tremendous power source into his life. In fact, the new nature that Christ supplies at salvation is the only power capable of the kind of temperament modification and selfless living every person needs. As the Scripture teaches of those who receive the gospel of Christ "It is the power of God," and "Old things have passed away; behold, all things have become new" (see 1 Cor. 1:18; 2 Cor. 5:17). Remember, it doesn't take place overnight and it isn't automatic. As we have seen, every man must cooperate with the Holy Spirit to make those necessary improvements. It's entirely up to you, but with Christ in your life, you have within you all the power necessary to do the job.

9

Accepting Your Partner's Contrasting Temperament

Self-understanding is only one benefit gained from knowing the theory of the four basic temperaments. In addition, it helps you understand other people, particularly those closest to you. Many a matrimonial battleground is transformed into a neutral zone when two individuals learn to appreciate each other's temperament. When you realize that a person's actions result from his or her temperament rather than a tactic designed to anger or offend you, it is much easier to accept the behavior. If your partner is quick on the mouth, you can be more accepting of his or her criticism and "barking." One wife I knew listened to her verbal husband's grumbling after he came home from work. Instead of saying anything, she just went to the door, opened it, and closed it again. He asked, "What's that all about?" She sweetly replied, "I thought you must have had your tail caught in the door, and I was just releasing it." He got the message!

"We are so hopelessly mismatched that we ought to get a divorce," lamented a couple one Tuesday evening in my office. To my question of "Where did you get that idea?"

they replied, "We have been to a Christian counseling center that gave us a battery of psychological tests, and that's the conclusion our counselor came to." I immediately responded, "That is the worst advice I have ever heard given by a Christian. It is unbiblical in your situation and will only compound your problems." The husband groaned, "Do you mean God wants us to be this miserable the rest of our lives?" "No," I replied, "there is a much better way! God is able to give you the grace to adjust to and accept each other's temperament." Since they knew nothing about temperament, I proceeded to show them my chart, and before long they could determine the true nature of their opposite temperaments. Upon my promise to counsel them, they agreed to cancel their scheduled appointment with an attorney the following Thursday and delay further talk of divorce. That was more than twenty years ago. If you saw that couple today, you would never dream that they had ever entertained ideas of splitting up. This chapter contains the principles I shared with them. I am convinced that any couple—with God's help—can understand and accept each other's temperament, ultimately reaching a perfect adjustment if they want to.

Why Opposites Attract Each Other

What could be more opposite than male and female? Yet they still attract each other after thousands of years. In fact, the future of the race is dependent on such attraction. Unfortunately, men and women fail to realize that their physical differences are only symbolic of the many other differences in their natures, the most significant of which are their temperaments. When I wrote this section for the first edition of this book, I was only beginning to show that opposites attract and could still resolve their natural differences. Fifteen years later, I was even more convinced of that principle and expanded on it in my book *I Love You, but Why Are We So Different?*

A negative is never attracted to another negative, and positives repel each other in any field—electricity, chemistry, and particularly temperament. Instead, negatives are attracted to positives and vice versa. I have found that almost universally true of temperaments.

Have you ever wondered what attracts you to other people? Usually it is the subconscious recognition of and appreciation for their strengths—strengths that complement your own weaknesses. Consciously or not, we all wish we could eradicate our particular set of weaknesses, and we blissfully admire the strengths of others. If given enough association with the person who sparks our attraction, we experience one of two things. Either we discover weaknesses in him or her similar to our own and are understandably turned off by them, or we discover other strengths we are lacking, which translates admiration into love. If other factors are favorable, it is not uncommon for such couples to marry.

Like temperaments rarely marry. For instance, a Sanguine would seldom marry another Sanguine, for both are such natural extroverts that they would be competing for the same stage in life, and no one would be sitting in the audience. Sanguines, you see, need an audience. Cholerics, on the other hand, make such severe demands on other people that they not only wouldn't marry each other, they probably would never date—at least not more than once. They would spend all their time arguing over everything and vying for control or authority in their relationship. Two Melancholies might marry, but it is unlikely. Their analytical traits find negative qualities in others, and thus neither would pursue the other. Two Phlegmatics would rarely marry, for they would both die of old age before one got up enough steam to propose. Besides, they are so protective of their feelings that they could go steady with a person for thirty years before saying or otherwise communicating "I love you." One Phlegmatic man had courted an exceedingly patient Christian lady for four years. Finally her patience snapped and she asked, "Have you ever thought about our getting married?" He replied, "A time or two." She countered, "Would you like to?" He answered, "I think so." "When?" He responded, "Whenever you would like." Years later he acknowledged that he had wanted to marry her for two years but was afraid to ask. Can you imagine how long they would have waited if she, too, had been a Phlegmatic?

In the Western world, where couples choose their own partners, we find that, in general, opposite temperaments attract each other. For a previous book, I surveyed several hundred couples who understood the temperaments and fed their responses into a computer. Less than .4 percent indicated that they matched the temperament of their spouses. Ordinarily, I found that Sanguines were attracted to Melancholies and Cholerics to Phlegmatics, although that is by no means universal.

Sanguines, who tend to be disorganized and undisciplined themselves, are apt to admire careful, consistent, and detail-conscious Melancholies. The latter, in turn, favor outgoing, uninhibited individuals who compensate for the introvert's rigidity and aloofness. The hard-driving Choleric is often attracted to the peaceful, unexcited Phlegmatic, who in turn admires Rocky's dynamic drive.

After the honeymoon, the problems from this kind of selection begin to surface. Sparky Sanguine is not just warm, friendly, and uninhibited—but also forgetful, disorganized, and undependable. Besides, he gets quite irate if his ladylove, a Melancholy, asks him to pick up his clothes, put away his tools, or come home on time. Somehow Rocky Choleric's before-marriage dynamic personality turns into anger, cruelty, sarcasm, and bullheadedness after marriage. Martin Melancholy's gentleness and well-structured lifestyle becomes nitpicky and impossible to please after marriage. Philip Phlegmatic's cool, calm, and peaceful ways often seem lazy, unmotivated, and stubborn afterwards.

Learning to adapt to your partner's weaknesses while strengthening your own is known as "adjustment in marriage." I hope it will comfort you to know that no matter whom you marry or what his or her temperament is, you will have to endure this adjustment process to some degree. Additional encouragement will be found in the fact that God, by his Holy Spirit, has given you ample resources to make a positive adjustment.

Eight Steps to Adjusting to a Partner's Temperament

Although the following eight steps for temperament adjustment were designed originally for married couples, with only minor variations they can be used for college roommates, brothers and sisters, fellow employees, or almost any interpersonal relationship.

1. *Admit to yourself, "I'm not perfect."* Nothing is more harmful in a fractured marriage than one partner who thinks so highly of himself he fails to see any of his own shortcomings and is occupied with the weaknesses of the other partner, usually making her out to be much worse than she is. Humbling yourself enough to admit that you are not perfect is the first step in accepting imperfections in others. It isn't enough just to say "I'm not perfect." You must really admit it to yourself. Once you realistically acknowledge that you brought weaknesses into this relationship that your partner must learn to live with, it will be easier to allow her the same human frailty. Anyone too proud to admit his or her own weaknesses is not only incurable but also extremely selfish.

2. *Accept the fact that your partner has weaknesses.* Repeatedly we have discerned through our study of temperament and temperament blends that *all* human beings possess both strengths and weaknesses. It cannot be otherwise until the resurrection, when we will be made perfect in Christ. The sooner you face the fact that anyone you marry will have weaknesses to which you must adjust, the sooner you can get to the business of adjusting to your partner. Resist all mental fantasies of "If only I had married _____!" or "If only I had married another temperament." That is not an option, so why not accept your partner's weaknesses?

After a seminar a man made the facetious comment, "I thought I married an angel, but soon after our honeymoon I found she wasn't." A humor-laden Phlegmatic standing nearby spoke up and said, "I can give you three good reasons why you should be glad you didn't marry an angel—one, they never have anything new to wear; two, they are always up in the air harping on something; and three, they are sexless!" Reason number three should be enough motivation for most men to begin accepting their wife's human frailties. Every happily married couple has had to come to grips with the fact that the other partner has weaknesses. It makes it easier when you understand that one of the proofs we are human is that we have serious weaknesses to cope with. Love does not depend on perfection; it depends on acceptance.

3. *Concentrate on and appreciate your partner's strengths.* Your partner does have strengths. That's what attracted you to him or her in the first place. So your problem now is twofold: (1) disillusionment at the discovery of weaknesses you didn't realize existed and (2) an inordinate concentration on them. Individuals regularly come in for counseling with all manner of complaints about their partners. When I ignore what they have said and ask, "Is there anything about your partner you do like?" they invariably reply affirmatively and soon list a few qualities for me. I write these on a card until we total eight or ten, then show the person 1 Thessalonians 5:18: "In everything give thanks; for this is the will of God in Christ Jesus for you." His or her assignment then is every morning and every evening to review the lists point by point and thank God for each item, thus fulfilling his expressed will for their lives. This not only cancels their obsession for dwelling on a partner's weaknesses but also helps them be grateful for his or her strengths.

One man to whom I gave this prescription for his lack of love for his wife reported that in three weeks he was "madly in love" with her again. When I asked, "Have you memorized your list of ten things about her for which you are grateful?" he replied, "Oh, I had those learned by the third day, but I've found fifteen other things about her I like also." Show me a man who predominantly thanks God twice every day for twenty-five things about his wife, and I will show you a man who dearly loves that woman regardless of her temperament. (Actually, ten items will usually do the trick.)

Everyone wants to be happy. I have never met an exception. But until a person turns on the spigot of gratefulness and gives thanks in everything, he will live in misery. You will never find a happy griper or a person who loves his partner after complaining about her all the time! Thanksgiving is the key to acceptance, love, and happiness.

4. *Pray for the strengthening of your partner's weaknesses.* God is in the temperament-modification business. By his Holy Spirit and through his Word he is able to provide the strengths your partner needs for the improvement of his or her temperament weaknesses, but it will never happen if you are on his or her back all the time. If a temperament weakness produces a consistent pattern of behavior such as tardiness, messiness, legalism, negativism, and so on, it may be advisable to talk lovingly to your partner about it once, but after that just commit the matter to God. If you take the place of the Holy Spirit in your partner's conscience, he or she will never change, but if you remain silent on the issue and love your partner as he or she is, then the Holy Spirit can get through to the person.

5. *Apologize when you are wrong.* Everyone makes mistakes! Fortunately, you don't have to be perfect to be a good person or partner. Earlier I defined a mature person as one who knows both his strengths and weaknesses and develops a planned program for overcoming his weaknesses. That presumes you will make mistakes. I must ask, then, Are you mature enough to take full responsibility for what you have done? If in anger you have offended your partner in word or in deed, you need to apologize. God in his grace has given us the example and the means for repairing mistakes and offenses. An apology reaches into another's heart and mind to remove the root of bitterness that otherwise would fester and grow until it choked your relationship. That is why the Bible teaches, "Confess your trespasses [faults or sins] to one another" (James 5:16).

6. *Verbalize your love.* Everyone needs love and will greatly profit from hearing it verbalized frequently. This is

particularly true of women, whatever their temperament. I once counseled a brilliant engineer, a father of five, after his wife left him for another man whose salary was one-third her husband's. After a bit of probing, I learned that he had not uttered his love for ten years. Why? He didn't think it was necessary. Verbalizing love is not only a necessity for holding a couple together but an enrichment of their relationship. In fact, he admitted he did not give his approval or encourage her even when she did something right. Few people can endure a love-starved relationship.

As we have seen, men must work harder at maintaining love than women. An industrious businessman, forced to take work home from the office, complained, "My wife will come into the den when I am up to my ears on some account, interrupt me by sitting on my lap and asking, 'Charlie, do you love me?' To be honest, right then I don't love anyone; I'm trying to get my work done. What do you do with such a woman?"

"Charlie," I said, "you ought to thank God for a wife like that! Most men wish they still had a sweetheart who cared that much for them. What's more important—that account or your marriage"? Naturally, he grinned sheepishly, and then I asked if he offered the same reaction when his children ran in for a little tender loving care. Acknowledging that he did, he asked what he should do. I answered, "Keep your priorities in order!" At those golden moments when your family needs reassurances of love, you have nothing more important to do. The work will keep, and you can return to it, but the opportunity to build a relationship of love comes all too infrequently. Take advantage of them whenever you can.

When our son Lee was five years old, we were involved in a church building program. I was extremely busy and unfortunately knew nothing about the Spirit-controlled life. I was also not aware that the third child in a family often feels insecure about his parents' love. Not only did Lee's brother and sister tease him a great deal, but—because he was probably the most gifted of our children and large for his age—he tried unsuccessfully to compete with them. His competitive fervor led him to exasperating extremes, and I'm afraid I was overly critical of him.

One night after the children went to bed, I was startled by the thought that Lee had not kissed me good night as the others had. Laying aside my books, I slipped into his room and looked down on his angelic features (little boys always look angelic when they are asleep). The covers were kicked off as usual, his little arm was tucked under his head, and I heard a faint little sob in his breathing. It was as if a knife pierced my heart! My son had cried himself to sleep, unassured of my love. I knelt at his bed, ran my fingers through his curly hair, and noiselessly cried out, "Dear God, what am I doing to my son? Every time I turn around I find myself criticizing him. He never seems to make his bed right or pick up his toys or clean up his plate. Just yesterday I bawled him out for kicking rocks, largely because he wore out a pair of shoes in three weeks." The harsh sound of my voice came back to me saying, "Lee, if you had to pay for your shoes, you'd take better care of them!" Just a few days before, I had found "LEE" carved on the mahogany doors of our console. Before spanking him, I asked why he did it. He confessed, "I wanted to get Larry into trouble, so I carved his name on the door." Unfortunately, at his age he could only write his *own* name. Now I realized that this was his boyish way of trying to capture that part of my heart that rightly belonged to him.

Kissing Lee on the cheek that night as I knelt there, partly to God and partly to him I prayed, "Forgive me for my selfish preoccupation, Son. With God's help I'm going to be a better father from this night on. Your little cares and needs will be important to me, and you can run into my heart whenever you like. Somehow I'm going to show you the love I really have in my heart for you. It's just been covered over by a lot of unimportant stuff lately. Please give me one more chance."

Fortunately for parents, little children are forgiving. I was the first one up the next morning and tenderly woke both boys. Before going to work, I lifted Lee up and gave him a big hug and kiss. I shall never forget the tight squeeze of both his little arms around my neck. He even waved to me as I drove away. That night I made a point of talking to him and asking about his day. I knew all was forgiven when, as I was reading the paper after dinner, he ran in, knocked it aside, and urged, "Daddy, let's wrestle." In a moment we were tumbling on the floor together. Oh, I haven't been a perfect father since then, but with God's help, today I have an adult son who is secure in my love. I am proud of him and we are good friends. In fact, we work together. I thank God for piercing my heart back then and causing me to reorder my priorities. And those pressing business matters that had come between us? I can't even remember what they were now.

We men have to work at loving, but it's worth it. Remember, everyone needs love.

7. *Accept your partner's temperament and work with it.* Whatever your partner's temperament, bear in mind that you made the choice. A man gave me a card that read, "Never criticize your wife; it's a reflection on your judgment." As long as you remain critical of your partner's temperament-induced behavior patterns, you will experience conflict. A woman reported recently, "My husband and I irritate each other." Why? Because neither would let the other be himself.

The closest temperaments I have ever counseled were a self-acknowledged CHLORSAN husband and a CHLORMEL wife. (Personally, I thought she was a MELCHLOR, but I don't argue with people about their self-evaluations.) In any case, she admired this dynamic, industrious, driving man—"except for one thing. He is sarcastically cruel to anyone who gets in his way, particularly the children." (I've found that Choleric husbands are often accused of being too harsh when disciplining their children.) He complained, "She is cold and unloving unless I'm perfect. I'm tired of getting loved as a reward for good behavior." (Leave it to a Choleric to tell it like it is!)

Two angry people living in the same house will inevitably produce conflict. That kind of problem must be approached two ways—he has to face his anger as sin and she has to trust God to accept him, whether he achieves victory or not. They should also treat each other kindly, of course, to avoid precipitating conflict. Usually one has little trouble picking a fight if he or she wants to, but Jesus said, "Blessed are the peacemakers."

It is absolutely imperative that both spouses learn how to approach each other in the light of their respective temperaments. Thankfully, not all couples are as different as my wife and I. No matter what needs to be done, we always come up with different ways of doing it. If we're taking a trip, Bev thinks we should take the northern route and I opt for the southern. She drives too slow by my standards and I drive too fast by hers. (We solved that by establishing a firm rule: "He that has the steering wheel makes the decision—the other keeps quiet.") We don't even shop alike. Bev buys just what we need; I hate to waste my time going to the store without filling up the cart. It used to irritate her that I always brought home far more than the grocery list; now she knows that it's the price of not doing the shopping herself.

We don't even make decisions in the same length of time. I can usually make up my mind in eight-tenths of a second; Bev likes to mull things over, analyze them from all sides, and then come to a conclusion. In this regard, I have learned that my snap judgments that usually work out in the long run are not always the best route to take. With that realization has come an increasing respect for her judgment because she thinks things through. When I am confronted with a decision, she has learned to suggest, "Let's think about it." At first it used to bug me; now I'm discovering that her delaying tactic often saves time. On the other hand, I have learned never to force her into a quick decision, for it will almost always be negative. I find that if I plan further in advance and say, "Honey, there's something I'd like you to think about—don't give me an answer now," she usually will come around to my way of thinking or offer a profitable suggestion to improve "our" idea.

Study your partner. Learn his or her likes, dislikes, prejudices, and weaknesses. Then try to avoid pushing or demanding in those areas. Isn't that love? Like paint, love covers a multitude of sins. Selfishness always demands its own way, but ruins a relationship in getting it.

8. *Expect God to improve your partner.* We have already said a good deal about maturity in this book. Every growing person matures. Because we all begin insecure and apprehensive, we are often overly defensive. As Christians, we own resources others cannot share. God the Holy Spirit is continually working on us in an attempt to mature us into that person he wants us to be. Your marriage partner today is not exactly the same person he or she will be in a few years, so you can afford to be patient.

One of my friends came to church one day with a black-and-white button on which was printed PBP GINFWMY. When I asked what it meant, he explained that he had just attended a Basic Youth Conflicts Seminar taught by Bill Gothard, where he had found the badge. It meant, "Please Be Patient. God Is Not Finished with Me Yet." That's great advice for partners! Don't forget, if your partner is a Christian, God the Holy Spirit is not finished with him or her yet—and all his modifications will be improvements.

10

Male Anger versus Female Fear

As we have seen in a previous chapter, opposites attract each other in marriage. Not only are their strengths opposite, but their weaknesses are also. One of the most serious areas of conflict arises when the man is of extrovertish temperament and prone to be angry and the woman tends to be fearful. This problem doesn't usually surface during the honeymoon, but after the couple returns to the normal pressures of life, sooner or later "It" takes place. Because of some pet peeve or source of irritation, the angry partner will blow up. (For the purposes of this chapter, we will assume that the angry partner is the husband. In some instances the wife has the anger problem. If this is true, her husband will inevitably face the fear problem, and we will deal with that in the next chapter.)

A pastor friend in Northern California called to ask if I would meet with a dedicated couple from his congregation who happened to be in San Diego trying to work out their marriage problems. This CHLORSAN husband and MELPHLEG wife had been married seventeen years and acknowledged two problems. First, both admitted, "We cannot communicate." Second, the wife added, "He turns me off sexually. I am absolutely dead toward him."

Sue's story was pathetic. Raised in a German immigrant family of five children, her father "ruled the roost with an iron hand." She lamented, "Mealtimes were always a terror for me because if Father got upset, he would pound his fist so hard that the dishes and silverware would leap off the table and clatter as they fell back down. I always promised myself that I would never marry a man like my father." When Bill came along, he seemed so sweet and kind that she fell in love with him and they soon married. "Three weeks after our wedding, it happened," she continued. "Something set him off, and he pounded his fist on the table so hard that the dishes and silverware leaped into the air. As they clattered down onto the table, I thought, 'I've married a man just like my father!'"

Anger and Fear Stifle Communication

Sweethearts rarely have trouble communicating before marriage. In fact, they can talk on the phone by the hour. But to destroy that relationship it takes only the angry action of one to set up a fear reaction in the other. Oh, they usually make up and renew their tenderness and communication, but the damage is done. Each has seen the other in his true light. Consequently, the spirit of free communication will be inhibited. The anger of one builds a formidable block in the wall that obstructs communication. The self-protection reaction of fear keeps the other from expressing himself or herself freely, and thus another block is added to the wall. Gradually, such outbursts and reactions build an impenetrable wall until the former lovebirds are not really communicating at all, apprehensive that the anger of one will be ignited or the fear of the other will cause added pain. Tears, silence, and pent-up feelings all play their part, and before long they need counseling because they can't communicate anymore. Lack of communication is not the problem. Anger and fear are the culprits! Unfortunately, this malady is so common that it warrants two chapters of consideration.

Pressure Doesn't Make Your Spirit!

Bill defended his actions by saying, "She has no idea of the pressures I'm under, and she takes my outbursts too seriously because of her background. What she doesn't realize is that all men have to let off steam. I don't really mean the things I say, but she won't forgive me when I apologize." In other words, Bill doesn't want to change. He expects Sue to live with an angry man just as her mother did.

What Bill doesn't recognize is that pressure does not make your spirit—it merely reveals it. What a man is under pressure is what he is! If you explode under pressure, you are admitting that underneath a carefully constructed facade you are an angry person. Some people have more tolerance and can take more pressure than others, of course, but if you are an angry individual, your weakness will show up sooner or later by the way you act, react, or think. And we all know that the home is potentially the world's greatest pressure cooker. That is why anger and its various forms of hostility are the family's number one problem.

One hostile husband told me, "Well, I have to find someplace where I can be myself." Yes, he did, and that was his problem—himself. A person at home always reveals his true nature. We can put up a front outside the home, but under the pressures of family living, the real individual manifests himself. I have found only one remedy. Let God change the real you so that your hours at home can be pleasant and those who love you most will not be threatened.

Anger and Masculinity

Men seem to have the strange idea that anger is a justifiable masculine trait. "Every man gets angry!" they exclaim. Some would insist that a man who doesn't have an anger problem isn't a real man. Nothing could be further from the truth. Man's natural tendency toward anger has probably started more wars, created more conflict, and ruined more homes than any other universal trait.

Anger seems to be man's way of expressing his frustrations, but it is a mistake to deem it a beneficial emotion. In fact, it inhibits sound judgment and thinking. A nineteen-year-old man who had a fight with his girlfriend backed out of her driveway and "laid a hundred and five feet of scratch" in front of her house. In seven minutes he was dead. His anger robbed him of good judgment until he floored the gas pedal at ninety-five miles an hour, failed to navigate a freeway curve, and sped straight into eternity. Anger struck again.

Norm Evans, the all-pro tackle for the Miami Dolphins for several years and later for the Seattle Seahawks, once confided, "It's really dangerous for a pro football player to get angry. In fact, that's when linemen sustain their most serious injuries." When asked to clarify that, he explained, "Anger is so harmful in football that if I can get an opposing lineman or end angry at me, he will concentrate more on beating me and forget to attack the quarterback, and that's my job—protecting the quarterback."

Mike Fuller, the fleet-footed safety and punt-return specialist for the Chargers, agreed. "The wide receivers are continually trying to make us angry each time they come into our area because they know that if they can upset us emotionally they can fool us on the next play." An angry person makes poor decisions, wounds those he loves with his tongue, overreacts, disciplines too severely, and continually does things that calm thought would not otherwise permit.

Bob Hutchins, former judo champion for Southern California and later a missionary in Mexico, told me, "I was just an above-average judo performer until I learned how to make my opponent angry. Then I could use his force against him. That's how I won the championship." Millions of men, like Bob's opponents, fall into the trap of thinking that you are not a man unless you get angry. In truth, anything you attempt when angry can be better accomplished when in full control of your faculties. That is particularly true of family living in relation to both wife and children. The most common complaint of the fearful wife concerns her husband's angry methods of disciplining the children.

Discipline, particularly spanking, administered in anger is almost always wrong. Even though the child deserves the punishment, if it is meted out in anger, the child tends to read the spirit of the parent and consider the spanking unjust. The parent would accomplish much more by waiting a few minutes to gain emotional control and then administering the punishment. In that way, the child receives the full benefit of its corrective instruction because he has no one else upon whom he can transfer the blame.

The three principle causes of child abuse today are alcohol, drugs, and anger. All tend to nullify a person's ability to control his actions. And all too often a small child pays the price through abuse.

What could cause any adult to so abuse a helpless child? Frustration due to anger! Brokenhearted parents have wept out the stories of their "abnormal behavior," registering amazement that they were capable of such action. They aren't basically abnormal; they just never learned to overcome their natural tendency to become angry. Consequently, when a sufficient level of frustration was reached, they lost control of themselves and committed an act they regretted for life.

A minister asked that I counsel his wife for an unrepentant affair she was having. Expecting to see a siren walk into my office, I was surprised to find a gracious, soft-spoken woman of forty-five who told this story through her tears. Her husband was a dynamic minister, successful in his church and admired by everyone. But he had one sin she could not excuse. He was an angry, hostile man whom she considered "overstrict and physically abusive of our three children. He cannot control his anger and has on one occasion beaten our oldest son unconscious." When the boy reached nineteen, he ran away and joined a hippie group. Brokenheartedly she said, "From that day on I lost all feeling for my husband."

An extreme situation like that never occurs suddenly. It had been building up for years, primarily related to major disagreements over disciplining the children. She had learned to live with his other angry explosions but could not endure his manhandling of the children. Too fearful to voice her real feelings, she witnessed her husband's angry frustrations worked out on the heads, faces, and backsides of their children. Although she only interrupted on extreme occasions, she acknowledged "dying a little" each time he abused them. As it turned out, her affair was not a real love problem but a retaliation to spite her husband.

When the minister came in, he was obviously desperate. I was never sure if he sought help because he really loved his wife or if he was just trying to save his ministry. When confronted with his hostilities, he retorted, "If a man can't let down and be himself at home, where can he?" I was silent for a long time. As he sat there thinking, he finally admitted. "That sounds pretty carnal, doesn't it?" Before leaving, he realized that his anger was as bad or worse than her adultery. Although this man was able to salvage his marriage, as far as I know he has never regained his son. In all probability, more sons have been alienated from their fathers because of Dad's anger than anything else. And the tragic part of it is that the son will probably treat his son the same way. Angry fathers produce angry children.

The Devastating Consequences of Anger

Anger, hostility, or wrath—or, as the Bible calls it, "enmity of heart" or "malice"—is as old as man. Doubtless you recall the first family squabble in recorded history, "Cain was very angry . . . and rose against Abel his brother and killed him" (see Gen. 4:5–8). Ever since that tragic day, millions have died prematurely, and countless marriages have broken up because of anger. The number of children subjected to emotional tension in the home due to the anger of adults staggers the mind. Any counselor will acknowledge that most of his emotionally scarred clients are the victims of someone's anger. It is a nearly universal emotional problem with devastating consequences—particularly in the home. Newspapers have reported many tragic stories of untimely deaths, one of which was a pro football player whose wife killed him in his sleep with an eight-inch kitchen knife. Only protracted anger that turns into the white heat of rage would make a person take another's life.

The only temperament that will not have an inherent problem with anger is the Phlegmatic, but since no one is 100 percent a Phlegmatic, even he will encounter the difficulty to a certain degree, depending on his secondary temperament. As we have seen, a PHLEGMEL will experience the least problem with it, depending of course on the percentages of his two temperaments. Sanguines, you will recall, are instantly eruptive and forgiving. Cholerics are eruptive and grudging. Melancholies take longer to explode, preferring to mull over self-persecution thoughts and harbor revengeful plans until they, too, are capable of unreasonable expressions of wrath.

The gravity of this problem cannot be overestimated! Of the 339 couples I have joyfully united as husband and wife during my years in the ministry, I am happy to say that only two dozen, to my knowledge, have divorced. Perhaps this is because I have asked each couple to make a sacred promise that before they ever spend a single night separated by duress, they will come to see me. Except for a few couples whose problem in the early days pertained to sexual difficulties that were resolved in a short period of time, *every other couple's problem was anger!*

Anger not only destroys home life but also ruins health. As I have noted previously, *None of These Diseases* lists fifty-one illnesses that can be caused by tension produced by anger or fear—high blood pressure, heart attack, colitis, arthritis, kidney stones, gall-bladder troubles, and many others. For years I have quoted Dr. Henry Brandt, who says, "Approximately 97 percent of all the cases of bleeding ulcers without organic origin I have dealt with are caused by anger."

At a seminar in Columbus, Ohio, a medical doctor identified himself as an ulcer specialist and reported, "I would take issue with Dr. Brandt—it's more like 100 percent!" At the same seminar a young internist informed me, "Yesterday afternoon I treated five patients with serious internal complications. As you were talking, I made a mental note that all five were angry people."

Doctors have warned us for years that emotionally induced illness accounts for 60 to 85 percent of all sicknesses today. What they mean is that tension causes illness. Anger, fear, and guilt are the primary causes of tension, so they are clearly the major culprits in poor health.

So many illustrations of real-life situations come to mind as I write about the appalling effects of anger that I scarcely know where to begin. I have seen it produce impotence in a twenty-seven-year-old athlete, make normal women frigid, render a twenty-four-year-old physical education teacher incapable of expressing love to her husband, and, in short, annihilate normal love responses. I have visited hundreds of people in hospitals who could have avoided the entire problem had they been relaxed in the Spirit instead of angry. I have even buried many before their time because, like Moses before them, they indulged the secret sin of anger.

In my opinion, the physical damage caused by anger is only exceeded by the spiritual harm it fosters. Anger shortchanges more Christians and makes more spiritual pygmies than any other sin. It has caused more church strife and turned off more young converts than anything else. It grieves the Holy Spirit in the life of the believer (see Eph. 4:30–32) and almost destroyed my own health, family, and ministry.

Anger Is Sin, Sin, Sin

In two of my previous books I deliberately identified anger as a sin and offered a scriptural remedy that not only changed my own life but has been used by thousands of others to resolve the problem. Since then, a number of writers have taken issue with my premise and tried to justify anger, insisting: "It is natural"; "Anger is universal"; "All

anger is not sin"; or, as one indicated, "The person who
never consciously feels any anger is emotionally ill." Some
counselors get so agitated that they write lengthy epistles
to correct my misunderstanding of the universal problem
of anger. One man was so irritated that he ended his letter
by saying, "You're wrong! Wrong! Wrong!"

Let me offer three reasons why such opinions do not
bother me (though I have tried to evaluate each new suggestion fairly).

1. The Bible, my base of reference, is extremely clear in
   condemning anger.
2. I am blessed with the hide of a rhinoceros.
3. It is essential to accept the sinfulness of anger in order
   to effect a cure.

Many Bible verses illustrate that God condemns anger in
the human heart. Consider these carefully:

"Cease from anger, and forsake wrath" (Ps. 37:8).
"Do not hasten in your spirit to be angry, for anger rests
    in the bosom of fools" (Eccles. 7:9).
"Better is a dinner of herbs [vegetables] where love is,
    than a fatted calf with hatred" (Prov. 15:17).
"Better is a dry morsel with quietness, than a house full
    of feasting with strife" (Prov. 17:1).
"It is better to dwell in the wilderness, than with a con-
    tentious and angry woman" (Prov. 21:19).
"A wrathful man stirs up strife, but he who is slow to
    anger allays contention" (Prov. 15:18).
"Whoever has no rule over his own spirit is like a city
    broken down, without walls" (Prov. 25:28).
"Make no friendship with an angry man, and with a furi-
    ous man do not go, lest you learn his ways and set a
    snare for your soul" (Prov. 22:24–25).
"He who is slow to anger is better than the mighty, and
    he who rules his spirit than he who takes a city" (Prov.
    16:32).

"Whoever hides hatred has lying lips, and whoever spreads slander is a fool" (Prov. 10:18).

"Hatred stirs up strife, but love covers all sins" (Prov. 10:12).

"But now you must also put off all these: anger, wrath, malice, blasphemy, filthy language out of your mouth" (Col. 3:8).

"Therefore, my beloved brethren, let every man be swift to hear, slow to speak, slow to wrath; for the wrath of man does not produce the righteousness of God" (James 1:19–20).

It is obvious from these verses that God condemns the sin of anger. That is why they say "cease from" it and "forsake wrath." History proves anger is the ultimate destroyer of interpersonal relationships—including our relationship to God. I do not believe anyone can walk in the Spirit until he lets God cure his natural tendency to be angry.

Is Anger Ever Justifiable?

Those who take issue with the premise that anger is a sin invariably introduce three arguments: (1) God became angry many times in Scripture; (2) Jesus was angry several times (no reader of the New Testament can forget the scene of his driving the money changers out of the temple!); and (3) one verse in the Bible reputedly condones anger—Ephesians 4:26 (which used to be my life verse!). Let's consider each of these objections.

1. God's anger is different from man's—it imposes holy wrath upon sin.

2. It is wrong to compare our Lord's anger at man's sin to man's anger, for Christ had a divine nature of holiness that man does not share; thus he could sustain a holy wrath without sin. His most severe anger, as I shall illustrate, involved righteous indignation against sin, never a response to personal rejection, insult, or injury.

3. Ephesians 4:26 states, "Be angry, and do not sin; do not let the sun go down on your wrath, nor give place to the devil." Since this is the only biblical text that seems to condone anger, we ought to examine it carefully. It carries three serious qualifiers: (1) do not sin; (2) do not let the sun go down on your wrath; and (3) give no place to the devil.

Qualifier number one certainly limits anger—sin not! It forbids any sinful thought or sinful expression of anger. People never visit my counseling room with emotional distress from that kind of anger, because "righteous indignation" (which is my label for anger without sin) does not create hang-ups. It is objective anger; that is, it is usually on behalf of someone else. Selfishness-induced anger—which is what most anger is—is always harmful.

Anger qualifier number two obviously demands that this innocent anger not linger past sundown. Those who terminate their anger at sundown will not cultivate emotional problems either.

The third qualifier suggests that if innocent anger is permitted to burn past sundown, it "gives place to the devil." Our Lord driving the money changers out of the temple is a good example of righteous indignation, or sinless anger based on concern for someone else. Even then, however, righteous indignation, which Ephesians 4:26 allows, can be dangerous if it is indulged too long, for it can give place to the devil. Abortion is an example. All Christians can be righteously indignant at the killing of the unborn. But if indulged too long, indignation can give place to the devil by causing a few activists to take the law into their own hands and commit some grievous sin.

The solution to the apparent conflict between the fourteen verses that condemn anger and Ephesians 4:26, which seems to condone it, is really quite simple. The Bible permits righteous indignation and condemns all selfishly induced anger. You experience righteous indignation when you see an injustice perpetrated on another. For example, when a bully picks on a child, you feel a surge of emotion (righteous indignation) and go to the aid of the child. You do not sin in this, nor is it difficult to forget such externally induced anger after dark. But when someone rejects, insults, or injures you, that is a different matter. Is your emotion without sin? And do you forget it after dark?

The Lord Jesus' earthly expressions of anger provide another example. When he drove the money changers from the temple, his action was impersonal (or righteous indignation)—"You have made my Father's house a den of thieves" (see Matt. 21:13). His anger at the Pharisees later was kindled because they were spiritual "wolves" leading the sheep astray, not because they were hurting him. In fact, when his beard was plucked out, or when he was spat upon and nailed to a cross, he showed absolutely no anger. Instead we hear those familiar words, "Father, forgive them, for they know not what they do." Our Lord never showed selfishly induced anger! Why? Because as a human emotion it is always a sin.

Those who use Ephesians 4:26 to justify the human frailty of anger tend to overlook an important fact. Just five verses further on we read: "Let *all* bitterness, wrath, anger, clamor, and evil speaking be put away from you, with all malice. And be kind to one another, tenderhearted, forgiving one another, just as God in Christ also forgave you" (Eph. 4:31–32, emphasis added).

It is quite clear from all of this that righteous indignation is acceptable, but personally induced anger is wrong. What is the difference? Selfishness! Selfishly induced anger, which is the kind most of us experience and that which causes so much personal and family havoc, is a terrible sin. That is why Scripture says, "Let all bitterness and wrath [all] and anger [all] be put away from you." As we shall see, it is curable—but only after you face it as a sin.

The Subtle Problems of Bitterness and Resentment

A woman once commented, "I never get angry; I just become bitter." Many others would admit the same about resentment. Let's understand something very clearly—the

Bible condemns all human bitterness, resentment, and indignation. They are just subtle forms of anger.

At a seminar several years ago, Bill Gothard made a statement to the effect that every couple he counseled for marital disharmony had either married without the approval of their parents or had developed a conflict with one or both parents that eventually created conflicts within the couple's relationship. When the person who had attended the conference shared that thought, I remember considering it a bit extreme. Since then, however, I have made this a standard inquiry concerning a couple's relationship to their parents. Without exception, I have found Mr. Gothard's formula to be correct. People who harbor bitterness and resentment toward a parent, brother, sister, or boss are bound to let it spill over and injure their relationship with others. Resentment and bitterness preserved in the recesses of the mind is like cancer; it grows until it consumes the whole person. That is why people who cannot forget an unfortunate childhood, rejection, or injury are invariably miserable people.

At a Canadian seminar, an emotionally overwrought man spoke to my wife after I had lectured on anger. (He wouldn't speak to me because I reminded him of his father.) He angrily justified his bitter spirit toward his parents because they rejected him as a child. One of the pastors thoughtfully stood close to my wife, just in case. Later he shared with us, "That man, who has a lovely wife and four children, is subjecting them to hell on earth. He has counseled with every minister in town and changes churches every year or so." He then added, "He is the angriest man I have ever known, and I consider him dangerous." Instead of the shock therapy, drugs, and psychiatric treatment to which he had been fruitlessly subjected, that man needed to get down on his knees, confess his harbored bitterness and wrath toward his parents, and let God replace his anger with love. Not only would it have transformed him, but it also would have benefited his entire family.

One of my favorite secular writers, a plastic surgeon, counselor, and lecturer, has authored three self-help books that have benefited millions. In one book he tells about two counselees with "choking sensations." One, a middle-aged salesman who suffered from an inferiority complex, occasionally woke up dreaming of being choked to death by his mother. The other was a young father who loved his wife but on two occasions awakened from a dream to find his hands clutching her throat with such a resolute grip that he was terrified. The good doctor accurately diagnosed both problems. The salesman hated his mother, and even though he had not seen her in years, she filled his thoughts. The young husband hated his father and subconsciously transferred his hatred to his wife. These cases may seem extreme to you, but they are not really unusual, for they demonstrate the natural result of harboring bitterness, resentment, and anger in your heart and mind. Remember this: Bitterness and love cannot burn simultaneously in the same heart. Bitterness indulged for those you hate will destroy your love for those most precious to you.

One of my most pathetic cases concerned a young mother of two who tearfully confessed to feelings of such anger at her infant when he screamed that she sometimes entertained "thoughts of choking him." She then added, "I'm afraid I will do something harmful to my baby." Upon questioning, we discovered that she had been rejected by her father and clung to bitter thoughts about that rejection. Her rancorous attitude was eating her up—in spite of the fact that her father had been dead for five years.

How to Cure Anger, Bitterness, or Resentment

Many years ago, after being an angry, hostile CHLORSAN for more than thirty years, I had a life-changing experience with God. Gradually my anger responses lessened from most of the time to only occasionally. Today they are so infrequent that I enjoy an inner peace that I wouldn't trade for that old hostile way of life, even for the youth it possessed. Since then I have shared the following remedy with thousands of people, many of whom will testify that it has changed their lives. It may not seem scientific to some, but I like it for two reasons: It is biblical and it works.

1. *Face your anger as sin!* The giant step in overcoming anger is to face it squarely as sin. The minute you try to justify it, explain it, or blame someone else, you are incurable. I have never known anyone to have victory over a problem unless he was convinced it was wrong! That is particularly true of anger. If you have any question at this point, then just reread the Scripture on pages (202–3) and consider such commands as "Cease from anger and forsake wrath" or "Let all bitterness and anger be put away from you."

2. *Confess every angry thought or deed as soon as it occurs.* This is giant step two, based on 1 John 1:9: "If we confess our sins, he is faithful and just to forgive us our sins and to cleanse us from all unrighteousness." Inwardly I groaned as I read the advice the plastic surgeon prescribed for the two men who came to him with anger-induced emotional problems. Essentially, he urged them to replace their hateful thoughts by concentrating on some successful or happy experience in life. I remember asking, "But what does that do for guilt?" Absolutely nothing! The blood of Jesus Christ alone, which is adequate to cleanse us from all sin, is available to all who call upon him in faith.

3. *Ask God to take away this angry habit pattern.* In 1 John 5:14–15 we have the assurance that if we ask anything according to the will of God, he not only hears us but also answers our requests. Since we know it is not God's will that we be angry, we can be assured of victory if we ask him to take away that habit pattern. Although secular man may remain a slave to habit, the Christian must not. We are admittedly victims of habit, but we need not become addicted to sins when we have at our disposal the power of the Spirit of God.

4. *Forgive the person who has caused your anger.* Ephesians 4:32 instructs us to forgive one another, "just as God in Christ also forgave you." If a parent, person, or "thing" in your life occupies much of your thinking, make a special point of formally uttering a prayer of forgiveness *aloud* to God. Each time the hostile thoughts return, follow the same

procedure. Gradually your forgiveness will become a fact, and you will turn your thoughts to positive things.

A charming illustration of this came to me after a seminar for missionaries in South America. A lovely missionary had been plagued with anger problems that almost kept her from being accepted by her board. A Christian psychologist challenged her that she must forgive her father, but she replied, "I can't." He said, "You mean you won't! If you don't forgive him, your hatred will destroy you." So in his office she prayed, "Dear heavenly Father, I do want to forgive my father. Please help me." She acknowledged having to pray that prayer several times, but finally victory came and with it the peace of God. She is a well-balanced and productive woman today because she forgave. You cannot carry a grudge toward anyone you forgive!

5. *Formally give thanks for anything that "bothers" you.* The will of God *for all Christians* is that we "in everything give thanks" (1 Thess. 5:18). Thanksgiving is therapeutic and helpful, particularly in anger reduction. You will not be angry or depressed if in every insult, rejection, or injury you give thanks. Admittedly, that may be difficult at times, but it is possible. God has promised never to burden you with anything you cannot bear (1 Cor. 10:13). Naturally, at times such thanksgiving will have to be done by faith, but God will even provide that necessary faith. Learn the art of praying with thanksgiving.

6. *Think only good, wholesome, and positive thoughts.* The human mind cannot tolerate a vacuum; it always has to dwell on something. Make sure yours concentrates on what the Scripture approves, such as things that are "honest, just, pure, lovely, of good report, virtue, and praise" (see Phil. 4:8). People with such positive thoughts are not plagued by anger, hostility, and wrath. It is essentially just a matter of subjecting every thought to the obedience of Christ—as we saw in chapter 3. Anger is a habit—a temperament-induced, sinful habit—ignited through the years by unpleasant distresses and circumstances that can control a person every bit as tenaciously as heroin or cocaine, making him react inwardly or outwardly in a selfish, sinful

manner. Unless you let the power of God within you change your thinking patterns, your condition will gradually ruin your health, mind, business, family, or spiritual maturity. In addition, it grieves the Holy Spirit (Eph. 4:30), robbing you of the abundant life which Jesus Christ wants to give you.

7. *Repeat the above formula each time you are angry.* Of the hundreds who claim that this simple formula has helped them, none has indicated that it happened overnight. In my case, I had over thirty years of practice, though it didn't take that long to gain victory. The first day I must have used this formula a hundred times. It was better the second day—only ninety-five times. Even today "the flesh" will attempt to assert control, but I have learned that victory is assured when I immediately brand the anger as sin, confess it, and follow the formula. If anger is a particular problem for you, use this formula for sixty days. Gradually God will make you a new person—and you will like the new you! So will others who know you, particularly your mate.

11

Male Fear versus Female Anger

The first negative emotion recorded in the Bible after the fall of Adam and Eve was fear. When God called, Adam hid himself from the presence of the Lord and explained, "I was afraid." Like it or not, every man since has experienced fear.

By this time, I trust that the notion that masculine man is fearless has been dispatched permanently. All men are assaulted by fear, and some temperaments struggle with it more than others. At times those fears become so intense that they inhibit many normal functions. In fact, most gifted people rarely reach the level of their capability because of fear in one of its many forms.

Distinguish in your mind between *fright* and *fear*. Fright is a God-given emergency alarm mechanism that works like a defense system. Because of our self-preservation instinct, emergencies trigger an emotional impulse to our adrenal glands, which pump adrenaline into the bloodstream, giving us superior strength, speed, and clarity of thought and action. Afterwards, our natural flushing system eliminates all ill effects of this excessive adrenaline. During such moments, superhuman feats of strength and courage are possible. For instance, a high school boy used that extra surge of power when the family Chevrolet fell off the jack, pinning his father to the ground. He lifted the car from his dad's chest, allowing him to slide out and be taken for medical help. The next day the teenager couldn't even budge the car. That was an encounter with *fright*.

Fear is the emotional result of negative, anxious, or worried thinking. And no matter how tough the man seems on the outside, his panic button is in ready position on the inside. Because of the universality of the problem, the Bible repeatedly challenges the Christian: "Fear not"; "Be anxious for nothing"; "Let not your heart be troubled."

As we have seen, opposites attract each other in marriage, so it is not uncommon for a man with a dominant fear tendency to marry a woman with a dominant anger trait. Such contrasting temperaments usually explain why a 110-pound woman can henpeck a 245-pound man. Just recently we stayed in a fine Christian home and watched a three-year-old Clara Choleric, who couldn't have weighed more than thirty pounds, bully her five-year-old MELPHLEG brother almost twice her size. Having discovered his natural fear zones, she jubilantly took advantage of them. That little "mighty mite," as Bev called her, was less subtle in her devious mastery over her brother than are many wives over their husbands, but the principle remains the same. A man does not cower in a corner or cry when attacked by his wife; he just clams up, grows sullen, or finds some place to hide out in order to avoid conflict. But her angry outbursts will precipitate his fears, and the impenetrable wall of conflict will stifle their communication. Gradually they will grow apart, develop independent interests, and watch their love die. If they stay together, the subsequent endurance contest will produce a miserable environment for raising children.

In men the most common expression of fear is retreat—from conflict, competition, challenge, risk, and in most cases, opportunity. Women seem to handle fear better than men, perhaps because society accepts worry, anxiety, insecurity, and hesitation (all forms of fear) by women. When the "weaker vessel" reaches the breaking point, she may cry or go to a friend for support. A man, unfortunately, isn't supposed to cry or be afraid, so he must always play the "manly game"—not only to others, but also to himself. Even if he has a friend to lean on, he finds himself reluctant to admit his weakness. Cold, naked fear may be gripping his heart, but he feels compelled to mask his despair and feign composure.

Because fear is a living entity, it grows like cancer until it influences every decision in a person's life. In extreme cases, the individual becomes neurotic and must seek professional help. Men who fail to conquer their fear and try to endure it will probably become inhibited vocationally, spiritually, physically, financially, and even sexually. The he-man may refuse to face his natural or temperament-induced fears and instead play the "ostrich game," pretending that somehow they will fade away. He fails to recognize that fear, like a petty thief who gradually becomes a hardened criminal, initially suppresses a man and eventually robs him of his God-given creativity and potential.

"How can I distinguish between a temperament-induced fear and a natural fear?" you may ask. There is little difference. All men entertain natural fears, but some temperaments endure them more than others. The Bible teaches that nothing confronts us that is not "common to man" (1 Cor. 10:13), and that is true of fear. Counselors for years have helped people by getting them to talk out their fears, exposing them to the light of day, for fear thrives on darkness and ignorance. In this chapter we shall discuss man's most common fears in the home, reducing them to life-size and then offering suggestions on how to cope with them. All men have faced these fears to one degree or another. An individual man's temperament and background will determine the importance he places on each.

Man's Greatest Fears

When my son Larry was twenty-five years of age, had two sons, a happy marriage, and was working with me in Family Life Seminars, we were chatting about this book. In an attempt to gain contemporary input, I asked, "What do you think is a man's greatest fear?" Without hesitation he replied, "Failure!" I soon realized, upon reviewing my list of man's fears, that they all involve failure.

1. *Fear of vocational failure.* One of the ten basic characteristics of manhood we studied earlier involved productivity. Every man has a need to be productive, not only in response to the urgings of his culture but also in accordance with his intuition. As he matures, this trait seems to grow in significance. He knows that the economic destiny of his family as well as the acceptance of his own self-worth are dependent on his productivity. Consequently, he develops a fear of vocational failure.

This vocational anxiety troubles the otherwise carefree youth and makes him restless until he settles on a satisfactory occupation. We have found that a college student who lacks ultimate goals rarely functions in accord with his potential and frequently creates more disturbance than others. But when he "finds himself," he develops a sense of purpose, becomes a better student, and cultivates a sturdy self-image. The man who never finds his niche is increasingly tormented by fear.

This solicitude for discovering the role in life for which he is best suited occupies a major part of a man's thought life until he finds it. The weight of responsibility in marriage will sharply augment his vocational fears. (The potential burden of such responsibility keeps many young men single—particularly as skill and training become more essential to productivity in a technically complex society.) A wife might not understand this vocational disquietude that nags men, for her natural instinct is to trust her husband to provide for the family. When an insecure husband asks, "What will I do if I lose my job?" his wife responds, "Get another." But the fear-inhibited man, with far less confidence in his ability than his spouse, inevitably retorts, "Where?"

If we could fluoroscope the sharply contrasting thoughts of a man and his wife, we would discover that the wife primarily dwells upon the home, children, and family; the man thinks more about his vocation. Such thoughts will occupy the greatest single block of his time—over two thousand hours annually for thirty-five to fifty years. Therefore, it warrants prayerful consideration of God's will and the paying of any sacrifice necessary to prepare for it.

I count it a great pleasure to know many families who struggled during those apprentice years so the husband could learn his skill, earn his degree, or gain his license in order to fulfill his destiny. Strenuous efforts to prepare for a vocation not only reduce a man's central fear but create a richer love partnership when they both enjoy the fruits of their labors.

2. *Fear of sexual inadequacy.* Sigmund Freud alleged that all men and boys suffer from a "fear of castration." That may be an extreme pronouncement, but what man has never allowed that terrifying thought to cross his mind? Though few experience physical castration, the sex drive creates such a mental preoccupation with the subject that the possibility of sexual inadequacy has plagued nearly all men. In some cases, fear of the problem can actually emasculate a man mentally. In our book *The Act of Marriage*, where my wife and I deal quite extensively with the increasing problem of male impotence, I related the story of a forty-eight-year-old man who failed to ejaculate once when he was forty years old and did not have the courage to try again for eight years. In all likelihood, his problem was not physical but emotional.

Our modern preoccupation with sex accentuates the problem because as a woman rightfully anticipates a more satisfying sexual experience with her husband, she places more pressure on him to perform. Young husbands often have the problem of premature ejaculation and thus leave their wives unsatisfied. Later in life an occasional bout with impotence will give a man the false notion that he is sexually washed up. Both dilemmas are compounded by fear of repetition, but in almost all cases they can be cured.

Male sexual ignorance is appalling! There is probably no more important subject in a man's life that he approaches with either minimal education or the wrong kind of information. Many a young man seems to consider it natural for him to be sexually capable. What he fails to realize before marriage is that satisfaction for a woman is much more complex than for a man. It takes longer to achieve and is an art to be learned. A husband is even more amazed to discover after marriage that if lovemaking is satisfying only to him, he feels threatened that he is not a good lover in his wife's eyes and in his own. Fear strikes again, ruining what otherwise could be an exciting and fulfilling experience.

It is a wise bridegroom or husband who humbly admits that men do not know all about sex just by virtue of being male. He should study some of the good Christian literature on the subject to learn this significant art, not just to eliminate a troublesome fear area in his own life, but to express his love meaningfully for his wife.

It is also a prudent wife who lets her husband know how satisfying she finds his lovemaking. Many misguided wives for some reason feel impelled to disguise their sexual pleasure in order to maintain some phony standard of wifely modesty. Communication should be limited to the two lovers, but he needs to be aware of her satisfaction. Such communication not only makes him a better love partner but also eliminates a potential male fear.

3. *Fear he will fail to be a good leader, particularly at home.* A married man expects to be the leader of his home. If he is not, he becomes frustrated and insecure. An angry man may erupt and demand his role in the family, creating turmoil. The more passive temperaments, rather than venting their spleen, will be more apt to endure their disappointments internally and hold their tongues.

Have you ever wondered what fear plagues most leaders? Criticism—by their peers, followers, or history. Dr. Paul Tournier reported in his book *To Understand Each Other* that a husband primarily fears being judged or criticized by his wife. Although that will remain a problem all through life, it is particularly true of a young husband.

Every young man needs to learn to be a leader through the process of leading, but he is destined to make mistakes! On occasion he will spend too much money, buy the wrong things, or make incorrect decisions. It is to be hoped that he will profit by the experience, but even if he doesn't, he can do without his wife's criticism—particularly if she is gifted with a caustic tongue. Monday-morning quarterbacks are always smarter, but their advice is irrelevant and immaterial. Hindsight may prevent future error, but its censure of past decisions serves little purpose. When her leader-husband makes a mistake, a loving wife can best preserve marital harmony by maintaining a sweet spirit and keeping her mouth shut. He should be allowed to milk all the educational benefit from his mistakes without her assistance.

The cause of one couple's serious communication problem was uncovered in my counseling room when the wife complained, "He never tells me anything about anything. I only find out about his plans when we are out with other people." He responded, "When I *do* tell you what I'm planning to do, you either find fault with it or dump cold water on it." No wonder he stopped communicating! Cholerics dread criticism as much as any other temperament, so he used the safety of the group to communicate his plans. Today that couple enjoys a growing partnership because she learned to keep her vexatious criticism to herself. It has been my observation that mates who have learned the art of listening, encouraging, and approving rarely complain about their partners not talking with them. Those who criticize, ridicule, or belittle their partners have to learn how to cope with silence.

Paul Tournier suggests that another fear that stifles communication is "unwarranted advice." He illustrates his point by telling of the wife who asks about her husband's day at the office and receives an account of various difficulties he has faced that day. She heatedly responds, "You absolutely must get rid of that ineffective associate. Stand up for yourself or he'll walk over you!" The wife has failed to consider unions, seniority, hiring a replacement, and a hundred other factors. Thus her "helpful" advice (or know-it-all attitude, depending on your point of view) is not desired, requested, or welcome. So wives, unless asked, don't offer your criticism or advice. Give your husband your love and patiently let him work out the situation. Remember, that is only a temporary issue that will soon be forgotten, but you are building a lifetime relationship with a man who is learning leadership. The Bible says, "Let every man [I think that means women, too] be swift to hear, slow to speak" (see James 1:19). Let your husband use you as a sounding board for his ideas, for by this means he can develop and refine them, but be careful not to call a domestic board meeting when he steps in the door each evening. Above all, display interest, understanding, and respect for his judgment; otherwise he will keep his thoughts to himself.

A great Christian leader, Dr. Henrietta Mears, used to say, "Leaders are made, not born." I am convinced that every man possesses some leadership potential, and most can develop more than they are using. The following simple suggestions will help at home and in business.

1. A leader has to know where he is going. Study the Word of God in order to discern the essentials of life. God will administer goals and objectives for you and your family.
2. A leader must recognize how to get there. The Bible promises that the man who meditates on the Word of God will be prospered in all that he does (see Ps. 1:1–3). God will direct your plans and inspire your thoughts through his Word.
3. A leader must be confident. This quality develops as you walk with God and follow his leading. The Word and his "still small voice" will impart confidence, and others will lean on your assurance.
4. Plan ahead; establish well-defined goals and standards.
5. Ask God to lead you to the best Christian associates, employees, or advisors, but take secular advice with a grain of salt. "Blessed is the man who walks not in the counsel of the ungodly" (Ps. 1:1).
6. Tell your associates exactly what is expected of them, but give them the freedom to function—including making mistakes—within the guidelines.

7. Inspect your associates' work from time to time to be sure they are staying within the guidelines. If not, it is the leader's job to confront them with their failings. (Some leaders scrutinize every detail of the process; others are result inspectors—it depends primarily on your temperament.)
8. Always anticipate success. Your affirmative spirit will be emulated by others.

The best advice I have ever read for a naturally fearful leader appears in God's counsel to young Joshua as he became leader of Israel:

> Be strong and of a good courage, for to this people you shall divide as an inheritance the land which I swore to their fathers to give them. Only be strong and very courageous, that you may observe to do according to all the law which Moses My servant commanded you; do not turn from it to the right hand or to the left, that you may prosper wherever you go. This Book of the Law shall not depart from your mouth, but you shall meditate in it day and night, that you may observe to do according to all that is written in it. For then you will make your way prosperous, and then you will have good success. Have I not commanded you? Be strong and of good courage; do not be afraid, nor be dismayed, for the Lord your God is with you wherever you go.
>
> Joshua 1:6–9

Notice that God instructed him three times to be strong and of good courage. That comes only from meditating regularly on the Word of God.

My most traumatic leadership experience occurred many years ago. Several ministers in town disparaged my idea that San Diego needed a Christian high school. Our church board of trustees, after two stormy meetings, finally voted three to two in favor of the project. Several members fought it vigorously, but finally it gained church approval. Ten days before the start of school, with thirty-two students registered, the principal resigned. We looked around frantically and "prayed without ceasing." On Wednesday night after prayer meeting, the school board met to discuss our next move, and we prayed an especially long period of time that night. Finally the chairman asked the question that loomed in every board member's mind: "Pastor, are you sure God wants us to start Christian High this year?" For what must have been one of the longest minutes in my life, I gazed into nine pairs of hesitant eyes. My response in that moment would make or break the founding of our school. When I prayed, "Oh, God, what should I say?" he assured me with the words, "Be strong and of a good courage. Have not I commanded you?" Suddenly I heard myself say. "I don't know how, but God is going to provide for our need of a principal." And he did—at 10:30 P.M. the night before school started! Christian High grew into two accredited high schools and once was the second largest Christian school system in the country, with over twenty-one hundred students. It has graduated more than three thousand young people, many of whom are in Christian work. Today after thirty years, the school is still prospering because God is faithful!

Every leader of a family, business, school, or corporation should pause long enough each day to read and meditate on the Word of God. It will make you a better, more confident leader.

4. *Fear of failing to maintain the respect of his wife, children, and associates.* The more you love someone, the more you crave his respect. The more you know someone, however, the harder it is to maintain that esteem because he knows your every weakness. That is why you must live the Christian life at home, because what you are at home is what you are. The family is a close-knit unit. If the father walks humbly and faithfully before God, he will earn his family's respect. He doesn't have to be perfect to earn a gold medal as "superior husband and father." The Christian life is a growing experience. During the process, we fall down, get up, and again walk in the Spirit. Although a Spirit-filled wife and her children can ask God to give them an increasing respect for the man in their home as they seek to obey him, this is one fear a man must conquer himself by maintaining a vital, personal relationship to God. Only in this way can he walk consistently before his family and associates.

5. *Fear of failing to protect his family.* While traveling around the world, I have become more acutely aware of life's insecurity without Christ. Practically every culture has its criminal element that doesn't hesitate to destroy the life and property of others. As I view a little house, perhaps far from civilization, out of the plane window, I often find it a symbol of the history of man. The wife and children huddle together, drawing on the man of the house for their sense of protection. What man, before he falls asleep, has not asked himself, "What would I do if suddenly in the night I was awakened by a vicious criminal?" In the pioneer days of America, such was certainly the case. For a time our nation was a safe place to live. Now, however, because of the godless, humanistic elite in government and education for the past forty or more years, we talk in terms of self-protection, judo and karate instruction, security systems, and so on—just to protect ourselves and our families from the criminal element in our once-safe cities.

In fact, all of life seems precarious. Drunk drivers are a constant menace on the road, air travel has its dangers, and even routine events can be hazardous (as when a U.S. astronaut slipped in the shower, fracturing his skull). The heroes of our present society, in my opinion, are the police officers, who with the rest of us must certainly commit themselves to God on a moment-by-moment basis. As an illustration of God's ability to take care of us, I think immediately of the young police officer, father of four, whose family was baptized in our church. While attempting to apprehend an armed robber as he came out of a building, the officer was shot five times. Amazing as it seems, none of the bullets did damage to a single organ of his body. A gunman who could hit him with five out of six shots yet not strike anything vital has to be the most inaccurate gunman on record—or Officer Robb had supernatural protection. (No wonder he felt God was calling him into Christian service and had something special for him to do.) Let's face it, a man has to lean on God today, as never before, for personal and family safety. Our times are in God's hands. As the prophet said,

"You will keep him in perfect peace, whose mind is stayed on You" (Isa. 26:3).

Fathers concerned with protecting their families should never overlook the threats imposed by TV, pornographic literature, X-rated movies, secular education, drug abuse, and other devices contrary to the principles of God. The Bible-believing (and teaching) church and the home—both institutions founded by God—are unique today. Their ways are not the ways of man (or shouldn't be), and they must be dependent on each other. As a father, I thank God that my four children were raised in a vital church with a dynamic youth program. Their lives have been wondrously enriched by it.

6. *Many other fears.* It is not possible to include all masculine fears: fear of failing to satisfy their parents' expectations, fear of sickness and death, fear of rejection, fear of losing youth or masculinity, fear of discrimination, and many others. All of man's fears can be resolved basically the same way—by yielding properly to the one legitimate fear in the Bible: "The fear of the Lord is the beginning of knowledge" (Prov. 1:7).

This "fear" is really a reverential awe of God that makes it possible for a man to include God in all the thinking, planning, working, living, and "being" areas of life. As that reverence for God is increased and enriched through regular Bible meditation, all other fears are reduced. Jesus Christ said:

> Therefore I say to you, do not worry about your life, what you will eat or what you will drink; nor about your body, what you will put on. Is not life more than food and the body more than clothing? . . .
>
> For after all these things the Gentiles seek. For your heavenly Father knows that you need all these things. But seek first the kingdom of God and His righteousness, and all these things shall be added to you. Therefore do not worry about tomorrow, for tomorrow will worry about its own things. Sufficient for the day is its own trouble.
>
> Matthew 6:25, 32–34

12

Special Note to Men Only!

A Southern California report on the family provided these astonishing statistics. Fifty years ago, one woman left her husband for every five hundred men who abandoned their wives. Today two wives run away from husbands for every man who leaves his wife. What caused such an astonishing reversal? Financial independence through a tremendous increase of women in the workforce (reports indicate that 71 percent of American married women work outside the home, providing one of the chief sources of exposure to sexual promiscuity outside of marriage), credit cards (if a wife is penniless and unhappy, she is no longer chained, for she can utilize the family charge card), and TV "soaps" that turn adultery into an "affair" and regard fornication as acceptable, which contributes to a general feeling that everyone should "do his or her own thing." These, of course, list just a few of the reasons I see no relief in sight, short of a national spiritual revival.

"The home is breaking down faster than at any time in human history" is an oft quoted statement in family-friendly sermons today. Dr. William Bennett's index of cultural indi-

Understanding the Male Temperament

cators for 1993 states that since 1960 the divorce rate "has quadrupled, tripling the percentage of children living in single-parent homes," which may account for the "200 percent increase in the teen age rate of suicide." Many sociologists estimate that over thirty million children will be raised by one parent during the first eighteen years of their lives because of divorce. Such cultural breakdown puts extra pressure on couples to make it when things get tough in their marriage. A nurse recently told me that she was raising three children without a husband—and all had different fathers. Married only one year to a "louse," she left him, then decided she wanted children. Naturally, it wasn't difficult for her to get pregnant. A TV documentary indicated that this is an increasing trend. If we continue, we will reduce our family commitment to the level of some pagan countries of the world—where only 30 percent of the population marry, and women have children by five or six different men. Having been raised by a single mother, due to the early death of my father, I can tell you it is not the best way for a child to grow up.

The Man Is the Key

In the midst of this "marriage shock" that is devastating so many homes, I have detected an interesting phenomenon. Christian homes are more robust than ever before. And I foresee them becoming even better as a result of the biblical training given to men at Promise Keepers meetings, Maximum Man conferences, and Dads Only meetings, as well as by a host of other Christian organizations that provide men the kind of training they need to be the best marriage partners and fathers they can be. Show me a home where the husband serves as spiritual leader, loves his wife and children, and directs his family as the Bible teaches, and I will show you a happy home.

As Christian fathers become better Bible students, they develop the confidence to lead their families in the ways of the Lord. Today more fathers are leading their families in the daily reading of God's Word in a translation they can understand than in the history of Christianity. Rarely is it necessary to counsel family members when Dad conducts daily devotions and the family takes an active role in a Bible-believing church.

Because of the leadership of godly fathers, the wholesome influence of the church, the many excellent books offering practical guidance for establishing Christian homes, and the numerous church-related seminars and Bible studies with an emphasis on the home, today's Christian young people are better equipped to be good partners and parents than ever before. True, they face temptations and pressures unshared by previous generations, but they also enjoy better resources to cope with them.

As more Christian men take their role in the home seriously and earnestly seek to fulfill their responsibilities to the family, I have great hopes for the future of the Christian home, even in today's decaying moral climate. I pray that men everywhere would understand that they are largely the key to the successful future of their families.

Love and Leadership

No man in his right mind would claim to understand women! And I am no exception. But spending a large part of my life counseling women has granted me insights to which the average man is not exposed. The most significant observation I have made is that the man is the key to the complex relationships of husband-wife-children-home. Women, of course, can create problems, but I have yet to find a Christian woman who will not respond positively to her husband if he treats her and their children properly. I have noted only two exceptions: (1) women subjected to years of bitter and cruel treatment who were drawn to someone else and refused to give him up and (2) women who have crossed the line of despair and lost all hope of happiness. But even some of these have responded to the love and tenderness of a loving husband. Just this year a godly man whose wife went off the deep end ten years ago, announcing, "I have lost all feeling for you—I want out of this marriage," saw her miraculously return. He had been a model of patience, love, and kindness, which finally brought her to repentance to God and then to him. Two months later they were remarried in a beautiful ceremony attended by their two married children.

Man is the key to a happy family life because a woman by nature is a responding creature. Some temperaments, of course, respond more quickly than others, but all normal women are responders. That is one of the secondary meanings of the word *submission* in the Bible. God would not have commanded a woman to submit unless he had instilled in her a psychic mechanism that would find it comfortable to do so.

The key to feminine response has two main parts—love and leadership. I have never met a wife who did not react positively to a husband who gave her love and leadership. Deep within a woman lies a responding capability that makes her vulnerable to that combination. It is so powerful, in fact, that many respond when they are only given love. (This is less likely when a woman is subjected only to leadership.) The combination of love and leadership is unbeatable.

An interesting facet of that two-sided key is that most men must consciously work on one or the other. The temperament that naturally exudes love must consciously make an effort to exercise consistent leadership. By contrast, the man gifted in leadership must concentrate upon a regular display of love.

A MELCHLOR husband accepted Christ during his second marriage. He grew spiritually and became the strong leader of his home, but the couple was not happy. His wife came in weeping about his sharp criticism of her. He evaluated her as "too fat, sloppy, disorganized, loud and talkative" to suit him. Basically, he had stripped her of all self-respect by repeated censure and made her a nonperson. Apparently, every night when Al came home, he would be immediately confronted with his SANPHLEG wife's undisciplined housekeeping carelessness and would therefore emote his displeasure, either verbally or through body language. She would respond from a wounded and defiant spirit, and usually the entire evening would become a disaster.

When we talked, Al admitted his disparaging remarks but justified them. I quickly turned to Colossians 3:19, which teaches, "Husbands, love your wives and do not be bitter toward them." I continued, "You see, Al, since a wife gains self-acceptance from her husband, your bitterness is destroying her self-respect. Consequently, her shortcomings under the present circumstances will never be resolved." When Al finally asked, "What do you suggest?" (and that question indicated a heart that honestly wanted to obey God's will), I returned to the scriptural admonition to love her and not be bitter toward her.

We worked out a plan together, and Al later shared the result. That evening, after prayerful thought all the way home, he walked in the house, put his arms around his wife, and said, "Joy, I love you. God has convicted me of the awful way I've been treating you. My bitter, critical spirit is going to destroy our home and marriage. Would you forgive me?" Needless to say, his responsive wife crumpled with tears into his arms. Within one week he detected improvement around the house. On her own she consulted a weight doctor, began to improve her appearance, and has gradually been transformed into a new person. They now enjoy one of the happiest love relationships I know. In fact, when two family members (on his side) later fell into difficulties, she suggested that they welcome them into their home and help them through their trials. Their relationship even weathered the storm of another family living in their home for long periods of time—and I consider that the acid test. The writer of Proverbs says, "Love covers all sins" (see Prov. 10:12).

A woman's need for love from her husband cannot be overemphasized. Four times Scripture commands men to love their wives. Why? Because it is the key to a happy home life. A woman will outperform her natural capabilities if she is given love. She is just made that way.

Husband—Test Your Love

Many husbands protest, "But I *do* love my wife!" When I hear the wife's version, it often goes, "He sure has a funny way of *showing* it." Women universally think that love ought to be demonstrated. And they are right! Love is an emotion that motivates to action. Love is not the action *per se*, but incitement to action. I would challenge you as a husband—on the basis of how you have treated your wife during the last two weeks—to test your love against the Bible's nine characteristics of love found in 1 Corinthians 13:4–8. Score yourself 0 to 11 on each of the following nine traits. Try to remain objective.

___ Patience		___ Kindness
___ Generosity		___ Humility
___ Courtesy		___ Unselfishness
___ Good Temper		___ Trust
___ Sincerity		___ TOTAL

Add up your total and throw in one free point to reach a potential 100. How did you do? If you scored 90 or over you are doing fine—keep it up. If 80 to 89, you need to work consciously on being more loving. A score of 70 to 79 signals that you are in trouble and your relationship is gradually deteriorating. At 60 to 69, your wife is unhappy and so are you.

A husband's love for his wife is a genuine reflection of his spiritual relationship to God. The Bible says, "He who does not love does not know God, for God is love" (1 John 4:8). It also warns, "He who does not love his brother whom he has seen, how can he love God whom he has not seen?" (1 John 4:20). We could legitimately modify that question and ask, "If a man doesn't love the *wife* he can see, how can he love God whom he has not seen?" The Bible clearly affirms that our love for God, which he pours into our hearts by his Holy Spirit, will flow out to others. The man who professes to be a good Christian but doesn't love his wife is kidding himself!

Four times God commands men to love their wives. Once, as we have seen, he adds "and do not be bitter toward them." The heart cannot harbor love and bitterness simultaneously, for one will cancel out the other. You are forbidden to be bitter and are commanded to love.

Of the nine characteristics of love listed above, the one that most charms and warms a woman's heart is kindness. I have observed an ordinary man with little of this world's goods enjoy the love of a woman because he was kind to her. In many cases, that is all he had to give, but it was sufficient. A woman seems to respond faster to kindness than to any other gesture from the heart. In fact, I have never known a woman to leave a husband who was kind to her. By contrast, I have seen a woman leave a man who heaped furs, diamonds, and cars upon her but failed in the one gift a woman seeks most—love expressed by kindness.

What is kindness? It is an unselfish spirit of thoughtful consideration administering to another's needs and desires. Loving-kindness prompts a man to make the bed or do the dishes just to help out or because his wife is tired or busy. It inspires a man to bring home flowers for no special reason, take his wife to dinner apart from special occasions, or change the baby before she asks. Each special gift loudly proclaims, "I love you, honey, and I'm sure glad you married me." Loving-kindness looks for an opportunity to bring pleasure into another's life. A husband who is kind to his mate will never lack for love.

The Other Side of Submission

Have you ever imagined what it would be like to be placed in submission to another human being on a twenty-four-hour basis, 365 days a year—for life? That is exactly what God demands of your wife. Obviously, some men seldom consider submission through wives' eyes, or they would stop treating them like second-class citizens. I can understand how the pagan native in the jungle can treat a woman like a slave, but I cannot understand how a self-centered man, insecure in his own identity, can treat her that way and call himself a Christian.

Submission is not servitude or slavery. It does not suggest that a woman is inferior or insignificant. A wise and loving husband will recognize that his wife is the most significant human being in his life. She is his partner, companion, lover, and friend. When so regarded, she finds it easy to "submit to her husband as unto the Lord" in everything.

Submission does not imply that a woman is incapable of having opinions, tastes, preferences, and good judgment. In fact, I have found that my wife is a more perceptive judge of colors and has better taste in clothes, furnishings, music, and many other areas than I. She is unquestionably a far better authority on our children. And even though I have learned to trust my judgment in most situations, I have found that corporate decisions are better than individual ones. We all recognize that two heads are usually better than one. I wish I had been mature enough to understand that when we were younger. But in my insecurity, I often insisted on my way at the expense of a more perceptive joint decision—not to mention a wounded spirit.

The young man who truly "loves his wife as Christ loved the church" will appreciate the other side of submission. In loving-kindness he will lead his family much like the president of a great corporation. When decisions have to be made, the president (or husband) will act as final authority, but he will weigh the thoughts and insights of all the vice presidents before doing so. The wise husband will heed his wife (and children as they get older), discuss matters with the family, and reach a corporate decision that they can all live with. The father who insists on rendering a long series of unilateral edicts may encounter vigorous resistance at home. His wife and children will find it much easier to comply with "the general's orders" if granted a hearing.

One reason the feminist movement caught on is that it has addressed an urgent need in the heart of most women— the need to be heard and respected. When you refuse to hear your wife fully, she will tend to think, "He doesn't really respect me as a person." If you communicate your respect for her intelligence and judgment, submission will be no problem in your home.

A brilliant attorney friend and his wife came in for counseling. She claimed she had lost all feeling for him. As I watched them interact, it was obvious what their trouble was. He did not communicate his love and respect for her, even in ordinary conversation. He was a CHLORMEL by temperament, which is a great temperament for a courtroom prosecutor trained to argue every little point to win a case. He won all the arguments in their marriage because he would interrupt her, overrule her, and contradict her. She, being a more passive or introverted temperament, was no match for him. Consequently, she gave up—on the outside. But she was angry, frustrated, and hurt on the inside. Nothing kills love like anger.

Fortunately my attorney friend is a practical man. When I told him she wanted her day in court, so she could express her opinion or how she felt about an issue, it dawned on him that he often told his friends how much he admired her mind and her judgment, but he rarely communicated that to her. By learning to leave his courtroom procedures behind, he taught himself what the Scripture says: "In honor, preferring one another."

It is a wise husband who learns to listen to his wife (amazingly enough, he often learns things), asking her what she thinks. One reason many couples rarely talk is because only one person usually does the talking. A good lover is a good listener.

Men, your love and leadership remain the keys to your home life. God has given you the power to lead your family in the ways of God, surrounding them with the love they seek from you, and he commands you to fulfill your responsibilities. Remember, he never demands what he will not supply.

"Husbands ought to love their own wives as their own bodies; . . . [nourish and cherish her] just as the Lord does the church" (see Eph. 5:28–29).

13

Every Good Man Wants to Be a Good Husband and Father

God has blessed me beyond my fondest expectations. I have enjoyed at least three different careers that turned out to be more successful than anything I could ever dream. I pastored churches for thirty-five years. I watched the church I led for twenty-five years grow into one of the leading churches in the nation, with a ministry of education from preschool through college. I have authored thirty-three books, with over ten million copies in English, some of which have been translated into thirty-one languages. I have received so many thousands of letters and testimonials of life-changing experiences of those who have read them that I can realistically hope that at least one million people have been genuinely affected by my books. As a Christian entrepreneur I have started sixteen different organizations, most of which are still operating—some better in my absence. Now I am a family-living and prophecy conference speaker and a Christian political activist with an office in Washington, D.C.

Some of the new conservative leaders in the nation's capital after the 1994 electoral revolution are personal friends.

Several men I have called by their first names for years are now good presidential prospects for the future. I don't say all this to brag, only to testify to God's faithfulness, for none of it could have been possible without his blessing. I say this only to prove I am a fulfilled man.

Yet none of the above is my source of greatest joy and fulfillment. That is reserved for something I share with Beverly, my wife of over forty years, who is still my sweetheart, companion, and best friend—our four children and nine grandchildren. They are not only a tangible expression of our love, they are also our greatest treasure. Perhaps a recent experience will illustrate. One of my pet administrative peeves is telephone interruptions. Not long ago I had called some Christian leaders to my office for a meeting. We had just started when my secretary indicated I was wanted on the phone. At first I responded, "Tell him I'll call him back." To my irritation she walked over and put a note on the conference table: "It is your son." I excused myself for a moment, picked up the phone, and heard the most wonderful voice from three thousand miles away say, "Hi, Dad! How are you? I am driving across town and I wanted to say Hi." My heart melted and for a moment I forgot the men who had come to my meeting.

Children really are "a heritage of the Lord." As the Bible teaches, they are our greatest treasure. Most men acknowledge that, but unfortunately they are not keenly aware of it in their twenties and early thirties when they are busy trying to establish themselves in their chosen vocation. It is not until after the children graduate from the home that fathers recognize those children really are their most treasured contribution to life.

I am not unaware that many fathers today have abandoned their children and that two thirds of the children in our inner cities are raised by single mothers because the father walked out on his paternal responsibilities. Nor am I unaware of the almost one million fathers or more each year who, "for the love of another woman," divorce their children's mother and for all practical purposes abandon them. That is why I titled this chapter "Every Good Man

Wants to Be a Good Husband and Father." A good man is one who puts his family ahead of his own selfish needs or desires.

In my many years of counseling, I have had the opportunity to glimpse inside the broken hearts of abandoned wives and children to see the havoc it wreaks and the scars it leaves on them, primarily because of the selfishness of the father. It is an old pattern. The couple fall in love and have children in the first fifteen years of life. The man starts to succeed in the business world, where he meets a lonely divorcée or single woman who seems more attractive to him than the mother of his children, who may not be as svelte as she was when they wed. If he doesn't get victory over his thought life, sooner or later he becomes intimate with "the other woman." Then he says, "I am no longer attracted to my wife." Of course he isn't. I have found that one cannot resolve marriage difficulties while a three-way relationship exists.

A doctor friend still thanks me for the "riot act" I gave him when he acknowledged, "I don't love my wife any more and think we ought to get a divorce." I looked him in the eye and asked, "Are you having an affair with one of the nurses in the office?" "No," he said, "it's one of the administrators at the hospital." He was willing to abandon his wife of twelve years and four children, not to mention his lifetime principles and spiritual life, for his new love. I pointed out that such behavior is selfishness personified. Sure, I could understand his alienation of affection; he had spent more time with his girlfriend at the hospital than with his wife who was home caring for his children. He had two choices: Leave his wife or leave the other woman. His selfishness would decide which. Then I asked, "If you let your selfish desires dictate, what will you do after you have lost vital contact with your family and then in twelve years find another cute young thing to love? Will you abandon your second family?" Fortunately, in his case he repented of his sin, abandoned "the other woman," and went home to be a husband and father. Today he has no regrets! Several times through the years he has said, "I can't believe I could have been so dumb! Today when I see that woman I can't believe I could have thought I was in love with her." She, by the way, has broken up two other families since he broke off their "affair."

"Love is blind" is not just a popular expression for the unmarried, it also describes all ages, even married men. Another more descriptive phrase is "There is no fool like an old fool." I have three friends, two deacons and a minister, who at the age of sixty-two left their wives for younger women. Unbelievably, all three tried to justify it by saying, "But I love her!" The Bible describes it as "lust, when it is conceived, brings forth sin" (see James 1:15).

Most married men, if they are honest, will admit that they have been attracted to another woman, at work or even at church. If a man deals with his thoughts immediately as wrong and an indulgence of selfishness to entertain fantasies about her instead of "ravishing himself with the breasts of the wife of his youth" as the Bible admonishes, it is no lasting problem. The decision to keep his marriage vows saves his wife, children, and even the "other woman" and her family much needless pain.

What a tempted man doesn't seem to understand is that his sex drive is so powerful that if he brings his mind into control and refuses to fantasize about other women, it is only a matter of time before his wife, the one and only legitimate object of his sexual expression, will become more and more attractive to him. Then the wonder of sex without guilt (married sex) will make her an increasing object of his love. Let's face it, sex is desirable for all men, and is essential for married men. God made man that way, not only for the propagation of the race, but to introduce him to the most exciting and pleasurable experience on earth and to help him keep that commitment he made to his wife at the wedding altar to "keep me only unto you so long as we both shall live." Keeping that vow provides a lifetime of enjoyment for both partners. Selfishly breaking that vow by sharing sex with another brings nothing but havoc and heartache into the relationship and is the principle cause of divorce today.

Hollywood may make it appear that all married people are bed hopping. Admittedly, some of the stars may live that way—and experience the resulting divorces and heartache that go with it—but that is not the way most Americans live.[3] I was not surprised by the 1994 sex survey that showed the vast majority of married couples did not have "affairs" outside of marriage. Instead, it was discovered that married people who kept their wedding vows had sex more frequently and more satisfyingly than those who broke them.

Good men do not break their wedding vows. Some may, in a time of weakness and selfishness, give in to temptation and be unfaithful, but it will be short-lived, and eventually a man's guilt will bring him to the cross of Christ where he can be forgiven—if he is willing to confess his sins as the Bible teaches and then do what our Lord said: "Go! and sin no more!"

Good men are not perfect. They are, however, forgiven and spend their life trying to be unselfish, not only in their sexual expression but in every area of life. All human beings have a problem with selfishness, depending on inherited temperament, childhood training, and spiritual commitment to obeying God's moral values. The happiest people in life are those who win the battle with selfishness most of the time.

How to Be a Good Father

Being a good father is not difficult; good men have been doing it for at least six thousand years. All men who have fathered children, however, have not been good fathers, which I contend every *good* man wants to be. History is filled with the tragic accounts of evil dictators, kings, gangsters, terrorists, and others who have brought much harm to other human beings. Most of these men were neglected or raised by bad fathers, some of whom even abused them.

If you are reading this book, you most likely want to be a good father—or want your husband to be. Let me give you some good news right at the start. You don't have to be a perfect father to be a good one. I learned that when my son Lee was only ten years old. I spanked him for something he was not responsible for. His day to bring the trash cans off the street was Monday. I spanked him on Thursday—his brother's day! So what does a father do? I was tempted to say, "Serves him right. Think of all the times that he got by with it." That idea didn't last long, so I went back into his bedroom and humbly apologized. I will never forget his response: "Oh that's okay, Dad, I know you're not perfect!" Then we hugged and he forgot it—I didn't, of course. In spite of that and other parenting mistakes, we are good friends. In fact, we are planning a three-day skiing trip this winter in the California mountains, just the two of us. I wish that relationship for every father.

While good fathers are not perfect, they do certain things that have an impact on their children's lives. The following are those I think are most important.

1. *Love them.* The greatest thing you can do for your children is give them your love. From infancy they need the reassuring voice of their father welcoming them into the world of men. Admittedly, at that early age they need mother's love more (and mother's food) and "mother constancy." But their earliest impression of men for good or bad will come from their father. That is why they need you to pick them up, shower them with affection, and rock them to sleep.

As they grow they learn one of the most important things in the world—self-acceptance—from parental love. Parents are like two giants in the emotional life of each child. If they are loved by their parents they grow up with a sense of self-acceptance. If they are not loved they start out life excessively insecure. Children learn they are significant because they are loved by their mother and father. Your love, properly expressed in early childhood, usually lasts into their teens, making those traumatic years a time of enjoyment. I have found that most angry, hostile teens felt unloved in childhood.

Some men have a difficult time showing affection, either because of their temperament or because they received very little love themselves as children. That can, however, with the Lord's help, be overcome by developing a spirit of determined unselfishness that can enable a man to meet the emotional needs of his children. Usually young children are easy to love; if you start early your ability will grow as they do. That is particularly true with your little girls. Most fathers don't realize that their relationship to their daughter is what establishes her attitude toward the opposite sex. If her father is warm and loving toward her, she will develop a positive attitude toward men. A good loving relationship with her dad is excellent preparation for her to enjoy a good sexual relationship with her husband someday. If she can run into her father's arms any old time and know that he will be there for her, she will not only have a good self-image, but she will be less likely to become promiscuous in her teens and will learn to respond readily to her husband after marriage. Most of the girls I have counseled who were sexually active early in life were usually love-starved at home, particularly by their father, or didn't have a resident father.

It is impossible to exaggerate the importance of giving your children your love. It is not only the greatest and most important gift, but it is one everyone can give, or learn to give, with God's help. Many times I have heard parents bemoan their inability to afford to give some of the material things of life to their children. Many feel badly that their income is not sufficient to send their children to college. What they don't understand is by giving their children their love, they are giving them the greatest gift in the world. One thing children can never get too much of is their parents' love.

2. *Love their mother.* Children are born insecure. They fear loud noises, falling, hunger, and almost everything. It is love that reassures them and helps them develop emotionally. The love between their parents is as important as the love they receive from their parents. As soon as they become old enough to reason, they can tell if their parents love each other. If they do, the children develop a strong

sense of emotional security. If, however, their parents are estranged, emote hostility toward each other, or are cold to one another, it intensifies whatever insecurities their temperament combinations bring to their personalities.

When children become teens, the best sex education parents can provide them is the warm sense of security that comes from seeing an affectionate relationship between the parents. They do not have to see their parents do anything indiscreet. They just seem to know there is something exciting Mom and Dad do in private that endears them to each other. True love cannot be hidden, particularly in the home. Cultivate your love for your wife, treat her with respect and preference, and your children will get the message. They will also learn standards of how married people treat each other. People who grow up in troubled homes where the parents don't get along well must work harder at their own marriages. The ideal is when both partners come from dedicated Christian homes where their parents loved them and each other. You can provide the mother of your grandchildren that kind of love as an example that will last them a lifetime.

Besides, as I've already pointed out several times, it's scriptural to love your wife. Four times in Scripture God commands husbands to "love your wife as Christ loved the church . . . and as you do your own body." Once it says, "and be not bitter against them." Always remember, you cannot be bitter at your wife and love her at the same time. Anger, bitterness, and resentment will stifle love and, if indulged long enough, will kill it. Many men have told me in counseling, "I no longer love my wife. My feelings are dead for her." There are only two basic causes for that: (1) alienation of affection (they have another love object that must be put off) or (2) anger or bitterness. If you have any trouble with this go back and read chapter 10 and practice the steps on overcoming anger. Then make a list of ten things about your wife that you like and thank God for them twice each day, and your love will return—it is natural.

Actually, you have no choice. God has commanded you to love your wife. She needs it, your children need it, and you need it. The good news is that God never commands us to do anything he will not enable us to do. Besides, every man wants love. The best way to get it is to give it. Another biblical principle is "Give, and it will be given to you" (Luke 6:38).

3. *Teach them to love God and accept Christ early.* Skeptics are not born, they are trained. All children naturally believe in God, but they must be trained to know him personally. Our Lord indicated that when he pronounced a curse on those who "cause one of these little ones who believe in me to stumble," he just assumed that little children believed. Consequently, we should start early introducing them to the truths about God. That is why the church puts so much priority on starting them early in the church nursery and why we start training them in the primary department, where every child's favorite song is "Jesus Loves Me."

You can supplement that childhood training at home by leading your family in daily Bible reading and prayer after dinner each night. Another good parent-child time is when you tell them a story, or when you talk to them and pray with them before bed. It lets them know you love God and you want them to also. This not only helps their emotional development, it also makes it easy to lead them to personally accept Jesus at an early age. Helping your child to bring God into their daily lives early in life will make it easy for them to live the biblical injunction "In all your ways acknowledge him" in adulthood.

Our first child was only four years old when she prayed to receive Jesus. It happened naturally. We had a large picture of Christ knocking at the heart's door hanging over the fireplace in the living room of our home. Many times we sat in front of the fire to have our nightly prayer sessions, and afterward we would sing songs familiar to her and her younger brother. One night she asked, "Why is there no handle on that door?" So I explained that the door represented a person's heart; the handle is on the inside. Jesus knocks and wants us to open the door to let him in. Then I quoted Revelation 3:20, where he says specifically, "Behold, I stand at the door and knock. If anyone hears My voice and opens the door, I will come in to him and dine with him, and he with Me." She looked at me and said, "Could I invite Jesus into my heart?" And of course we said she could, and she did. The interesting thing is that, in spite of how very young she was, she assures me that she has never doubted her salvation from that date. Later she married a minister and together they have served the Lord for many years. Her brother did not receive the Lord until he was seven. Children are different, but parents who teach them early to love God often see them accept Christ at a young age.

If your child is in the fourth grade and has not yet made that decision, his or her salvation should be your number one priority in prayer until he or she does. Children raised in Christian homes who do not receive Christ before the teen years are often open to rebellion and skepticism thereafter.

4. *Spend quality time with them.* Love always takes time to convey. You cannot convey your love for your children without spending quality time with them. Since most fathers are away at work during the day, you had best get into the habit of spending the evening with your children. Unfortunately, most men say they don't know what to do with children. Usually that is a cop-out. We can figure out what to do if we really want to, from changing their diapers, holding them while feeding them, spoon-feeding them when they get to that stage, or doing whatever the situation calls for. Most wives love it when the father comes home to give hands-on care of the child while they finish preparing the evening meal.

When your children are somewhere between two and three years old, you can begin looking at picture books and reading the Bible and other wholesome stories to them. It may get boring for you to read them the same story over and over, but children love repetition. Reading to them reg ularly sets them up for learning to read in early childhood. Educators find that the best thing any parent can do to help prepare a child to become a good reader is to read stories to them when they are very young. That piques a reading curiosity in your young child's mind that drives them to become a good reader later on. And remember this: Becoming a good reader is the very foundation to all education. If you can read well you can learn almost anything. So quality time spent reading to your children as often as possible does two things: It conveys your love and it prepares them to learn to read early and well.

Naturally, as your children get older you have to learn to do other things with them—sports, games, garage work, something that proves you care enough to spend quality time with them. I have performed over three hundred weddings in my years as a pastor. Many stand out special in my mind. One was the beautiful virgin daughter of one of the leaders in the church who was marrying a dedicated Christian young man. She and her father were whispering daughter-father talk as she glided down the aisle. Then, just as her father was ready to place her hand on the groom's arm, she raised her veil and kissed her dad warmly on the cheek. I was reminded of that in mid-November of 1994 when I read Columnist Donna Britt's conclusion that "Daddy's girls" rarely become teenage unwed mothers. Then she said, "Growing up with a close father, a girl receives a firsthand education of the heart, and is far less likely to be swayed by the first boy who attempts to snow her with compliments." I couldn't agree more. But that kind of loving relationship, what every good father desires, takes quality time.

5. *Teach them to honor and obey their parents and other adults.* The Bible only gives two commands to children: "Obey your parents in the Lord, for this is right. Honor your father and mother" (Eph. 6:1–2). I wish I could tell you that children automatically obey and honor their parents. Instead, quite the opposite is true, depending on their temperament.

Sanguine children are fun-loving con artists who can ignore your standards or lie their way out of taking responsibility for their own behavior. Choleric children are defiant and rebellious. They always test your rules—make sure you don't flunk their tests. Melancholy children are sensitive to rebuke or chastising. They usually accuse their parents of being harder on them than on their siblings. Phlegmatic children almost never rebel openly, but if they don't want to do something, they won't do it. Obviously, every child is a challenge. Perhaps that is why God gave them two parents—to get control of them early. You will enjoy them more later in life if you give them loving discipline in their early years.

The Bible tells us that "Rebellion is bound up in the heart of the child and the rod of instruction will drive it far from him." It also says, "He that loves his son will chasten him." Susanna Wesley understood this principle when she raised her seventeen children, two of whom shook England for God and then came to the Colonies and had a powerful spiritual influence on our country. She claimed, "The child that is not taught to obey their parents in the home will neither obey God or man outside the home."

Obviously, obeying parents and showing honor (or respect) for adults is not intuitive, it is taught. Perhaps that is why there are so many undisciplined, self-indulgent people in our society today; we have had almost four decades of psychobabble about parents allowing their children to be expressive of their thoughts and feelings rather than abiding by biblical standards of discipline.

A loving father will start the disciplining process early by refusing to allow his children to get by with sassing or expressing anger, particularly toward their mother. Those traits do not go away naturally; they have to be trained out of the child, not by angry discipline, but by consistent discipline. One Sunday night after church we visited a young couple in our congregation. On the way home I predicted that our friends would have trouble with their children ten or so years in the future. At the time all three were under five years of age. They were undoubtedly the sassiest kids I had been around in a long time. Through the years they have brought great heartache to their parents. Children must be taught to obey and honor their parents by those same loving parents. It is an act of love that will save them much heartache all through life. Child psychologist Dr. James Dobson once said, "The time to disarm that teenage time bomb is before he is five years old."

God has given men a lower registration of voice that tends to command respect easier than a woman's. It is a wise father that uses that gift gently but firmly to demand that his children never sass or talk back to their mother. Not only will she love him as he demands they respect her, his children will also learn discipline and one day rise up to call him blessed. It is important, however, that all such discipline should be done without anger. All too frequently parents ignore discipline opportunities when the children are little and wait until their own frustration level rises to the point where they are rightly motivated to take action but with the wrong emotion. Anger, as we saw earlier, is a harmful emotion. *Never* discipline your children in anger. That is when parents go too far, spank too hard, and in some cases unintentionally administer child abuse. Such children often grow up with no self-confidence or become excessively rebellious. All discipline should be administered in love and once finished, the matter forgotten. It should never leave the child feeling you have rejected him. Instead, he should understand it is that specific behavior that is unacceptable. When parents emote anger in the process of discipline, the child becomes confused and the discipline is likely to be ineffective. The thin line of difference is that the child should always understand your love is unconditional but the specific behavior for which you are correcting him or her is not acceptable.

6. *Teach them to feel good about themselves.* All children start out as little people without skills or abilities in a complex world of big people whom the children think know everything and can do anything. Depending on their temperament, this problem can plague them all through life, particularly Melancholies and sometimes Phlegmatics. Perfection is seldom good enough for the former, and the latter are often so passive they elicit little praise yet inwardly yearn for it. Of course, they gradually grow up to learn that no one can do everything, but by then the damage is often done. That is where children surrounded by father and mother love have it all over others. They know they are important and that their parents love them.

One thing you can do to help your children gain self-acceptance is to teach them to do things, but watch them to see what they have an affinity for and help them learn it well. That is why I stress reading to them early in life. Then as they go to school, go over what they are studying, and when they start reading, let them read to you, then ask them to tell you what they have read. This can develop in them a lifetime interest in learning.

If your son is musically inclined, give him some lessons if possible. If he is athletic, teach him a sport. My son could tell early that his son, Randy, had a knack for tennis, so he spent good money he could ill afford to give him lessons. It paid off the first day he went to high school, when the coach said, "No ninth graders can play on the first team." Randy raised his hand and respectfully challenged the coach by saying, "I can beat half the best players on the first team." The coach was intrigued and let him try. Sure enough, he could beat five of the ten upperclassmen and made the first team. If there is anything Randy is not, it is insecure.

I have two other grandsons who excel at racing motorcycles and mechanical repair, another at soccer. It is much easier to help a child learn self-acceptance and self-confidence if they know in their heart they can do something well. That is particularly true of Christian young people because our lifestyle is different by the standards of the world. But if they know they can do something well, it helps build their general self-esteem. Besides, the self-discipline they learn in becoming proficient at something will spill over into other areas of their life.

One thing fathers should be aware of is that your favorite sport or hobby may not be theirs. Don't try to impose your love of sports on a boy who has no affinity for athletics. Don't be like my wrestler friend who wasted years trying to make his sensitive and frail son into a wrestler when the kid abhorred violence. Today he is a violinist, and his dad is proud of him. Always remember King Saul, who made the mistake of trying to put his giant armor on little David. Eventually David had to throw off the armor and use what he was skilled at—the sling that killed the giant. Let your sons and daughters be themselves; don't try to force them into your mold. Instead, be sensitive to their gifts and interests and help them succeed at them. It takes time and effort, but it is well worth it—you're preparing a life.

7. *Avoid undue criticism.* All children are inept. That is the price they pay for being little people in a big world. While they are learning coordination, logic, and common sense, they will naturally make mistakes. They usually feel bad enough about their mistakes without hearing the man they love and want to please most criticizing them unduly for everything they attempt. That just shatters their self-confidence and often retards their progress.

It is much better to be encouraging of their efforts and suggestive in a positive way. We had a neighbor who always yelled his favorite expression at his son: "Don't be so stupid!" You can imagine what that did to the boy's self-confidence. I am not surprised he grew up to be a teenage rebel.

Children need discipline and correction, but they do not need condemnation. Most children, particularly Melancholies and Phlegmatics, need constant encouragement. But if their father, or even their mother, has that perfectionist tendency (unduly critical), they can leave their tender self-image shattered. If either of their parents is a Choleric who indulges his or her naturally critical and angry temperament by being overly critical, it can also have devastating effects on the development of the children. One of the most frequent mistakes parents make is underestimating how important they are to their children. Always try to be approving and encouraging so when you have to be critical of some specific behavior, it comes after many positive expressions of approval.

8. Provide them a spiritual atmosphere in the home. Fathers, even more than mothers, can set the spiritual tone of their home. If Dad indicates they are going to have daily devotions, prayers at bedtime, grace at mealtime, and regular attendance at church, it will be done. Such an environment is ideal for children to grow up in, for it brings their religious faith and practice right into the home. I have already touched on the fact that nothing is more reassur-

ing to children than hearing their parents pray regularly for them and for their hearts' concerns.

I remember well the time during family devotions when I asked the children for their prayer requests. Our seven-year-old, Lori, asked that we pray for "Susie's cat, she has a broken leg." I'll be honest with you; I don't like cats. Yet here I was, having to pray for an animal I didn't even like. That is when it dawned on me that I wasn't just praying for a cat, I was praying for Lori's prayer request. Many years have passed, yet even today as the mother of four, Lori will still call on occasion, just to have her dad pray for her. Through the years we have prayed about tests, school, where to go to college, boyfriends, jobs, and houses. It all started in the spiritual environment at the table after dinner.

Don't wait until you're faced with a crisis to bring God into the everyday circumstances of life. God has challenged us to acknowledge him in all our ways, and he will direct our paths (see Prov. 3:6). Add to your prayer and Bible reading good music in your home. Music has a profound effect on a person's emotions and is also a good teaching tool. You will find that the atmosphere you bring your children up in will be the kind your grandchildren will be raised in also.

9. *Lead them to be active in your local church.* The church is the family's best friend. It is the one institution that proclaims the same moral values you are teaching at home. It is also the only institution today that consistently communicates your faith and the biblical principles it is based on. Children raised in an active Bible-teaching church by parents who try to live in the home the principles the church teaches are much easier to raise, particularly when they get to the teen years. A 1994 survey of Southern Baptist youth of Texas indicated that 72 percent said they do not drink alcohol, 85 percent said they had not had sexual intercourse—compared to 51 percent of girls and 67 percent of boys in public school, including both churched and unchurched, who admit to being sexually active. You could safely conclude from these statistics that keeping your young people active in church will make them three times less likely to become sexually active—and that sur-

vey was taken before churches began to stress the "virtue until marriage" campaign that has received some national press coverage.

Another result of that survey that is important to parents is that 95 percent said they don't use illegal drugs and 80 percent said they do not smoke. Just having your children select their friends from among young people with committed lifestyles like that should be incentive enough for all fathers to keep them active in a Bible-believing church. There are, of course, many other reasons, including exposing them to the faithful preaching of the Word of God and opportunities to close out the world for a few hours and learn to worship the Lord in praise, song, and prayer. All of this is conducive to their committing their lives to Christ during their most formative years. They certainly get no such opportunities from school or community sponsored activities.

I hope you have selected your church carefully for its faithfulness to the Word of God and its ministry to children and youth. At times they will need your encouragement to keep regular in church attendance and youth activities. Don't be surprised that at some time they will rebel, saying they don't like the kids in the youth group. When that happens, get to know the kids they do like. I can almost guarantee you will not like the influence those young people have on your teen. That is when they need a parent like my single mother, who told me, "Young man, as long as you park your feet under my table, you will abide by my rules— and I say that those boys at school are having a bad influence on you, so I want you to break off with them and select your friends at church." Her authority was based on 1 Corinthians 15:33, where Paul said, "Evil company corrupts good habits." I probably would not have happily spent over half a century in Christian work without a mother like that! Although I thought of her as a narrow-minded fanatic at the time, today I call her blessed.

Church attendance should never be optional; it should be a way of life. And if you lead the way, it will be. Every time the doors are open, your family should be there. Since the church is the family's best friend, you should use your church to help you in raising your children to love and serve God.

10. *Teach your children to be unselfish.* All good fathers want their children to be happy in life. And, whereas getting a good education and finding the right vocation and life partner are important, the most important thing for them to learn is to be unselfish. It is impossible to be lastingly happy and be selfish. Most personal and family misery today is caused by selfishness. I have counseled more than twenty-five hundred people for marriage problems. The one thing they all have in common is that they are selfish. That basic sin is the scourge of the human race and the predominant cause of divorce. To make matters worse, children raised by selfish parents become selfish themselves and perpetuate that misery. Selfishness allows an angry partner to explode and pour out his wrath on his partner. His selfishness allows his fears to draw him back into a shell of self-protection or explode in retaliation, hardly a good environment in which to raise children.

Frankly, I do not know any way to overcome selfishness short of a genuine conversion experience with Jesus Christ. Even then it is not automatic; that is why I stress the Spirit-filled life. As you cooperate with the Holy Spirit within you, his power can give you victory over the universal tendency of selfishness. I address this in more depth in my book *I Love You, but Why Are We So Different?* Selfishness can be overcome, but it takes supernatural power to do so. That supernatural power is, of course, available to any Christian. One thing that helps is for a child to see unselfishness in the lives of his parents. In addition, he needs to be corrected early for expressions of selfishness and to be taught that it is unacceptable for a Christian or for a member of your household. As the apostle Paul said, "Be followers of me, even as I also am of Christ," the ultimate example of unselfishness. So you can say in your heart to your children, "Learn unselfishness from me as I have learned it from Christ my Lord." This takes effort and courage, but it is worth it for you and for your children.

Good Fatherhood Is a Choice

Becoming a father is not difficult. It takes only a few moments, and any man can do it. That is why we have six billion people on this planet. Becoming a *good* father takes time, effort, and personal sacrifice. But it is the most worthwhile thing a man can do. Unfortunately, many men are too selfishly preoccupied to make the decision to be a good father. Granted, it will occupy between twenty and thirty years of your life, depending on how many children you have and how far they are apart. There will be times when you will think, "Will this period of life never end?" But there will also be many times of true enjoyment and satisfaction. The Bible calls children "a heritage of the Lord." Don't wait until they are married and gone before you enjoy those childrearing days. Savor them by deciding, "I am going to be a good father!"

God, of course, wants you to be a good father and, naturally, so does your wife, and probably your parents. God has promised, "Train up a child in the way he should go, and when he is old he will not depart from it" (Prov. 22:6). That doesn't mean that at a time of rebellion he might not throw off the traces and disappoint you by some of the bad choices he makes for his life, because God gave him a free will too. But when he is old, he will come back to walk with God. Some men reading this book are saying, "I am praying it won't be too long." Trust God and keep praying; he or she will come back—I could give many thrilling illustrations of that.

But there are some who will read this book who realize that they may not have been good fathers. You can make the choice now and still have a powerful impact on your child's life. Have you ever thought of King David as a father? He was a great king in Israel, but he was a bad father the first period of his life. Actually, he had two families. The first was evidently neglected, for they turned against everything he had stood for during the first fifty years of his life. That is seen in Absalom, the heir to his throne, who rebelled and tried to take the throne from his father. Amnon raped his sister Tamar, and Absalom avenged her by killing him. This is hardly what we would call a good or godly family life. Evidently David had not taught his children the principles of God for happy living. But that is not what he did with his second family. After he repented of his sins, including his dereliction as a father, he made a decision to raise Solomon to be a king. He must have changed his treatment of this son, for when Solomon was writing the book of Proverbs he said this of his father:

> When I was my father's son . . . he taught me . . . let your heart retain my words; keep my commands, and live. Get wisdom! Get understanding! . . . Do not forsake her . . .
>
> Hear, my son, and receive my sayings, and the years of your life will be many. I have taught you the way of wisdom; I have led you in right paths. When you walk, your steps will not be hindered, and when you run, you will not stumble. Take firm hold of instruction, do not let her go; keep her [wisdom], for she is your life.
>
> Proverbs 4:3–13

What Solomon was saying here is, The wisdom I give in these proverbs I learned from my father, "early, at his knee."

Don't wait, like David, until your second family to make the decision to be a good father. That opportunity in David's life came after great suffering. Be a good father now. Not only will you obey God, but you will raise your children to be all they can be. And isn't that what you want for them, and for yourself? And for the glory of your heavenly Father?

14

Success without Perfection

Every man wants to succeed in life. Perfection, however, is never the prerequisite to success. A baseball player who carries a batting average of .333 is superior. Few are aware that such an average concedes failure .667 of the time. Most professions are not that forgiving, but I know few that demand perfection.

Whatever your profession, you want to succeed. That is natural and commendable. The Bible clearly charts the route to success, as we have already seen. But that narrow path to success is replete with detours, most prominent of which is the unbalanced life. Many men today, even dedicated Christian workers, are extremely successful in their professions but fail with their wives, children, or both. I am convinced that if men establish their priorities in accord with God's principles, they will accomplish far more and fulfill the totality of their lives. Note the Bible's standard for a man's relationships and priorities.

A Man's Priorities

1. Your Relationship to God

But seek first the kingdom of God and His righteousness, and all these things shall be added to you.

Matthew 6:33

You shall love the LORD your God with all your heart, with all your soul, and with all your mind.

Matthew 22:37

It is absolutely essential to maintain a regular quiet time, meditating upon the Word of God and talking to him, in order to sustain this love relationship as your number one priority. If you do not, the things of the world and the pressures of life will gradually dull the keen edge of your love for God.

2. Your Love Relationship to Your Wife

Husbands, love your wives, just as Christ also loved the church and gave Himself for it.

Ephesians 5:25

This love, too, must be cultivated, as I indicated in chapter 12. Some parents fear that children will become jealous of a strong love relationship between their parents, but quite the opposite is true. Dr. James Kilgore, in his book *Being a Man in a Woman's World,* points out that "children in therapy made progress when those children began to perceive that the relationship between father and mother was closer than the relationship between either of the parents and their children. Mom and Dad ought to have the strongest commitment to each other and the children ought to be aware of that in an emotionally healthy home." The child can readily understand when he is the number two love object in his parents' hearts and is positively affected by it. By contrast, children who become number one in the love of a parent often became unnaturally sex obsessed. Those who become the number one love object of the par-

ent of the opposite sex are vulnerable to adapting the homo-
sexual lifestyle.

In addition, the love relationship between parents is an
educational experience. The children will more often treat
their partner some day in the same way they see their parents treating each other. Your grandchildren will be influenced someday by the love you show their grandmother
now.

3. Your Relationship to Your Children

And you, fathers, do not provoke your children to wrath, but bring
them up in the training and admonition of the Lord.

Ephesians 6:4

As discussed in the last chapter, the Bible makes it clear
that a man is responsible for the training of his children,
and when that priority becomes less than number three in
his life, both he and the children suffer. Probably the hardest gift for a man to confer upon his children is his time. I
have already confessed mistakes I made during the early
years of my children's lives. That is the major fact of my life
I would change if I could renew the past. Fortunately, the
Lord revealed that deficiency before it bred fatal consequences among my children.

Even more important than a man's time, however, is his
children's need for love. The most emotionally crippled
young people today come from homes where they were literally starved for the love of their parents. Unsaved men
may use temperament and background to justify their lack
of affection, but a Christian man is without excuse.

The devastating effect of the lack of a father's love was
demonstrated one night as I came down the steps of an airplane in San Diego. In front of me was a young man of about
twenty-four who suddenly began twitching and jerking for
what seemed an unexplainable reason. I first thought that
he was having a seizure. Then I spotted an eight- or ten-
year-old boy at the foot of the steps, waiting to welcome
his brother (I guessed) on his return home. Like all junior
boys, his big liquid eyes were transparent in their yearning

to be engulfed in his brother's love. But the closer the older boy came to the younger, the more he twitched, and finally I realized that he was incapable of a genuine expression of love. When he greeted his brother, the best he could do was to reach out his arm and touch him on the shoulder. From my position above and behind him, I could see the hurt in the little fellow's eyes. I initially thought, How selfish of the older boy not to supply the hunger for love which his younger brother felt. But then I reflected on the cause of such an abnormal incapacity for affection. I can only imagine the heartbreaking rejections to which the older brother must have been subjected during his years of childhood—probably warping him for life. An affectionate father in the home, administering large doses of love, would have prevented such a tragedy.

4. Your Vocation

But if anyone does not provide for his own, and especially for those of his household, he has denied the faith and is worse than an unbeliever.

1 Timothy 5:8

The Holy Spirit of God is the best personnel director I know. He never puts round pegs in square holes. By seeking his leading, you will be guided into the proper use of your natural strengths and talents as you surrender your professional life to him. He is interested not only in the kind of work you do but also in the place you do it.

5. Your Responsibility to Both Parents

"Honor your father and mother," which is the first commandment with promise.

Ephesians 6:2

This command is operative throughout life. Many Christians today, led into the pitfall of committing this responsibility to the government, seriously neglect their parents in their old age. A good relationship to your parents will both improve your relationship to your wife and teach your children how they should treat you in the twilight years of your life.

6. Your Relationship to the Church

The church, a place where you not only feed on the Word of God but prepare to serve him, deserves a vital place in your family's life. Today it is more important than ever that the church be the family's best friend. Families need a bulwark against the many agencies of influence attacking the family and its values—from big government that overtaxes and overregulates to public education that undermines Christian principles by teaching the irresponsible lifestyle of secular humanism to the entertainment industry that will corrupt your child's mind emotionally and morally. It is important that parents conscientiously lead their children to be involved with every activity the church provides that is appropriate for their age group.

The church is the one major agency of influence that is supportive of the values you are trying to teach your children at home. For that reason, wise parents use their church to help them raise their children to love and serve God.

I cannot say too much in favor of providing your children with a Christian school or home school education. The Bible teaches, "Beware lest anyone cheat you [or your children] through philosophy and empty deceit, according to the tradition of men" (Col. 2:8). Today most public schools are cheating America's children out of a pro-Christian educational philosophy by teaching a near-exclusive philosophy of humanism that is just a step away from atheistic socialism. Consequently, it is 180 degrees in opposition to the philosophy you want for your children. And it is going to get worse!

Goals 2000, that for now is the law of the land, is federalized education—that is, it is doing away with traditional local control of education in our country in favor of one made up in Washington, D.C., by world secularists.

The most important organ of your child's body is the brain. As the brain goes—its philosophy—so goes the child. Youth experts like Josh McDowell and Bill Gothard tell us that the church is losing 35 to 50 percent of our children to the world before they graduate from high school because of twelve thousand hours of secular humanistic indoctrination in the public schools. Christian school or home school offers a better education, better environment, better adult role models, and a 100 percent better philosophy of life. For the sake of your children, your family, and your heritage, consider—if at all possible—a Christian education for your children.

7. Your Relationship to Neighbors and Yourself

You shall love your neighbor as yourself.

Romans 13:9

Every man has a responsibility to exemplify before his neighbors the fruits of the Christian life. Throughout the years, the most effective church evangelistic tool has been our members leading their neighbors to the Savior. You may be the only Christian some of your neighbors will ever be exposed to. Find some time in your busy life to share the most important thing in your life with them—your personal faith in Jesus Christ.

Follow God's Leading

If you study these priorities, you will find that of necessity some will take precedence over others at certain periods. That is understandable, but don't err by giving your vocation precedence over everything else. The price men pay for that mistake is much too dear. Rather, look to the Lord for guidance. If you faithfully keep your priorities in focus, God will take care of your vocation and grant the fulfillment every man desires: a successful family and home.

You don't have to be perfect to enjoy that fulfillment, but you do have to maintain the right priorities.

Shortly after my fiftieth birthday, while flying on a DC-10 enroute to San Diego after a seminar, I took a hard and honest look at myself. It was a sobering and revealing experience! I'll let you take a peek inside at the "inner me."

The first thing I discovered was that I am really an ordinary guy! My grades in high school were low, and I was so disinterested that I graduated *in absentia*. Academic proficiency improved somewhat in college, but still I graduated only *magna cum lucky* (337 in a class of 517). At eighteen, I washed out of pilot training and became a waist-gunner on a B-29. As an athlete, I failed to impress the professional scouts. Oh, I made the second-string Air Force football team at nineteen, but even the coach laughed when I came out for practice. (After all, who needed a five-foot-seven 155-pound middle linebacker?) In basketball, a game for giants, I quickly discovered that my competitive spirit was no match for height and talent. If it hadn't been for the fact that I was the pastor of the church that owned the gym, I would never have been allowed to play—but even then I was always chosen last. I did enjoy playing shortstop on the baseball team, but I could never learn to hit fast pitching. My best golf score ever was eighty-five, but that's because we encountered a torrential rainstorm and quit on the seventeenth hole. I found the church bowling team a pleasant experience, but had to endure the humiliation of coming home three fourths of the time knowing that my wife had outscored me by ten to twenty-five pins.

The one sport in which I display some skill is skiing, both snow- and waterskiing, but already some of my grandchildren ski circles around me—and so do their parents. I really excel in only one sport: football spectator. Win, lose, or draw, I must be the Chargers' and the Redskins' number one fan!

I did finally learn to ride my motorcycle well enough in the desert to go on eighty- to one-hundred-mile treks without killing myself, but that was because of the patience and encouragement of my friend, Skeeter Hollenbeck, a champion motorcycle racer. I do a respectable job of flying my twin-engine plane—but that's a matter of survival, and I must confess that if I hadn't taken half again as much instruction as the average man, I'd probably be an insurance hazard.

At the risk of disillusioning you further, I must confess that I am mechanically inept. My family and I discovered long ago that it was always cheaper to take my car to a mechanic, for every time I raise the hood, I foul up the engine. When it comes to carpentry, I specialize in wood butchery. I couldn't cut two boards the same length if my life depended on it. Even my wife knows better than to tell me that the sink is leaking. By the time I finish the task, not only is the kitchen a mess but we also have to shut off the water and wait for the plumber. Gardening has never brought me accolades either, for I can kill any growing thing in three months. Now we live in a condominium, and I'm not responsible for the outdoors.

Professionally, I do a little better, but being absolutely honest, I'm not a world-beater as a preacher either. Take away my overhead projector and I'm like Samson after his haircut—as weak as any other man. And no one ever accused me of being a model pastor; if it weren't for the fantastic associates God sent me, I'd probably have been fired many years before I resigned after twenty-five years of ministry in the same church. Oh, it's true that with several best-sellers on the market I have had some success as a writer, but as much as it grieves me to admit it, if it weren't for the editing transfusions Dr. Jim DeSaegher gives my rough drafts, people would ask, "Tim LaWho?"

You may think I'm kidding about all this, but if you knew me, you would realize that I am actually an average guy. And that's what I observed when I looked inside myself on that plane ride home. But as I started down the steps that night, I noted that my whole family was waiting for me, eagerly anticipating a special dinner in celebration of my birthday. Bev was there with our two married kids, our three grandchildren, and our two other children, Lee and Lori, who were still single at that time. Suddenly I felt very grateful to God. "Tim," I said to myself, "you are a rich man! Who could ask more out of life than the love and companionship of a wonderful woman and the devotion and fellowship of your own children?" More than fifteen years after that day, I can see even more clearly that nothing else really matters—not to me, anyway, and I have found that God has designed all of us similarly. A man fulfilled at home is a man fulfilled in life. Nothing else will really take the place of family solidarity and love—that's why God has provided it.

As I stepped down from the plane that night to receive the affectionate greetings of my family, one other thought came to mind—how thankful I was to God for *all* his blessings. My thoughts raced back to that experience at the age of twenty-one, when I finally surrendered my life 100 percent to Jesus Christ. I wanted to be an attorney; God wanted me to be a minister. That is without a doubt the best bargain I ever made! He has enriched everything in my life, and I am convinced that is exactly what he wants to do for every human being. I can confidently challenge you, not only on the basis of my own personal experience, but also on the authority of God's Word, that if you surrender everything you are and have to God and to the best of your knowledge obey him in all things, he will enrich and fulfill your life in the areas that really count.

The same can be true for you, for God's Word has promised this:

> My son, do not forget my law, but let your heart keep my commands; *for length of days and long life and peace they will add to you.*
>
> Proverbs 3:1–2 (emphasis added)

Certainly you will encounter problems in life, but as a child of God you are not left alone, for your heavenly Father guarantees divine help and guidance. He has further promised this to the man who seeks his aid:

> He shall call upon Me, and I will answer him; I will be with him in trouble; I will deliver him and honor him. *With long life will I satisfy him,* and show him My salvation.
>
> Psalm 91:15–16 (emphasis added)

Notes

1. William Rusher, "Thunder across the I.Q. Horizon," *Washington Times,* 12 November 1994. Quoted in Richard Herrnstein and Charles Murray, *The Bell Curve.*

2. Tim LaHaye, *How to Study the Bible for Yourself* (Irvine, Calif.: Harvest House Publishers, 1976).

3. Robert Michaor, University of Chicago, Graduate School of Public Policy, National Opinion Poll, *Washington Times,* 7 October 1994.

Additional Reading

Hallesby, O. *Temperament and the Christian Faith*. Minneapolis: Augsburg Publishing House, 1962.

LaHaye, Beverly. *How to Develop Your Child's Temperament*. Irvine, Calif.: Harvest House Publishers, 1977.

———. *The Spirit Controlled Temperament*. Irvine, Calif.: Harvest House Publishers, 1966.

LaHaye, Tim. *I Love You, but Why Are We So Different?* Irvine, Calif.: Harvest House Publishers, 1991.

———. *Spirit-Controlled Temperament*. Wheaton: Tyndale House Publishers, 1966.

———. *Transformed Temperaments*. Wheaton: Tyndale House Publishers, 1971.

LaHaye Temperament Analysis

Have you ever wondered why you act the way you do? The key is your temperament. But do you know what temperament you are—or what your secondary temperament is? Do you know how to recognize your weaknesses and the steps to overcoming them? Are you living a Spirit-filled life according to the Word of God? If you can't answer all of the above questions, you need to take the LaHaye Temperament Analysis!

This analysis has been designed to

- identify your primary and secondary temperaments
- provide a description of your predominant characteristics
- give information regarding your vocational aptitudes and possible vocations suited just for you
- recommend ways to improve your work habits
- list your spiritual gifts in order of their priority
- suggest where you can best serve in your church
- provide steps for overcoming your ten greatest weaknesses
- offer counsel on marital adjustment and parental leadership
- give special advice to singles, divorced persons, pastors, and the widowed

Special Offer: As a reader of this book, you are entitled to receive the LaHaye Temperament Analysis for $19.95 (a $10.00 discount off the regular price of $29.95). If you would like to take advantage of this discount, simply write to me at Family Life Seminars, P.O. Box 2700, Dept. UMT, Washington, D.C. 20013–2700, enclosing your check or the appropriate credit card information. Or call 1-800-962-1022.

Dr. Tim LaHaye is a noted author, minister, and nationally recognized speaker on Bible prophecy. The founder of Tim LaHaye Ministries, he has written more than forty books. His current Left Behind series is the all-time best-selling Christian fiction series with more than eighteen million copies in print. LaHaye and his wife, Beverly, have been married for over fifty years.